HOPE IN
TIMES
OF FEAR

HOPE IN
TIMES
OF FEAR

THE RESURRECTION
AND THE
MEANING OF EASTER

✳

TIMOTHY KELLER

VIKING

VIKING

An imprint of Penguin Random House LLC

penguinrandomhouse.com

Grateful acknowledgment is made for permission to reprint the following:

"Seven Stanzas at Easter" from *Collected Poems*, 1953–1993 by John Updike, copyright © 1993 by John Updike. Used by permission of Alfred A. Knopf, an imprint of the Knopf Doubleday Publishing Group, a division of Penguin Random House LLC. All rights reserved.

Lyrics from "Building Block" by Noel Paul Stookey, copyright © 1977 by Public Domain Foundation, Inc. and benefitting the nonprofit: musictolife.org. Used with permission.

All Scripture quotations, unless otherwise indicated, are taken from the Holy Bible, New International Version®, NIV®. Copyright © 1973, 1978, 1984, 2011 by Biblica, Inc.™ Used by permission of Zondervan. All rights reserved worldwide. www.zondervan.com. The "NIV" and "New International Version" are trademarks registered in the United States Patent and Trademark Office by Biblica, Inc.™

LIBRARY OF CONGRESS CATALOGING-IN-PUBLICATION DATA

Names: Keller, Timothy, 1950– author.
Title: Hope in times of fear : the resurrection and the meaning of Easter / Timothy Keller.
Description: New York : Viking, [2021] | Includes bibliographical references.
Identifiers: LCCN 2020040699 (print) | LCCN 2020040700 (ebook) |
ISBN 9780525560791 (hardcover) | ISBN 9780525560807 (ebook)
Subjects: LCSH: Jesus Christ—Resurrection. | Hope—Religious aspects—Christianity.
Classification: LCC BT482 .K445 2021 (print) | LCC BT482 (ebook) | DDC 232.9/7—dc23
LC record available at https://lccn.loc.gov/2020040699
LC ebook record available at https://lccn.loc.gov/2020040700

Printed in the United States of America

1 3 5 7 9 10 8 6 4 2

BOOK DESIGN BY LUCIA BERNARD

Bible quotations in this volume are from the New International Version (NIV) unless otherwise specified. Some other translations are occasionally cited. They include: CEV (Contemporary English Version); ESV (English Standard Version); KJV (King James Version); RSV (Revised Standard Version); NASB (New American Standard Bible).

To Ray and Gill Lane,

Christian friends for decades,

Faithful laborers in the Lord's vineyard,

Whose supernatural gifts of hospitality have

Succored us for many years.

CONTENTS

PREFACE

✳

When I had thyroid cancer in 2002 I read an eight-hundred-page masterwork, *The Resurrection of the Son of God* by N. T. Wright. It was not only an enormous help to my theological understanding but, under the circumstances, also a bracing encouragement in the face of my own heightened sense of mortality. I was reminded and assured that death had been defeated in Jesus, and that death would also be defeated for me.

Now, nearly twenty years later, I am writing my own book on the resurrection of Jesus, and I find myself again facing a diagnosis of cancer. This time I have pancreatic cancer, and by all accounts, this condition is much more serious and the treatment a far bigger challenge.

I am also writing in the midst of the worst world pandemic in a century. Many people are living in fear of sickness and death. My apartment in New York faces some of the great hospitals of the city, and especially during the height of the virus, every window blazed all night and the wailing sirens and red flashing lights came at all hours. Hopes for an early solution to the virus and a quick turnaround have been dashed again and again.

But the pandemic has brought more problems than just sickness. There may be major disruptions for the worse in nearly every sector of our society that will last for years. We may be in for unemployment unknown since the Great Depression, the failure of innumerable businesses, the painful contraction of whole industries, massive tax shortfalls jeopardizing the lives of millions who rely on government services and retirement, and crises for both private and public education. And that's just the list that comes mind now when I am writing in the very earliest days of the crisis. There will inevitably be others that we cannot yet foresee. In any case, the most socially and economically vulnerable will pay a higher price. On top of everything else, the social isolation has brought despair and a sense of hopelessness to millions.

In the midst of skyrocketing deaths from the coronavirus, protests over a different kind of death erupted into the streets during the early summer of 2020 following the murder of George Floyd by police in Minneapolis. The demonstrations happened in over two thousand U.S. cities and around the world, drawing millions of people, making them the largest such social protests in our history, far larger than those during the civil rights movement of the 1960s under Dr. Martin Luther King, Jr.

Nearly all the current protests have been focused on the ongoing racism in our society at large. But being old enough to remember the civil rights movement protests firsthand, I have been struck by a contrast. Our recent protests and calls for social justice, as encouraging as they are in so many ways, have little of the same sense of hope that that the earlier movement had.

In Dr. King's masterpiece, his "I Have a Dream Speech," he says:

> This is our hope, and this is the faith that I go back to the South with. With this faith, we will be able to hew out of the mountain of despair a stone of hope. With this faith, we will be able to transform the jangling discords of our nation into a beautiful symphony of brotherhood. With this faith, we will be able to work together, to pray together, to struggle together, to go to jail together, to stand up for freedom together, knowing that we will be free one day.[1]

King's reference to cutting a "stone of hope" out of a mountain of despair is a reference to Daniel 2:34–35,45. The chapter was a divine vision of the future, given to the king of Babylon in a dream. In that vision the idolatrous kingdoms of this world are smashed by a small rock "cut out" of a mountain "but not by human hands," which then grows into a mountain of justice and peace that fills the earth. Christian interpreters have understood the stone as the kingdom of God, a supernatural work ("not by human hands"), starting as quite a small thing, seemingly powerless, yet eventually toppling all proud regimes that perpetuate evil and oppression. Dr. King used the image with great rhetorical skill, but the image is more than rhetorical. "The kingdom of heaven is like a mustard seed," Jesus says in Matthew 13:31–32, "Though it is the smallest of all seeds, yet when it grows, it . . . becomes a tree, so that the birds come and perch in its branches."

Dr. King did not let the financial and political powerlessness of African Americans in the U.S. dash his hopes. The hidden systemic racism and the overt racial exclusion and violence that the civil rights leaders faced in the 1950s and 1960s were enormous. But he knew that God moves in this way—from small beginnings and weakness through sacrifice and service toward change. Dr. King was not merely a sunny optimist. Read his speeches and letters and you can see anger and realistic fears about the movement, but the note of hope remains.

It has often been pointed out that the civil rights movement was led by African American pastors and Christian leaders, and so the biblical references that fill their speeches and calls to do justice were not mere grandiloquence. They were statements of faith and hope rooted in God.

Death, pandemics, injustice, social breakdown—we again desperately need a stone of hope.

And there is no greater hope possible than to believe that Jesus Christ was raised from the dead. Saint Paul says he was "crucified in weakness, yet he lives by God's power" (2 Corinthians 13:4). If you grasp this great fact of history, then even if you find things going dark, this hope becomes a light for you when all other lights go out. That's why Paul can add, "Likewise, we are weak in him, yet by God's power we will live with him."

This is a book on the resurrection of Jesus. I am not trying to do the same exhaustive work on the historical sources and evidence for the resurrection that N. T. Wright did—nor am I capable of it. Early in the volume I try to summarize much of his work, which I don't think can be bettered at the present time. Because I am a preacher and not an academic, I am concentrating on the resurrection as a key to understanding the whole Bible and to facing all the challenges of life—suffering, personal change, injustice, moral clarity, and the uncertainty of the future.

Theoretically everyone knows that they could die at any moment. But a diagnosis of cancer or heart disease or the threat of a pandemic transfers us into the realm of those who know it as an immediate reality. During a dark time for most of the world, and for me personally, as we all long and grasp for hope, there is no better place to look than the resurrection of Jesus Christ.

INTRODUCTION

In his great mercy he has given us new birth into a living hope through the resurrection of Jesus Christ from the dead . . . and so your faith and hope are in God.

—1 PETER 1:3,21

A New Age of Anxiety

Even before the COVID-19 pandemic of 2020 and its aftermath, the Western world had been experiencing a growing crisis of hope.

For at least two centuries Western cultures had been animated by a powerful hope that history was progressive, that the human race was moving inevitably toward creating a world of greater and greater safety, prosperity, and freedom. In short, there was a strong belief that overall every generation of human beings would experience a better world than the previous generation. This is one of the legacies of the European Enlightenment, whose many figures predicted that human reason, ingenuity, and science, once freed from superstitions of the past, would inevitably bring in a better future.[1]

But then came the twentieth century. In 1947 W. H. Auden wrote his book-length poem *The Age of Anxiety*. The poem is about four persons in a bar in Manhattan talking about their lives and about life. It won the Pulitzer Prize but is seldom read. What grabbed attention was its title, which seemed to capture the cultural moment. In less than four decades the world had passed through two world wars, a pandemic, and the Great Depression and, at the time, it was heading into decades of a nuclear-armed Cold War between the West and communist nations.

Yet when the Cold War ended in 1989, the older belief in inevitable human progress seemed to revive. Some even declared "the end of history," meaning that the lethal struggles between the great ideologies—fascism, communism, and Western-style democracy—were finally over. The fears of warfare that could bring about worldwide conflagration were diminished. International capitalism, fueled by globalization, went into high gear and many economies seemed to be thriving. The Age of Anxiety was over; the earlier optimism of the Enlightenment was rekindling. The number of people who said that children today will grow up to be better off than their parents' generation went up to over 50 percent of the population.[2]

One leading thinker who has provided an empirical basis for this optimism is Steven Pinker of Harvard University. His books *The Better Angels of Our Nature: Why Violence Has Declined* and *Enlightenment Now: The Case for Reason, Science, Humanism, and Progress* assemble data to argue that across the world there is decreasing violence, warfare, and poverty, as well as lengthening life spans and improving health care.[3]

Pinker confines himself to empirical measures of comfort and safety, but Yuval Noah Harari makes stronger claims. In his 2017 bestseller *Homo Deus: A Brief History of Tomorrow* he argues that in ancient times human beings turned to God or to gods only because they did not have control over the world in which they lived. But we have that control now.

> At the dawn of the third millennium, humanity wakes up to an amazing realization. Most people rarely think about it, but in the last few decades we have managed to rein in famine, plague and war. Of course, these problems have not been completely solved, but they have been transformed from incomprehensible and uncontrollable forces of nature into manageable challenges. We don't need to pray to any god or saint to rescue us from them. We know quite well what needs to be done in order to prevent famine, plague and war—and we usually succeed in doing it.[4]

The title of the book *Homo Deus* conveys its basic conclusion. It is not merely that we no longer need God. Humanity now *is* God. We are our own hope for the future, our own God. We can have not just hope but confidence in a bright future because we have all the resources within ourselves to bring it about.

The Loss of Hope

Pinker and Harari, despite having many followers, are not capturing the spirit of the age as did Auden. By the middle of the first decade of the twenty-first century the numbers of people believing in a better life for their children began to decline again.[5] Pessimism about the future for our children and society has only deepened over the past fifteen or twenty years, as a variety of polls and surveys show.[6]

There are many reasons. Some point to a polarization and fragmentation in society that goes far beyond the usual political partisanship. There is a growing tribalism that reveals a culture in which there is a vacated center, a loss of any shared idea of common public good. There is a profound loss of social trust that appears to be undermining all the institutions that have held our society together.

There is another category of threats to our future that come not from a lack of scientific and technological progress but, ironically, as the result of it. For example, pandemics may be impossible to contain because of our mobility through air travel and because of the globalization of our economies, all due to modern technology. Our polarization and loss of trust in what to believe is now acknowledged to be, to a great degree, fueled by social media. Then there is the threat of climate change and the never-ending possibility of international terrorism, both heightened by scientific advances. The very things that were supposed to save us from terrible perils have created new ones.

Andrew Sullivan points to another category of reasons for the increasing sense of anxiety and hopelessness characterizing our age. Sullivan professes to be a great admirer of Pinker, and in a review of his book *Enlightenment Now*, he finds no fault in any of its empirical conclusions. But Sullivan then adds: "[Pinker] doesn't have a way of explaining why, for example, there is so much profound discontent, depression, drug abuse, despair, addiction, and loneliness in the most advanced liberal societies." He notes: "As we have slowly and surely attained more progress, we have lost something that undergirds all of it: meaning, cohesion, and a different, deeper kind of happiness than the satiation of all our earthly needs."[7]

Yuval Harari believes that people turned to God for hope in the past because of an inability to understand or control the natural environment. But religion addressed something much deeper than that. The human dilemma from time immemorial has not only been about how to control nature "out there" but—the far more difficult challenge—how to control nature "in here," that is, the many enigmas and problems of human nature itself. We hunger for meaning and purpose. We find that things that we thought would bring us satisfaction do not. We are shocked at the evil things other human beings—and we ourselves—are capable of doing. What can we do about *us*? As Sullivan indicates, controlling external nature is not enough, and there is plenty of evidence in a year of the COVID-19 pandemic that we are far from having done even that.

Pinker and Harari believe that leaving religion behind is an important part of human progress. But the prominent philosopher Jürgen Habermas over the last twenty years has taken a different position. He recognizes the limits of secular reason for providing moral absolutes and motivations to sacrifice one's selfish interests for the good of others. Habermas, though not a Christian, believes that religion can provide a basis for the sacredness of all human life and a motivation for sacrificial love in human relationships. These are things mere science cannot give us.[8] The greatest threat to our hope for a better world is not the natural environment but the various evils that continually spring from the human heart. Science cannot eradicate human evil—in fact it can give it more tools to use for its own ends. And by "evil" we don't mean only the horrendous eruptions such as the

Jewish holocaust. We mean the ordinary cruelties of self-interest in business, racial bias, arrogance and pride, dishonesty and corruption, and the innumerable daily acts of selfishness that pull society downward.

The Hope of the Resurrection

One of the reasons for the remarkable rise of Christianity in its earliest centuries was that it offered resources for hope in the face of the numerous urban pandemics that were devastating the Roman world. Kyle Harper, a historian who has written on ancient pandemics, was interviewed and asked about how Christianity kept thriving and growing in the bleakness of those times. He said:

> For [Christians], it was a positive program. This life was always meant to be transitory, and just part of a larger story. What was important to the Christians was to orient one's life towards the larger story, the cosmic story, the story of eternity. They did live in this world, experience pain, and loved others. But the Christians of that time were called to see the story of this life as just one of the stories in which they lived. The hidden map was this larger picture.[9]

The Christian "hidden map" went far beyond ordinary religious consolations. For example, other religions spoke of the uncertain possibility of a better hereafter if our moral performance was sufficient. The Christian hope exceeded such quavering wishful thinking in every way. The biblical word *elpida*, translated as the weaker English word *hope*, means profound certainty. Christians view even the hardest circumstances as part of a history guided by God at every turn toward not merely some kind of afterlife but toward the resurrection of our bodies and souls into new, remade heavens and earth.

And all this hope centers on one explosive event—the death and resurrection of Jesus Christ. That is what Christianity offers a world that has lost hope.

The Christians to whom Peter wrote had already "suffered grief in all kinds of trials" (1 Peter 1:6) and were now in the midst of a "fiery ordeal" (1 Peter 4:1). But Peter reminds them of this: "He has given us new birth into a living hope through the resurrection of Jesus Christ from the dead. . . . so your faith and hope are in God" (1 Peter 1:3,21). The fact of the resurrection means we have a hope for the future not based on scientific advance or social progress but on God himself (1 Peter 1:21). And this is not simply an intellectual belief but, as Peter says, it is a "living hope," a vital part of the new spiritual life that comes into Christians by the Holy Spirit through what the New Testament calls "the new birth." Faith in the resurrection implants that hope into the root of our souls. It becomes such a part of who we are that we can face anything.

But what *is* this faith in the resurrection that can become a living hope, burning within us like a warming and energizing fire? And how do we get it?

Knowing the Resurrection

The first step is to believe that the resurrection of Jesus Christ really happened. The resurrection is of little use as a mere symbol. And as we will see, belief in the resurrection was as difficult for people in Jesus's day as it is for us. Ancient and modern worldviews alike believe that resurrections from the dead simply can't happen. The evidence for Jesus's resurrection was formidable. It answered people's intellectual objections then and still can do so today.

However, accepting the bare fact of the resurrection does not automatically make it a living hope for us. We must understand not only that it happened but also, just as important, what it means. Many of us will have trouble thinking of any time that we heard an extensive treatment of the resurrection from the pulpit outside of Easter Sunday. In mainline Protestant pulpits the resurrection is usually seen as a general concept, a symbol that somehow good will triumph over evil. And when the resurrection is preached in evangelical church pulpits, the sermon often consists of a lengthy argument that it really happened. Yet it is one thing to know about the resurrection, and it is another thing, as Paul says, "to *know the power* of his resurrection" (Philippians 3:10), to know it personally and experientially. Surprisingly, the church has not given us much guidance in that.

In my own church tradition, Presbyterian and Reformed, classic systematic theologies give far more attention to Jesus's death on the cross than to this resurrection. Charles Hodge, the Princeton theologian, spends 127 pages on the cross and only four on the resurrection. Other theological treatments are similar.[10] Sam Allberry writes that many Christians, while believing in the resurrection and rehearsing that belief every Easter Sunday, "then effectively stick it back in a drawer for the rest of the year" because they are "at a loss to know what to do with it."[11] Verses like Romans 4:25—"he . . . was raised for our justification"—show us that it is not just the death of Jesus but also his resurrection that saves us. Yet when most Christians give a "gospel" presentation to explain how we can be saved, they talk exclusively about the cross and make the resurrection an afterthought or leave it out altogether.

The Good Invasion

The resurrection is not a stupendous magic trick but an invasion. And the event that saved us—the movement from cross to resurrection—now remakes the lives of Christians from the inside out, by the power of the Spirit.

The cross and the resurrection together—and only together—bring the future new creation, the omnipotent power through which God renews and heals the entire world, *into our present*. When Christ paid the debt of sin on the cross, the veil in the temple was ripped from top to bottom (Matthew 27:51). That veil represented the separation of humanity from the holy presence of God. That presence had once made the earth a paradise and now, because of the death of Christ, that presence *can* come to us, and because of the resurrection of Christ, it *does* come to us. The risen Christ sends us the Holy Spirit, and both Christ and the Spirit are the "firstfruits" (Romans 8:23; 1 Corinthians 15:20–23), the "earnest" (Ephesians 1:13–14; 2 Corinthians 1:22,23, 5:5 KJV), a first installment, a down payment on the future triumph over death and of a new, remade material world. This renewing power from the future is only here partially, but it is actual and substantial—and has entered the present world.

The "incomparably great power" with which God raised Jesus from the dead is in us now (Romans 8:23; Ephesians 1:19–20). So we are to live in the "light" of the future "new creation" (Romans 13:11–13; Galatians 6:15; cf. 1 Corinthians 6:1–2). That is, we are to participate in that future resurrection life in the way we live now. If Jesus was raised from the dead, it changes everything: how we conduct relationships, our attitudes toward wealth and power, how we work in our vocations, our understanding and practice of sexuality, race relations, and justice.

Also, the cross and the resurrection together—and only together—give us the basic shape or pattern by which Christians now "live in light of the new creation." The cross and resurrection is the Great Reversal. Christ saves us through weakness, by giving up power and succumbing to a seeming defeat. But he triumphs—not despite the weakness and loss of power but *because of it* and *through it*. The Great Reversal becomes "a dynamic" that "opens out onto a rhythm of life, an ethic, and a way of looking at and living in the world" and every aspect of life.[12] By living this principle, death and resurrection, we renew human life here—only partially, but substantially. The "already but not yet" presence of the new creation avoids both naivete and cynicism, both utopianism and defeatism.

An Outline of the Book

This is the basic thesis of the book—that the resurrection, the Great Reversal, brings us both the power and the pattern for living life now connected to God's future new creation.

To unfold this theme, I will begin in chapter 1 by looking at the resurrection as a historical fact. It is of course much more than that, but it is not less. Modern skepticism about the supernatural makes it difficult for people to believe in the historical, bodily resurrection of Jesus. But without the miracle of the resurrection our infallible confidence in a future triumph over evil and death vanishes. Then, in the following four chapters I will explore how the resurrection as the Great Reversal is the key for understanding the plotline of the entire Bible, as well as the operating principle for the life of a Christian. In the sixth and seventh chapters I will examine how personal resurrection faith begins by looking at five famous case studies: Mary, John, Thomas, Peter, and Paul. In the final five chapters I will look at specific areas of life and explore how the resurrection gives us unique resources for living faithfully and distinctively in each one.

Perhaps the most ordinary, daily benefit of the resurrection is this. To follow not a dead, revered teacher but rather a risen Lord is to have him actually *with* us. In Revelation 3:20 Jesus says he "stands at the door and knocks" and that if "anyone hears my voice and opens the door," he will come in and eat with them "and they with me." It is commonly thought that this is an invitation to nonbelievers to "open their hearts to Jesus," but in the context of Revelation 3 Jesus is speaking to the church, to Christians. To eat with someone was and is to have fellowship with them. Jesus is saying to believers that there is a potential for rich, intimate communion with him, for knowing him and knowing his love, that is generally untapped.

Because of the resurrection, he is not a deceased writer we know only through his books. He is alive and he is calling to us. "Here I am!" he says to you (Revelation 3:20). Open up and love him and listen to him. Those who do so will "awaken from despair and put away the imaginations of darkness."[13]

HOPE IN
TIMES
OF FEAR

CHAPTER I

CERTAIN HOPE

Now, brothers and sisters, I want to remind you of the gospel I preached to you. . . . For what I received I passed on to you as of first importance: that Christ died for our sins according to the Scriptures, that he was buried, that he was raised on the third day according to the Scriptures, and that he appeared to Cephas, and then to the Twelve. After that, he appeared to more than five hundred of the brothers and sisters at the same time, most of whom are still living, though some have fallen asleep. Then he appeared to James, then to all the apostles, and last of all he appeared to me also, as to one abnormally born. For I am the least of the apostles and do not even deserve to be called an apostle, because I persecuted the church of God. But by the grace of God I am what I am, and his grace to me was not without effect. No, I worked harder than all of them—yet not I, but the grace of God that was with me.

—1 CORINTHIANS 15:1,3–10

The heart of the Christian faith is the gospel. "It is the power of God that brings salvation," Paul says in Romans 1:16. The gospel is infinitely rich and can be expounded at great length, as we see in the books of Galatians and Romans. But the value of this passage in 1 Corinthians is that Paul gives us the gospel briefly, and this enables us to get a clearer view of all of its constituent aspects and points. The passage tells us that Christianity is a historical, reasonable, and gracious faith.

A Historical Faith

The gospel begins with the reporting of certain historical events. Christianity is rightly seen as a life-changing experience, but it will transform you only if you accept as facts that certain events occurred in history.

When I was in college I took courses studying the religions of the world. Looking back on my studies, it became clear than no other faith started by saying, "Above all and before everything else, you must believe that these historical events happened." Certainly all the religions had origin stories and accounts of various heroes of the faith. But such stories were provided primarily as examples to emulate. The main message was "Live in this way and find the path of wisdom and you will find unity with the infinite."

Christianity opens not with "Here's how you have to live," but "Here's what Jesus did for you in history." First, he died for our sins and was buried, and second, he was raised to life on the third day and he appeared to many eyewitnesses.

An Ahistorical Faith?

One reason to stress the historicity of the crucifixion and resurrection is to provide a note of caution about the ongoing effort that started two centuries ago to create a liberal Christianity that is more like other religions.

In the early part of the nineteenth century there was a movement to remove the supernatural elements from Christianity in order to align it more with modern sensibilities. Friedrich Schleiermacher taught that Christianity was not a matter of faith in historical events but rather an internal feeling of dependence on God. Albrecht Ritschl taught that we could no longer believe in miracles, and so we had to reread the reports of Jesus's incarnate birth, death, and resurrection not as historical events but as legends and parables and examples of how to live. The basic reasoning of this movement went something like this: "There are many superstitious, miraculous elements in the Christian faith. Modern people can't believe these things actually happened. So if we are going to appeal to the modern world, we will have to reinterpret them as fiction, but fiction that preserves the essential principles of living that are in the Christian faith."

How did this program of modernization treat Easter, the doctrine that Christ was raised bodily from the dead? The new account went like this: "We can't believe in a literal, physical, historical resurrection anymore. Ah, but we still have the *idea* of Easter. Doesn't nature itself teach you that after winter comes spring? That even in a disaster and after death there can be new beginnings? That even in our misfortunes we can discover lessons and we can grow and we can begin afresh? That's the principle of Easter."

Liberal Christianity has taught that it doesn't matter whether these events in the story of Jesus's life actually happened. All that matters is that Christians be good, ethical people who love others and make the world a better place. This is an effort to create a non-historical faith, one that isn't grounded in what God has actually done in history, but only in what we do and how we live. Liberal Christianity even tries to read itself back into history as the original, true Christianity. It claims that the original Jesus was simply a human teacher of justice and love. Only decades later did these miraculous, supernatural elements get introduced into the legends about his life, and only then was he presented as a Son of God who rose from the dead. In this telling, the original faith was not about miraculous historical events but rather was simply an ethic of love.

This narrative, however, is not actually an updated version of Christianity. Rather, it is the creation of a different religion altogether. Christianity's unique message—that you are saved not by what *you* have to do but by what *God* has done—is swept away. The crushing weight of self-salvation is put squarely back onto the believer, whereas the historical gospel took that burden off of us.

The stark difference between liberal Christianity and the original faith was put famously by H. Richard Niebuhr. He described liberalism thus: "A

God without wrath brought men without sin into a Kingdom without judgment through the ministrations of Christ without a Cross."[1] And, he could have added, without a resurrection. Liberal Christianity—a message of simple ethical love and hope—could never have turned anyone's life, much less the entire Roman world, upside down.

The electrifying original message was this: God's power has come from outside of history into this world. Jesus died for our sins in our place so that through faith we can know his love and receive a guarantee of eternal life—all by grace, as a gift. He also rose from the dead to bring into history the powers of the age to come, in which we will all be resurrected and every tear will be wiped away (Hebrews 6:5; 2 Peter 3:13; Romans 8:18–25). Because Jesus's death for sin and resurrection happened in history, everything has changed. *Everything.*

In 1 Corinthians 15:14 Paul says, "If Christ has not been raised, our preaching is useless," and the Greek word for *useless* is *kenos*, without power. Paul is saying that mere ethical exhortations—that "we need to work against injustice" or "we need to keep up hope in the face of anxiety"—as right as they are, are nonetheless *impotent* if Jesus hasn't been raised from the dead in history. If he was raised, we have not only every reason in the world to work for the good, but also the actual inward power to do so. But if he was not raised, then, both the ancient philosophers and modern scientists agree, the world will eventually burn up, and no one will be around to mourn for it, and nothing anyone does will in the end make any difference.

Liberal Christianity, though now in steep demographic decline among believers, is nonetheless highly popular with the modern media, which sees it as the only viable version of the faith.[2] But a non-historical faith—a non-supernatural faith—simply won't do. It did not change lives and the world at the beginning, and it won't do so now. As John Updike wrote:

> *Make no mistake: if He rose at all*
> *It was as His body;*
> *If the cells' dissolution did not reverse, the molecule reknit,*

the amino acids rekindle,
the Church will fall.
It was not as the flowers,
each soft spring recurrent;
it was not as His Spirit in the mouths and fuddled eyes of the
eleven apostles;
it was as His flesh; ours.
The same hinged thumbs and toes,
the same valved heart
that—pierced—died, withered, paused, and then regathered
out of enduring Might
new strength to enclose.
Let us not mock God with metaphor,
analogy, sidestepping, transcendence,
making of the event a parable, a sign painted in the faded
credulity of earlier ages:
let us walk through the door.
The stone is rolled back, not papier-mâché
not a stone in a story,
but the vast rock of materiality that in the slow grinding of
time will eclipse for each of us
the wide light of day.
And if we have an angel at the tomb,
make it a real angel,
weighty with Max Planck's quanta, vivid with hair, opaque in
the dawn light, robed in real linen
spun on a definite loom.
Let us not seek to make it less monstrous,
for our own convenience, our own sense of beauty,
lest, awakened in one unthinkable hour, we are embarrassed
by the miracle,
and crushed by remonstrance.[3]

A Reasonable Faith

Because Christianity is a historical faith, it is also a reasonable one, and 1 Corinthians 15 is brimming with reasons to believe. Many modern theories have been developed to explain away the claim of the resurrection, but these verses provide answers to them all.

One of the oldest theories is that the legends of Jesus's resurrection developed only many decades after the actual events had faded from living memory. But the 1 Corinthians text is itself an important piece of evidence against that view. Verses 3–7 are now seen by most New Testament scholars as not an original Pauline composition but rather an early gospel summary used by the earliest church in its evangelism and instruction which Paul is citing. As he says in verse 3, these words were "received," not created by him, and then "passed on" to others. Scholars also show that the vocabulary in these verses—"according to the Scriptures," "on the third day," "the Twelve" are not terms Paul uses elsewhere in his writings. So this was a gospel summary that was already in widespread use by Christians all around the Mediterranean world when Paul wrote. Since this letter to the Corinthians was written only fifteen or twenty years after Jesus's death, the eminent biblical scholar James Dunn concludes that "we can be entirely confident" that this summary in 1 Corinthians 15:3–7 "was formulated . . . within months of Jesus's death."[4]

That disproves the theory that Jesus's resurrection was a legend developed only after all the people who were present at his death were gone. Instead, this text demonstrates that almost instantly thousands of Jewish men and women were worshipping Jesus as the Savior and risen Lord (Acts 2:41). Unlike the Romans, the Jews "did not believe that a man might become a god. . . . [Such] claims [were] as stupefying as they were . . . repellent. . . . Not merely blasphemy, it was madness."[5] A growing movement of Jews who worshipped a human being as the Son of God was completely unprecedented. And it happened immediately after Jesus's death. Something momentous must have happened to bring this about. If it was not the resurrection, what else could it have been?

Paul also says Jesus was raised "on the third day," which undermines a second modern theory, that the earliest followers of Jesus did not literally see the resurrected Christ with their eyes but only experienced his continued presence with them in their hearts. "The third day" shows that Jesus's resurrection was an actual event with a time stamp.

Paul then goes on at length to report that the risen Jesus appeared "to Cephas (Peter), and then to the Twelve. After that, he appeared to more than five hundred of the brothers and sisters at the same time, most of whom are still living, though some have fallen asleep. Then he appeared to James, then to all the apostles, and last of all he appeared to me also, as to one abnormally born" (1 Corinthians 15:5–7). This list challenges a third modern hypothesis, namely, that the resurrection was a hoax. The problem is not only that Peter, Jesus's brother James, and Paul himself all claimed to have literally seen Christ back from the dead. Jesus also appeared to five hundred people at one time. There were literally hundreds of corroborating eyewitnesses.

Contemporary readers might think that in Paul's day everyone was highly credulous and superstitious. So if you wanted to claim that the founder of your religion had risen from the dead, all you'd have to do is say, "He rose, and you must believe it because I say so." Instead, Paul writes as if his readers would be unwilling to accept such a claim without evidence— much like people today. So over 75 percent of the words in this gospel presentation are dedicated to listing the eyewitnesses of the resurrection. When he gives their names and says "most of [them] are still living," he is inviting anyone to seek them out and hear their eyewitness testimony for themselves. In other words, Paul is *not* what has been called a "fideist," someone who says, "I have no arguments or reasons for you; you must just take a wild leap of faith in the dark and believe what I'm telling you despite the lack of evidence."

We might ask why an ancient audience would be so slow to believe in something like the resurrection. Surely people in those days *were* less skeptical about claims of miracles than people are today? But in his book *The Resurrection of the Son of God*, biblical scholar N. T. Wright explains at length that both Greco-Roman culture and Judaism of that time had strong beliefs that made the claim of an individual bodily resurrection incredible. Jews of Jesus's day either did not believe in resurrection at all or believed only in a general resurrection of the righteous at the end of time when the whole world was renewed. What they did not think possible at all was a single, individual resurrection in the midst of history while evil, suffering, and death continued as before.[6] This then refutes a fourth modern belief, that Jesus's followers were so grief stricken and desirous for him to be alive that they convinced themselves he was resurrected. Wright makes the strongest case that this could not have happened. Such a resurrection was too unimaginable for Jews. It was only the evidence of the empty tomb and all the eyewitness accounts that overcame their deep skepticism about the claim of resurrection.

> Any first-century historian should recognize . . . that whatever it was that the early Christians were expecting, wanting, hoping and praying for, this was *not* what they said, after Easter, had happened. . . . Something had *happened*, something which was not at all what they expected or hoped for, something around which they had to reconstruct their lives.[7]

Paul's Evidence for the Resurrection

In Acts 26 Paul spoke to King Agrippa and Festus, the Roman governor. He talked about Christ's death and resurrection. In the middle of his discussion, Festus cried, "Paul, your great learning is driving you insane" (Acts 26:24). Paul's response was respectful but surprisingly confident.

> "I am not insane, most excellent Festus," Paul replied. "What I am saying is true and reasonable. The king is familiar with these

things, and I can speak freely to him. I am convinced that none of this has escaped his notice, because it was not done in a corner."

(Acts 26:25–26)

Paul says that his faith in the resurrection is "reasonable"—a word that refers to careful, rational thought. He is not making mere assertions but is offering arguments. Paul can also say confidently to Agrippa that he knew the facts of Jesus's death, of the empty tomb, and of the reports of the eyewitnesses to the resurrection, because these things were "not done in a corner." They were public knowledge and so there was substantial evidence for what he was saying.

Paul is doing in 1 Corinthians 15 for all readers, present and future, what he did before Agrippa and Festus. To summarize, he provides two main arguments for the resurrection.

First, the tomb was empty. The gospel summary does not merely say that Jesus died but also "that he was buried." That would be redundant unless to make the point that this was not a "spiritual" event, that the body was gone and the tomb empty.[8] The fact of the empty tomb is accepted by most scholars, including those who don't accept the resurrection. It was extremely important to Jews to bury people and not leave bodies out simply to decay.[9] And the text of 1 Corinthians—as well as this gospel summary—proves that the very earliest Christians believed and proclaimed Jesus's resurrection from the dead. Therefore, "it is hard to imagine belief in a risen Jesus getting very far if one could easily point to the grave in which he was still present."[10]

The second main argument is that a large number of people, across a diversity of circumstances, testified that they had seen the risen Jesus. We are not talking about one single sighting, or several appearances in one remote location where they could be staged. Peter Williams gives the list:

The resurrected Jesus is recorded as appearing in Judea (Mt 28:9; Lk 24:31, 36) and in Galilee (Mt 28:16–20; Jn 21:1–23), in town (Lk 24:36) and countryside (Lk 24:15), indoors (Lk 24:36) and outdoors (Mt 28:9,16; Lk 24:15; Jn 21:1–23), in the morning (Jn 21:1–23) and the evening (Lk 24:29,36; Jn 20:19), by prior appointment (Mt 28:16) and without prior appointment (Mt 28:9; Lk 24:15,34,36; Jn 21:1–23), close (Mt 28:9, 19; Lk 24:15,36; Jn 21:9–23) and distant (Jn 21:4–8), on a hill (Mt 28:16) and by a lake (Jn 21:4), to groups of men (Jn 21:2; 1 Cor 15:5,7) and groups of women (Mt 28:9), to individuals (Lk 24:34; 1 Cor 15:5,7–8) and groups of up to five hundred (1 Cor 15:6), sitting (Jn 21:15 implied), standing (Jn 21:4), walking (Lk 24:15; Jn 21:20–22), eating (Lk 24:43; Jn 21:15), and *always* talking (Mt 28:9–10, 18–20; Lk 24:17–30, 36–49; Jn 20:15–17, 19–29; 21:6–22). Many are explicitly close-up encounters involving conversations. It is hard to imagine this pattern of appearances [recorded] in the Gospels and early Christian letters without there having been multiple individuals who claimed to have seen Jesus risen from the dead.[11]

Many have sought to explain away these eyewitness accounts. The most common theory is that they were simply made up by the New Testament writers. But here in this well-attested, early public document, Paul says that most of these witnesses were still alive and readily accessible. Such claims would have been impossible if the witnesses never existed. In addition, as is often pointed out, the gospels claim that the very first witnesses of the resurrection were women. Since women in that patriarchal culture were not allowed to give evidence in court,[12] there would be no plausible reason that the gospel writers would have invented them. The only historically plausible reason that women would have been recorded as seeing the risen Christ is: they did.

As previously noted, some explain the resurrection appearances as psychological wish fulfillment or hallucinations or ecstatic visions on the part of the witnesses. But the variety of times and circumstances of the encounters makes that highly unlikely. For example, how could five hundred people have the same hallucination at once?[13] And as Wright has argued, the Jewish worldview made it inconceivable that a single person could be resurrected in the middle of history. It would have neither occurred to Jesus's disciples to make up such an idea nor to think they could get other Jews to believe it if they did. It would have required some extraordinary, impossible-to-deny, powerful evidence to get first-century Jews to overcome all they had been taught and to believe that Jesus was the resurrected Son of God. According to 1 Corinthians 15, that is exactly what they received.[14]

So we are left with two hard-to-refute facts: that the tomb was empty and that hundreds of people claimed to have seen the risen Christ. If we had only the empty tomb, then we could plausibly claim the body was stolen. If we only had the testimonies, we could say they had to be fantasies. Together, however, they give evidence that something extraordinary happened. N. T. Wright says that if you rule out a resurrection, you have a formidable challenge—to come up with a historically possible alternate explanation for these two facts, as well as for the birth of the church itself. He writes:

> The early Christians did not invent the empty tomb and the meetings or sightings of the risen Jesus. . . . Nobody was expecting this kind of thing; no kind of conversion experience would have invented it, no matter how guilty (or how forgiven) they felt, no matter how many hours they pored over the scriptures. To suggest otherwise is to stop doing history and enter into a fantasy world of our own.[15]

The Gospels' Evidence for the Resurrection

To these two most basic pieces of evidence we can add a third, one to which we alluded in the introduction and that comes from the gospels' resurrection accounts themselves. We could call this category "the strangeness of the risen Jesus." In his Gifford Lectures, John Polkinghorne says that the inability of the first eyewitnesses to recognize the resurrected Christ was remarkable. He argues that if people of that time (or ours) were to make up a story about someone resurrected, they would have drawn from the two kinds of legends about people returning from the dead, depicting him as either "a dazzling heavenly figure or a resuscitated corpse."[16] N. T. Wright agrees. There were stories in the Jewish apocalyptic tradition of figures appearing "in blinding light or dazzling radiance, or wreathed in clouds." Daniel 12:2–3 describes the resurrected at the end of time as "shining like the brightness of the heavens." 1 Samuel 28 tells about King Saul speaking with the ghost of the dead prophet Samuel, who appears as "a ghostly figure" (verse 13). Surely if Jewish gospel writers wanted to make up a story to teach that Jesus had risen from the dead, they could have drawn on those accounts and depicted him as too bright to look upon or as a frightening phantasm. Instead the risen Jesus appears to be completely ordinary—"as a human being among human beings."[17]

On the other hand, Polkinghorne says that if the gospel writers conceived Jesus not as being divinely transformed or as a spirit but merely as resuscitated, brought back to life as Lazarus was, then surely he would have looked exactly the same. There is no indication that anyone had any problem recognizing Lazarus after he was resurrected (John 11). Yet in these resurrection narratives Jesus looks different enough that his disciples don't recognize him—until they do. The closest analogy would be meeting a childhood friend in your fifties whom you have not seen since you were both in your teens. You would not recognize her at first, until you looked more closely. So here Jesus is being shown to have a resurrected body—very human and continuous with his former body (he still has wounds where the nails were used in his crucifixion, John 20:27)—but now transformed.

Wright adds that Jesus's body is also "trans-physical." It can be touched, and he can eat a fish (Luke 24:36–43), and yet twice the gospels speak of him entering through locked doors (John 20:19,26). Jesus is neither a ghost nor a dazzling apparition, nor does he have a revived, normal human body. There simply was nothing like this in Jewish and Greco-Roman literature and legend for the gospel writers to draw on. These were wholly new conceptual categories, major departures from anything any religion or culture had ever imagined before. It was an entirely new way to think of body and spirit.

Wright and Polkinghorne argue that it is extremely unlikely that anyone fabricating stories about the resurrection would have conceived of a risen Christ like this. No one could have thought this up. "This would be a strange motif to recur in stories that were merely made up," concludes Polkinghorne. "It seems likely to me that, on the contrary, it is the kernel of a genuine historical reminiscence."[18]

Finally, we can add a fourth kind of evidence for the resurrection from the history of the early church. N. T. Wright looks at the inexplicability of the early church's resurrection faith. Modern people assume that ancient people believed that resurrections from the dead were possible "but that now, with hundreds of years of scientific research on our side, we know that dead people stay dead." But Wright then adds that this modern way of understanding ancient people's views "is ridiculous." He argues: "The [historical] evidence was massive and the conclusion universally drawn. . . . Ancient paganism contains all kinds of theories, but whenever resurrection is mentioned the answer is firm negative: we know that doesn't happen."[19]

But what about Judaism? Wright says that a majority of first-century Jews believed in a bodily resurrection of the righteous at the end of time. And yet Christians' belief in the resurrection almost overnight developed "remarkable modifications" or what he calls "mutations." Unlike in Judaism, which contained a range of beliefs and emphases (and skepticism) about the resurrection, *all* Christians immediately believed in the resurrection, and it was central to their faith. Judaism had speculated that resurrected people would have a resuscitated but basically identical body. But as we have seen, Christians believed the resurrected body would be physical but have a range of new properties and powers. Judaism had also taught that if the resurrection happened, it would all happen at the end of history, but Christians insisted that it has already happened to one person in the middle of history. Finally, no Jews believed that the Messiah would die and rise again, nor that any human being could possibly be the Son of God. Yet the early Christians, most of them Jews, did believe just that.[20]

In all these ways the belief of the early church about resurrection was a radical departure in the history of human culture and thought. And there was no debate within the early church over this—this new belief was instant. Wright says: "These mutations are so striking in an area of human experience where societies tend to be very conservative, that they force the historian . . . to ask, 'Why did they occur?'" If historians tackle that question, they will find it difficult to find a plausible explanation for Christians' overnight break with all other beliefs including their own upbringing. Wright concludes that it is "impossible . . . to account for the early Christian belief in Jesus as Messiah without the resurrection."[21]

Can We Know That the Resurrection Happened?

Does all this *prove* beyond a shadow of rational doubt that the resurrection of Jesus Christ actually occurred? As Wright and others point out, no event in past history can be empirically proven the way something can be tested in a laboratory. We can't know that William the Conqueror invaded England in 1066 in exactly the same way we know that a compound liquefies at such and such temperature. However, once we make that distinction, we can still say we know that things in history happened if there is a great deal of historical evidence that they did.

So what about the resurrection? If you ask historians to answer the question "What explanation do you have for the rapid development of this new view of resurrection and for the explosive growth of the church?" they must answer historically. Even if they hold a philosophical presupposition that disbelieves in miracles, they still have to find some alternative explanation that is historically possible and, as Wright argues, that is not at all easy. "No other explanations have been offered, in two thousand years of sneering skepticism . . . that can satisfactorily account for how the tomb came to be empty, how the disciples came to see Jesus, and how their lives and worldviews were transformed."[22]

What this means is that, on the one hand, the use of human reason alone cannot force us to believe in the resurrection. There is room for intellectual doubt of most any historical event. On the other hand, we can see that belief in the resurrection of Christ is *not* a blind leap of faith. It has left an enormous footprint, as it were, in history. This is why it "poses that kind of challenge to the larger worldview of both the historian and the scientist." Resurrection faith is not blind belief that rejects human reason—it "transcends but includes what we call history and what we call science."[23]

Indeed, almost nothing important that we base our lives on can be demonstrably proven. Our moral values, our beliefs about human nature, our beliefs about whether the material universe was its own cause or was created by God—all of these fundamental assumptions about reality come through a combination of reasoning, evidence, and faith.[24] Can we *know*, for example, that all human beings have equal dignity and human rights? Although there is much evidence for that belief, human rights cannot be scientifically proven so that any skeptic would be forced to accept them. And can we *know* that the resurrection happened? Even if you come to believe, on rational grounds, that the resurrection of Jesus probably happened, you still must exercise faith to become a Christian.[25]

A Gracious Faith

So while Paul has emphasized the historical and rational side of Christianity, he does not mean that it is sufficient to merely give mental assent to doctrines and principles. We must appropriate these truths personally, by faith. Belief or nonbelief in the resurrection is never merely an intellectual process. We are not computers. We are flesh-and-blood human beings, and when we confront the claim of the resurrection, we address it not only with logic but with a lifetime of hopes and fears and preexisting faith commitments. And we will never be able to accept it until we see our need for God's grace.

That is why immediately after the summary of doctrine in 1 Corinthians 15:3–8 Paul adds a testimony of how these truths changed him personally.

> For I am the least of the apostles and do not even deserve to be called an apostle, because I persecuted the church of God. But by the grace of God I am what I am, and his grace to me was not without effect. No, I worked harder than all of them—yet not I, but the grace of God that was with me.
>
> **(1 Corinthians 15:9–10)**

What was it that made Paul into a completely different person? Three times he uses the word *grace*. The man formerly known as Saul in no way thought he needed mercy and forgiveness. He was, in his mind, far more zealous for the truth and for God than anyone he knew (Philippians 3:6). But when life humbled him and he saw his flaws and insufficiency and that he needed God's grace, that made him open to claims and truths to which he was previously closed.

Before we become Christians, most of us also think of ourselves as sincere seekers after the truth. We feel like we're pretty good people. But most Christians, like Paul, look back on their lives and see that they had never really been sincere seekers after truth at all. They had wanted a truth and a God that fit their desire to be in charge of their own lives. And yet God came after them, found them, and graciously helped them see their own blindness and their unwarranted distrust of him.

This is what happened to Paul. He thought he knew who God was and who Jesus was, and he got it all wrong. There is a 1992 movie titled *Hero* starring Dustin Hoffman. Hoffman plays Bernie LaPlante, who, at the risk of his life, rescues fifty-five people out of a crashed, burning airplane. The plot of the rest of the movie hinges on the fact that he is such an unheroic, unimpressive character that no one believes he did it. Instead the public chooses a more photogenic and attractive person and convinces itself that he was the one who saved everyone. All the people around Bernie LaPlante say he couldn't possibly have done that. But he did. They thought they knew him. But they didn't. Their eyes were blinded by superficialities and they could not discern true heroism.

Paul (like the rest of us) was just as spiritually blind to the nature of salvation. He thought that he could save himself, that he could make God bless him because of his zeal and righteousness. And he thought that Jesus—that uneducated, homeless, unemployed carpenter who died a cursed criminal's death—could not possibly have been a Savior. Nor could he have been raised from the dead. Not only did Paul get it all wrong, but looking back he knew he had *wanted* God to be a God he could control, and that he had *wanted* Jesus to be a false teacher. That put him in the driver's seat of his life. He had not been a sincere seeker after truth. He deserved to be judged and condemned by God.

Instead he was confronted by God, forgiven for everything, and made an apostle! Despite how spectacular Paul's turnaround was, he insists that, in the end, all of us are in the same basic spiritual condition. He writes:

> There is no one righteous, not even one; there is no one who understands; there is no one who seeks God. All have turned away, they have together become worthless; there is no one who does good, not even one.
>
> **(Romans 3:10–12)**[26]

When he says "no one is righteous," he does not mean that there are not millions of people who, like Paul, are leading moral lives. What he denies, however, is that in so doing they are actually seeking the true God. Unless we come to see our spiritual blindness and our need for God's help, we are all, like Paul, living good lives primarily for ourselves, in order to stay in control of our lives. We do so with distorted views of God we have devised out of our own self-interest.

Paul was brought to see the inadequacy of his conceptions by a visual encounter with Jesus. For the rest of us, there are other ways that we may be "mugged by reality."

The COVID-19 pandemic of 2020 was something that modern people, with their faith in science and technology, did not believe could happen. It brought death to our doors in ways we thought would be impossible in modern times. There have been a variety of responses to the threat. Many, to prove their fearlessness and freedom, refuse safety precautions of any kind. Some have been highly self-protective without regard for others. There were bitter fights between parents and teachers over whether schools should reopen. Each side accused the other of self-preservation at the expense of other people's lives. During the crisis many churches took their Sunday and other gatherings online, and to their surprise they often got many times more viewers than they had members. It meant that at least some people were "looking in" who previously had not thought they needed spiritual resources. What we all need in such frightening times is faith in the resurrection.

In 1527 the bubonic plague was spreading across Europe, and Elector John (Luther's sovereign) ordered Luther to leave in order to save his life. Instead, Luther remained and stayed to minister to the sick and dying. He eventually turned his own home into a field hospital. In the midst of it, Luther wrote a public letter—"Whether One May Flee from a Deadly Plague." It is a remarkably prudent and nuanced document but, above all, it exhibits a fearlessness in the face of death. He begins by saying some Christians believed they should flee and others that they should stay. Luther responds that both can be right.

First, "to flee from death . . . is a natural tendency, implanted by God and not forbidden. . . . Appropriate it is therefore to seek to preserve life and avoid death if this can be done without harm to our neighbor."[27] Luther argues that to risk your own life needlessly, just to supposedly demonstrate your freedom from fear, is proud and reckless. Your life is not your own—it is God's—and all human life is precious. The Bible demands quarantine for infected people (Leviticus 13–14), and so it is wrong to refuse the precautions and measures necessary to stop the spread of disease. Therefore, to "distance" and do everything to preserve your life and those of others is right and good.[28]

On the other hand, if Christians find themselves in situations where their retreat from the plague would leave anyone else defenseless to it, for the same reason (the infinite value of human life) they should stay. "Christ does not want his weak ones to be abandoned [by the strong]."[29] If the sick in your home, neighborhood, or town would not get sufficient care because of your withdrawal then you should not go. In particular, Luther argued that ministers, mayors, judges, "and the like" must stay and "remain steadfast before the peril of death."[30] He knew the disorder into which communities can descend if "frontline" workers abandon their posts out of self-preservation. "To abandon an entire community . . . to all kinds of danger such as fires, murder, riots, and every imaginable disaster is a great sin."[31] Luther concludes that it may be right to flee the plague and it may be wrong to flee, and that therefore all people should assess their situation and no one should condemn the other for their decision. How different from the combination of panic, recklessness, and constant recriminations that we have seen in our own world during the pandemic.

The foundation of Luther's remarkably calm yet realistic response to the plague was his complete lack of fear of death. Fear of death can lead you either to a strident protestation of your freedom from safety precautions as a way to conquer your anxieties or else to a panicky capitulation to them. If the fear is conquered, however, it enables you to then ask the important question with more objectivity: What is the most loving thing for me to do in my circumstances? And then you can do it.

Luther explains where that fearlessness comes from. The gospel has given us freedom from "the real and spiritual pestilence" of sin and Satan through the death of Jesus. And now we can regularly "reverently meditate . . . upon death and the resurrection."[32]

We can draw strength from the resurrection, however, only if we believe it happened.

In May of 1970, when President Richard Nixon escalated the Vietnam War by sending U.S. troops into Cambodia, many university campuses held "student strikes." I was at Bucknell University, where for many days students gathered on the central quadrangle with an open mic where anyone could come and speak. It was a peaceful time of intense discussion and dialogue. Only months earlier I had found vital faith in Jesus myself, and I was part of a fairly tiny group of ten to fifteen Christians who sat together on the quad and wondered how to break into the conversation. Finally one of our number made a sign and put it up, and all day one or two of us sat under it at the edge of the crowd. It read:

THE RESURRECTION OF JESUS CHRIST IS INTELLECTUALLY
CREDIBLE AND EXISTENTIALLY SATISFYING.

Most people ignored it, and one or two gave us only expletives. But I had many good conversations that week. That was when I came to realize that each doubter faced two issues—the rational and the "existential" or the personal. One female student admitted that she didn't need to look at the evidence because it wouldn't matter to her even if it happened. She didn't need a savior. A male student said something like "But I don't want the universe to be like that, and I doubt that it is."

When Paul met the risen Christ, it challenged him *both* rationally and personally. He not only had to overcome his deep rational doubts that a resurrection could happen in the midst of history, and that such a weakling could be the Messiah. He also had to see that his righteousness was insufficient, that he was spiritually lost, and that nothing less than the death and resurrection of the Son of God could save him. Only when Paul, who thought he was the best, finally came to see he was *the least* (1 Corinthians 15:9) did he become someone great.

Look at the remarkable self-image Paul had, grounded in the living hope in Christ's death and resurrection for him. Paul does not say that he *was* the least of the apostles but now is the most successful. Nor does he say he is an unworthy sinner and therefore of course he's not really accomplished much of anything. No, he says he *is* the least of the apostles (and "the worst of sinners," 1 Timothy 1:16), and at the same time says he has borne the most fruit. We know little of such a self-image. We think that either you think highly of yourself or you think little of yourself. Paul is able to hold together two true assessments, namely, that in himself he is still a flawed, sinful man deserving of rejection and that at the very same time, in the grace of God, he is loved and fruitful. How can Paul do that? How can Paul say in one place, "I'm the worst of sinners," and then confidently laugh in the face of death, challenging kings who could snuff out his life, and lead this history-changing movement?

You may think, "If I thought I was the worst of all sinners, I would be on the verge of suicide." If you say that, you still don't fully understand the gospel. When you believe that in Jesus Christ the Father loves and fully accepts you, then you can admit your sin and weakness and at the same time know he's going to forgive you and use you in spite of it. That's the reason why Paul has his incredible self-image. It's astonishing. There's nothing like it.

Did the resurrection happen? Yes, but you will be able to accept it only if you let it confront not only your reason and head but also your self-image and the commitments of your heart.

CHAPTER 2

FUTURE HOPE

"The time has come," he said. "The kingdom of God has come near. Repent and believe the good news!"

—MARK 1:15

The resurrection of Jesus Christ actually happened. But a fair question is—"So what?"

The Bible records several miraculous resurrections (1 Kings 17:17–24; 2 Kings 4:32–37, 13:20–21; Matthew 27:52–53; Mark 5:35–43; Luke 7:11–17; John 11:39–44; Acts 9:40, 20:9–10). They are all dramatic and moving, and they give testimony to the power of God. But is that all Jesus's resurrection is, a proof that God exists and that Jesus is the Son of God? I devoted the first chapter to the argument that the resurrection is at least that, but the rest of this book is dedicated to showing that it is infinitely more.

It has been common for Christians to believe that the cross alone saves us from our sins. Then the resurrection is viewed as a wonderful miracle that proved Jesus was the Son of God, but nothing more than that. I became a Christian during my undergraduate years and, looking back, I realized that I adopted that same attitude. I was glad to argue for the historical evidence for the resurrection, but I did not see it as something that affected how I lived my daily life now. I had not noticed Paul's statements that Jesus was "raised . . . for our justification" (Romans 4:25) and that to be a Christian is to "know the power of his resurrection" (Philippians 3:10). These verses are saying that the resurrection of Christ is a source of salvation, life, and power to us right now. But I hadn't grasped the magnitude of the promise.

It was not until I entered seminary in preparation for ministry that I learned something that I should have been taught as a new believer. The resurrection was indeed a miraculous display of God's power, but we should not see it as a *suspension* of the natural order of the world. Rather it was the beginning of the *restoration* of the natural order of the world, the world as God intended it to be. Since humanity turned away from God, both the human and natural worlds have been dominated by sin and evil, disorder and disease, suffering and death. But when Jesus rose from the dead, he inaugurated the first stage of the coming of God's kingdom power into the world to restore and heal all things.

The resurrection means not merely that Christians have a hope *for* the future but that they have hope that comes *from* the future. The Bible's startling message is that when Jesus rose, he brought the future kingdom of God into the present.[1] It is not yet here **fully** but it is here **substantially**, and Christians live an impoverished life if they do not realize what is available to them. So Paul prays for the Ephesians that "the eyes of your heart may be enlightened in order that you may know . . . his incomparably great power for us who believe. That power is the same as the mighty strength he exerted when he raised Christ from the dead and seated him at his right hand in the heavenly realms, far above all rule and authority, power and dominion, and every name that is invoked, not only in the present age but also in the one to come." (Ephesians 1:18–21)

The resurrection began the kingdom of God, and if God is going to "enlighten the eyes of our hearts" with regard to the wonder of what he has given us, we need to understand what the kingdom of God is.

The Prophecy of the Kingdom

In the Hebrew Scriptures, God is described as the King reigning over all things (Psalms 93:1, 103:19). In one sense we can say that everyone in the universe is under God's rule and therefore is in his kingdom. But the Old Testament prophets spoke of a future divine kingdom that would be established at the end of history. Isaiah predicted that a descendant of David (Isaiah 11:1) would arise, uniquely filled with God's Spirit (verses 2–3). He will rule, bringing not only justice for the poor and the oppressed (verses 4–5) but also unity among the nations and the races (verses 10–11). But the vision goes on to speak of things even more remarkable. Under his rule:

> *The wolf will live with the lamb,*
> *the leopard will lie down with the goat,*
> *the calf and the lion and the yearling together;*
> *and a little child will lead them.*
> *The cow will feed with the bear,*
> *their young will lie down together,*
> *and the lion will eat straw like the ox.*
> *The infant will play near the cobra's den,*
> *and the young child will put its hand into the viper's nest.*
> *They will neither harm nor destroy*
> *on all my holy mountain,*
> *for the earth will be filled with the knowledge of the Lord*
> *as the waters cover the sea.*

(Isaiah 11:6–9)

The literary form and the language are poetic, but the message is completely clear. This kingdom will not only bring political peace and social improvement, nature itself will be healed. The violence and bloodshed of nature will be over, along with aging (cf. Isaiah 65:20), disease, and death itself. A parallel prophecy says: "He will swallow up death forever. The Sovereign Lord will wipe away the tears from all faces" (Isaiah 25:8). This is Eden restored.

The world was created by God to be a place of perfect harmony under his rule. Every thing was cohesively woven together with every other part of creation. There was no disharmony between the body and the soul or between our feelings and our conscience. There was no conflict between individuals or the genders. The body never became disharmonious within itself—there was nothing like the disintegration of the body through disease, aging, and death. There was also perfect harmony between humanity and the animals and the environment. There was no broken relationship of any kind.

But sin, which at its heart is resistance to God's kingly authority, broke the unity between God and humanity, and that led to the breaking of all other relationships, to the "unraveling" of creation. Everything in the world—every aspect of life—is now subject to futility and decay (Genesis 3:17–19; Romans 8:20–21). Our relationships with God, one another, ourselves, and nature fell apart. War and crime, racism and poverty, anger and despair, famine and plague, aging and death are all the results of this great disintegration. God created us to glorify and enjoy him supremely, and when we turn away and love anything more than him, breakdown is the result. Where God is not acknowledged as King, there is darkness and death.

But the prophets insist that one day the Lord himself will return to the earth (Isaiah 40:3–5), and he will be called "Wonderful Counselor, Mighty God, Everlasting Father, Prince of Peace" (Isaiah 9:6). Psalm 72 describes how the true king's presence brings all of creation to flourishing (verses 1–7). God's kingly reign will bring the complete healing of creation, the reunification of humanity, and the end of physical decay and death (verses 8–14). Isaac Watts's famous hymn "Jesus Shall Reign," based on Psalm 72, is a classic:

> *Blessings abound where'er he reigns;*
> *The pris'ner leaps to loose his chains;*

The weary find eternal rest,
And all the sons of want are blest.

Where he displays his healing power,
Death and the curse are known no more;
In him the tribes of Adam boast
More blessings than their father lost.

In his most famous hymn, "Joy to the World," Watts paraphrases Psalm 96. In striking language, he announces that the kingdom of Christ means the complete reversal of all the curse of sin pronounced by the Lord on the earth in Genesis 3:18–19 ("It will produce thorns and thistles for you . . . for dust you are and to dust you will return."):

No more let sins and sorrows grow,
Nor thorns infest the ground;
He comes to make his blessings flow
Far as the curse is found!

The kingdom of God, then, "means the renewal of the world through the introduction of supernatural forces."[2] It will heal the entire world and all the dimensions of human life. From the throne of the coming King flows new life and power, such that no disease, decay, poverty, blemish, or pain can stand before it.

Near the end of the Old Testament, Daniel adds to all the other prophecies about the kingdom that it will include a bodily resurrection to eternal life (Daniel 12:1–2). And so by the time Jesus announced that he was the Messiah, the expectations were that that Messiah would heal the world, abolish all evil and suffering, and resurrect all believers into fullness of life—a life not only of endless quantity but of unimaginable quality, freed from the disintegrating effects of sin.

But Jesus told his listeners that, while the kingdom of God was at hand

(Mark 1:14–15), it would not come in a way that anyone was expecting. What Jesus told them could not have been more shocking.

The Already-but-Not-Yet Kingdom

In Jesus's day everyone who believed in the coming kingdom of God had a firmly established picture of what that would look like. "We now live in the age of sin, evil, and death. But when the Messiah, the true king, arrives that age will pass away completely and the new age of the kingdom of God will begin."

So everyone thought that the kingdom of God would come like this:

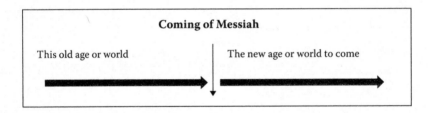

Jesus, however, confounded all of these expectations. He claimed to be the Messiah foretold by the prophets (Luke 4:14–20). He taught that with him the kingdom of God had arrived (Luke 17:20–21). He claimed that he brought the new covenant and the Spirit (cf. John 6:45 with Jeremiah 31:34 and Isaiah 54:13); that to believe in him delivers us from death (John 11:25–26); that the "exodus" by which God will liberate the whole creation from slavery to death and decay is through him (Luke 9:31); and that he was building the prophesied new temple (John 2:19–21). In other words, Jesus claimed in the greatest detail that every feature of the reign of God had begun with his first coming.

And yet. Jesus is just as clear that the kingdom of God has *not* come in all its fullness. He taught his disciples to ask God in prayer for the kingdom to come (Matthew 6:10). He told them that "the kingdom prepared for you since the creation of the world" would not be given until Judgment Day (Matthew 25:34). Many of Jesus's parables of the kingdom stress the incompleteness or the hiddenness of the kingdom of God. Because it is still future, the kingdom of God is like a seed that that grows largely out of

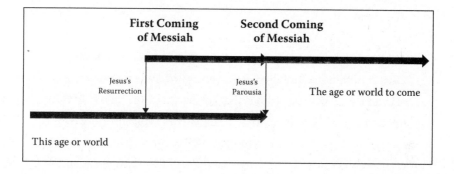

First Coming
of Messiah

Second Coming
of Messiah

Jesus's
Resurrection

Jesus's
Parousia

The age or world to come

This age or world

sight, invisible to human eyes, and yet will eventually grow into the greatest of trees (Matthew 13:31–33).

Jesus revealed a very different coming kingdom than the one they were expecting.[3]

The kingdom of God is already here, but not yet in its fullness. We must not underestimate how present the kingdom of God is, but we must also not underestimate how unrealized it is, how much it exists only in the future. Because the kingdom is present partially but not fully, we must expect substantial healing but not total healing in all areas of life.[4]

The implications of this are significant. If we overstress the "already" of the kingdom to the exclusion of the "not yet," we will expect quick solutions to problems and we will be dismayed by suffering and tragedy. But we can likewise overstress the "not yet" of the kingdom to the exclusion of the "already." We can be too pessimistic about personal change. We can withdraw from engaging the world, too afraid of being "polluted" by it. John Stott suggests more applications:[5]

Knowledge of truth. God has spoken. In a time in which many insist that no one can know any truth for certain, our King *has* given us his Word. But on the other hand, we must be humble about our ability to understand the Word perfectly. In those areas where Christians cannot agree, we should be less triumphalistic. The "not yet" means more charity in nonessentials, more humility and dialogue and tolerance and openness in areas of disagreement.

Personal change and growth. The Holy Spirit has come into us already, subduing our fallen nature and our selfishness. The presence of the kingdom includes that we are made "partakers of the divine nature" (2 Peter 1:3 ESV). The "already" means more confidence that anyone can be changed, that any enslaving habit can be overcome. But on the other hand, our fallen nature remains in us and will never be eliminated until the fullness of the kingdom arrives. We must avoid pat answers, and we must not expect quick fixes. The "not yet" means more patience and understanding with growing persons; it means to not be condescending nor impatient with lapses and failures.

Church change and growth. The church is the community of the King. The "already" means confidence that God can bring revival and transformation through the local church. But the "not yet" means error and evil will never be completely eradicated from the church. We must not, then, be harshly critical of imperfect congregations, nor jump impatiently from church to church over perceived blemishes.

Social change. Christ is even now ruling over history (Ephesians 1:22ff.). Through "common grace" he gives the world the institutions of family and government restraining evil, and he gives strong consciences and gifts of art and leadership and science to many to enrich the world. Alongside trouble and pain, God has given improved health care and medical advances, growing defense of human rights, the abolition of slavery, many protections for working people, and so on. The "already" means that Christians can expect to use God's power to change social conditions and communities. But on the other hand, the kingdom is not yet here in its fullness. There will be "wars and rumors of wars." Selfishness, cruelty, terrorism, and oppression will continue. Christians harbor no illusions about politics nor expect utopian conditions. The "not yet" means that Christians will not trust any political or social agenda to bring about full righteousness here on earth.

In general, those who believe that the kingdom is *only* "not yet" will be extremely pessimistic and negative about change in people, the church, and society. Those who believe that the kingdom is *already* here will be overly optimistic and naive about the possibility of revival, change, and transformation.

Paul's instruction about the kingdom of God perfectly matches the teaching of Jesus. He repeatedly speaks of Christ as the "firstfruits" (1 Corinthians 15:20) and the "firstborn" (Colossians 1:18) from the dead. In the Old Testament the firstfruits constituted the earliest part of a crop that was offered in thanksgiving to God. But the term signified not just that it was a gift but that it was a "pledge of the remainder," a promise or "assurance of a full harvest." This means not merely that the resurrection of Jesus points to our future resurrection. It guarantees it.[6]

In the resurrection we have the presence of the future. The power by which God will finally destroy all suffering, evil, deformity, and death at the end of time has broken into history now and is available—partially but substantially—now.[7] When we unite with the risen Christ by faith, that future power that is potent enough to remake the universe comes into us.

The Freedoms of the Kingdom

What, practically, does this mean? What does Christ as the resurrected one give to us for life now? The rest of this book will answer that question. But we can begin with the idea of freedom. To be brought out of one kingdom into another, as Christians are (Colossians 1:13), means to be freed from things that once controlled us.

First, the risen Christ, the King, brings us freedom from the fear of guilt and shame. The resurrection is a powerful sign to our consciences that Jesus fully paid the penalty of our sin on the cross. It brings us a freedom that the cross by itself could not give us.

Two illustrations can help us here. If you have committed a crime and the debt to society is two years in jail, you go to jail or prison for two years. How do you know the debt is fully paid? When the doors that barred your way are open and you can walk out. The Bible says that "the wages of sin," the penalty for breaking God's law, "is death" (Romans 6:23). But Jesus took that penalty, that curse of the law, for us (Galatians 3:13) and paid it in full. How do we know he actually paid the debt in full? Because the door of death opened, and he went out.

A second illustration is the idea of a receipt. If you are in a large department store, you may purchase an item at a cashier's station deep inside the store. What if you get to the exit and are stopped by a store employee who questions you about the merchandise you are carrying? You whip out your receipt and say, "This proves that the price has been paid in full." And with that you are free to go. In the resurrection God stamped "Paid in full" across history and across your life. It is an assurance that the debt of sin has been paid.

Paul says, "If Christ has not been raised, . . . you are still in your sins" (1 Corinthians 15:17), which means that because Christ *is* raised, we are not "in our sins." Rather, as Paul says over one hundred times in his letters, you are in *him*, in Christ. Your sins are covered and the Father loves you "even as" he loves Jesus (John 17:23). The Father looks at you and he sees a treasure. To the degree you live in consciousness of that, to that degree you are free from shame for anything in your past. You are free from what people say. Otherwise, you're taking your identity from what people say about you and how you're doing, and so you're up and down. At night you toss in bed because somebody snubbed you. The next day you're elated because you did well. But if Christ is risen and you have put your faith in him, you are not in your sins.

It doesn't matter who you have been or what you have done in your past. Think of Paul. What did he have in his past? He could remember the cries of innocent people and the looks on their faces as they died, like Stephen (Acts 7). Do you have anything like *that* in your past? Even if you did, it is no match for the grace of God. That is why, in the midst of describing the resurrection, Paul can jump quickly to the new truth that "[only] by the grace of God I am what I am" (1 Corinthians 15:10).

God said in the resurrection, "This payment is sufficient. You *never* have to pay for these things again. *Never.*" Do you understand that? Do you have your receipt? Do you look at the resurrection and say, "That's God's way of saying to me I'll never have to pay for any of these things again?" There is no condemnation for those who are in Christ Jesus (Romans 8:1).

> *Well may the Accuser roar*
> *Of ills that I have done:*
> *I know them all, and thousands more:*
> *Jehovah knoweth none!*[8]

Second, because it brings freedom from guilt and condemnation, the resurrection brings freedom from the fear of death (Hebrews 2:14–15). Not only does the resurrected Christ gives us a look at our own future resurrected bodies, but his resurrection guarantees and proves that this will be our future too. In 1 Corinthians 15:23–26 Paul declares that when

Christ rose from the dead he began to reign (verses 24–25) and that he will continue to reign until "all dominion, authority, and power" is destroyed and until "all . . . enemies [are] under his feet. The last enemy to be destroyed is death" (verses 24–26). This kingly triumph over death is partially—but not fully—here now. Even though we still must physically die, nevertheless death cannot separate us from God and his world of love. Indeed, death now can only infinitely enhance our experience of the love and joy of God's presence.[9] George Herbert addresses death, though what was once "an executioner" is now merely "a gard'ner," "an usher to convey our souls beyond the utmost stars and poles."[10] And at the end of time, when the kingdom is fully come, death will be completely destroyed. Meanwhile, for those who believe in the risen Christ, death is defanged. It no longer removes you from love. On the contrary, it can only bring you more love than you could imagine.

Third, the death and resurrection frees us from other "authorities" that would enslave us. In Colossians 2 Paul writes:

> Having canceled the charge of our legal indebtedness, which
> stood against us and condemned us; he has taken it away, nailing
> it to the cross. And having disarmed the powers and authorities,
> he made a public spectacle of them.
>
> **(Colossians 2:14–15)**

When the world looked at Jesus dying on the cross, it saw only weakness and defeat. If Jesus claimed to be a king, his campaign seemed to have ended in utter failure. But in reality, Paul says, Jesus triumphed doubly. On the cross Jesus destroyed our "legal indebtedness"—the debt we owed God for our sin. This was the barrier between us and God, but it has been removed. And then, "having disarmed the powers," Jesus also made a "public spectacle" of their defeat. As most commentators argue, this can only be a reference to the resurrection and ascension of Christ.[11] The resurrection displayed unmistakably to the world that Jesus had paid our debt to divine justice, opening a door to a life without the crushing weight of self-salvation and making it possible for God's renewing presence to enter the lives of those who acknowledge him as Lord and Savior.

We can understand these "powers and authorities" both cosmically and personally. Until we enter the kingdom of God, who saves us by grace, all of us live in the kingdoms of false gods to whom we look for significance and security, for identity and meaning. We have to live for something, and whatever it is that we live for to justify our existence, that thing essentially controls us. As Rebecca Pippert writes: "Whatever controls us is really our god. . . . The one who seeks power is controlled by power. The one who seeks acceptance is controlled by the people he or she wants to please. We do not control ourselves. We are controlled by the lord of our life."[12]

There are also cultural false gods. Societies make corporate idols out of military might and war, material prosperity and comfort, sexuality and romance, technology and science, or state power. At the cultural level these become ideologies of nationalism, capitalism, sexual liberation, technocracy, and socialism. Each of these can become a "power and authority" in our lives. The more we look to them for happiness, significance, and security, the more they enslave us. The cross freed us in principle from these powers, these idols. But the resurrection brings into our lives the power we need to live this freedom in practice. The resurrected Christ sends the Spirit, which makes Jesus real to our hearts so that the old authorities and powers lose their grip on us.[13]

This same freedom from cultural idols that was offered to the Colossians is offered to us today. So the death and resurrection of Jesus frees us from the dominion of all other kingdoms. When we repent and believe (Mark 1:15) and are born again (John 3:3,5), we are transferred into this new realm of freedom (Colossians 1:13).

The Verdict of the Kingdom

These freedoms—from authorities, shame and guilt, and death itself—are rooted in a great gift that the resurrection brings us.

All our lives we have been receiving evaluations of our behavior and of our selves. Parents, teachers, coaches, spouses, and friends give us good or bad grades, tag us with "likes" or "dislikes," pepper us with good and bad verdicts on our looks, intelligence, politics, and character. We love the good appraisals but they can never overcome the wounds that the negative ones inflict. We believe the criticisms far more readily and remember them far more vividly than the praise.

On the last day God will judge all the inhabitants of the earth according to their works, "according to what they have done" (Romans 2:6). But Christians are assured that on that day, "whoever . . . believes . . . has eternal life and will not be judged" (John 5:24). On that day we will be told that God loves us even as he loves his only Son (John 17:23–24). There, finally, at last, we will receive the good verdict that sinks deep into our hearts and overturns all the bad ones. All guilt and shame will be gone forever.

But the gospel tells us that Christians do not have to wait until the end of time to hear that healing word. When we believe in Jesus we are at that moment justified by faith, pardoned, and accepted (Romans 3:21–24; 2 Corinthians 5:21) When we are born again we actually receive the praise of God (Romans 2:29). How is this possible? Paul writes: "Since we have now been justified by his blood, how much more shall we be saved from God's wrath through him!" (Romans 5:9) See how he connects the word on the final Judgment Day with the verdict of justification that we receive now. What this means is summed up by Michael Horton:

> According to the New Testament . . . the age to come has indeed broken into this present age. . . . Jesus has been raised as the beginning of the general resurrection, and . . . *the future verdict of the last day [is] brought forward into the present.*[14]

The reason why we can be justified by faith apart from our works is because, through the resurrection of Christ, we are connected to that future moment and we are told *now* that "there is no condemnation for those who are in Christ Jesus" (Romans 8:1).

This great gift from the future comes into us now and frees us from shame, from the insecurity and anxiety that drives us to serve the idols of money, sex, and power, and from the fear of death and judgment day.

As a pastor, I've spoken to people nearing death who express guilt and shame for things they had done. But I've spoken to far more people who were wracked with regret for the things they had *not* done. They realized at the end that much of their lives had been simply wasted and that their lives warranted a negative verdict. This regret assails nonreligious persons as much as, if not more than, religious ones. As my wife and I have passed the age of seventy and as I have entered cancer treatments, we have ourselves felt this burden of sins of omission.

We live with this invisible weight. When we are younger we may say, "Nobody has the right to tell me how to live! Nobody has the right to make me feel guilty. Only I judge myself." But even within that framework, as the years mount, we see that we have not lived up to our own standards. The burden, barely noticed at first, gets heavier as the years go by. For more religious people that may be guilt over specific sins they have done; for nonreligious people it may be a less specific shameful sense of not being the persons they should be.

But all Christians know that our verdict is in—and has been in since the moment we united by faith with the living, resurrected Christ. We are accepted in the beloved Son. There is a famous episode in John Bunyan's *The Pilgrim's Progress* when the pilgrim walks along, straining under a huge weight on his back. It is a great burden of self-salvation—which consists of both the guilt for specific sins and the shame of knowing he will never live up to the moral standards to which he is obligated.

> Up this way therefore did burdened Christian run, but not without great difficulty, because of the load on his back.
>
> He ran thus till he came at a place somewhat ascending, and upon that place stood a Cross, and a little below in the bottom, a Sepulcher. So I saw in my Dream, that just as Christian came up with the Cross, his Burden loosed from off his shoulders, and fell

from off his back, and began to tumble, and so continued to do, till it came to the mouth of the Sepulcher, where it fell in, and I saw it no more.

Then was Christian glad and lightsome. . . . It was very surprising to him that the sight of the Cross should thus ease him of his Burden. He looked therefore, and looked again, even till the springs that were in his head sent the waters down his cheeks. . . .

Then Christian gave three leaps for joy, and went on singing:

. . . Blest Cross! blest Sepulcher! blest rather be
The Man that there was put to shame for me.[15]

Bunyan shows us a man whose burden of sin and shame is loosed by the cross but then consumed by the empty tomb. His final song of joy shows that what frees him is not just the sight of the cross and tomb but the knowledge of a man bearing the burden of our guilt and shame and then, having paid it himself, rising triumphant to give us forgiveness and the beginning of a new resurrection life that will continue forever.

The Presence of the King

The resurrection means that we do not merely follow the teachings of a dead leader. Rather, we have vital, loving fellowship with a living Lord. Jesus the King is present with us. We will spell out the ways we experience him. But we should begin by understanding that we can be saved only by a risen, living Savior, not by one who is dead. Romans 4:25 says that Jesus "was delivered up for our trespasses and raised for our justification" (ESV). How does a resurrected Christ save us? Theologian John Murray, in his commentary on Romans, explains.

First, he writes: "The righteousness of Christ by which we are justified (Romans 5:17–19) . . . can never be thought of in abstraction from him as a reservoir of merit stored up."[16] There is a danger that when Christians talk about being justified in God's sight, we imagine righteousness as a kind of virtue bank account that someone transfers money into. It makes salvation a mechanical or mercenary process. Instead, Murray says, "it is in union with Christ [*himself*] that we are justified." It is *in* Jesus that there is no condemnation (Romans 8:1). Only when we are united with him, through faith and the Holy Spirit, do we become a loved and accepted child of God. "Only as a living Lord can he be the object of faith. . . . Only as the living one can Christ . . . be made to us righteousness from God (1 Corinthians 1:30)." To be saved is not to get infusions of power and or points of merit— it is to get him, Jesus Christ, "the Righteous One" (1 John 2:1). Our salvation is radically personal and supernatural.

Second, Murray points out that Christ now stands before the Father as our advocate, representing us so that our prayers for forgiveness are always accepted (1 John 1:8–9; 2:1–2; Hebrews 7:25) and so that all things work together for our good and nothing can separate us from his love (Romans 8:28–30, 33–39). Only a risen Christ can intercede for us. So we are not saved merely by the cross. Rather, "The death and resurrection of Christ are inseparable."[17]

"For if, while we were God's enemies, we were reconciled to him through the death of his Son, how much more, having been reconciled, shall we be saved through his life!" (Romans 5:10)

The Once and Future King

Many branches of the human family are full of legends of great kings in the past who, when they ruled, brought their people a golden age. When these kings ruled with justice and wisdom and compassion and grace and power, everything was right in the world. The Robin Hood legend is about holding the fort until the true king returns. *The Lord of the Rings* is basically about restoration of peace, justice, and prosperity because the rightful king takes the throne. On the tomb of King Arthur is written: "Hic iacet Arthurus, rex quondam, rexque futurus" ("Here lies Arthur, the once and future king"). The promise is that this good king who had brought about the "one, brief, shining moment" of Camelot would someday come back and make things right.

The odd thing about those legends is that the actual record of kings in history is abysmal. It is a record of tyranny and of slavery. Over the years almost all kingdoms have been toppled in favor of democracies. And Christians have been very much behind this move. As Harvard scholar Eric Nelson tells us, democratic nation-states arose in early modern Europe because of Christians' reading of the Bible.[18]

And yet these legends of a true king still have enormous purchase, as we see from the blockbuster films, year after year, that are based on these older stories or narratives like them. Not only that, in countries that still have some kind of royalty, those royals are idolized. And in countries like the United States where there are no kings, we create them out of athletes, billionaires, supermodels, and film stars. It is often seen how this need to create heroes and celebrities is toxic both for the objects of the adulation and the subjects. But as C. S. Lewis writes, this need to crown *some*one and adore them stays strong because "spiritual nature, like bodily nature, will be served; deny it food and it will gobble poison."[19] What does he mean?

There is evidence that deep in the human heart is a desire to crown a king. The Bible says we know, but suppress (Romans 1:18–19), that we were created to serve and adore a king. The Bible tells us that there once was a King, and his beauty and his love and his compassion and his power and his wisdom were like the sun shining in full strength. If we can't serve him, we will *have* to build our lives around and serve something. Spiritual nature will be served. It's not a question of being free or not. No one is free—everyone is serving someone or something. Instead the question is: Are you serving the true King, who will forgive you and liberate you to be all you were created to be? Or will you serve something that will never absolve you for your failures and will never fulfill your heart?

This is the good news: This King will return and take his throne, and everything sad will come untrue. We will see him face to face finally. And yet "the rightful king has landed, you may say landed in disguise, and is calling us to take part in a great campaign of sabotage" against the forces of darkness.[20] We are not only free but freedom fighters, in service of our once and future King.

CHAPTER 3

GLORIOUS HOPE

Then Jesus said: "Did I not tell you that if you believe, you will see the glory of God?"

—JOHN 11:40

The History of God's Glory

The resurrection not only brings the future into the present but also brings heaven to earth. It reunites people with the glory of God. This is one of the most important themes that run through the Scripture. To trace it out helps us see how all the books of the Bible fit together into a single, coherent story.

The Bible begins in the Garden of Eden, a place God created where he could live with humanity. But because of sin, we were banished from God's presence—a flaming sword was put at the entrance of the Garden (Genesis 3:24). This was a graphic representation of the truth that the penalty for sin is death. The way back into the presence of God was blocked by justice. There was a debt that had to be paid. There was no way back into the presence of God without going under the sword.

After delivering the Israelites out of slavery in Egypt, God brought them to Mount Sinai to meet with him. God's presence came down on the mountain, and the result was lightning and thunder, fire and thick smoke, and a violent earthquake (Exodus 19:16–18). When God spoke to the people, it sounded like an intolerably loud trumpet blast. They were warned not to touch the mountain or else the presence of God would "break out" and kill them (Exodus 19:19–24). The raw, unmediated presence of God was unbearable, and the people begged to *not* have God speak to them "or we will die" (Exodus 20:19). Only Moses was willing to "approach the thick darkness where God was" (verse 21).

Moses, however, wanted not less of God's presence but more of it. With extraordinary boldness, he asked: "Now show me your glory" (Exodus 33:18). But God replied: "You cannot see my face, for no one may see me and live" (verse 20). The way back into the Garden, into life with God, was not open. The cherubim's sword was still there. Sinful human beings cannot bear the presence of God—it is as fatal to us as the surface of the sun.

Despite this, Moses still asks that somehow God's "Presence" (literally, his "face") would go with the Israelites as they journey (Exodus 33:14–17). And so in the wilderness God created a movable sanctuary—the tabernacle where people could draw near to meet him (Exodus 25:22).

The tabernacle was God's way of beginning to restore what had been lost. Many features of the Garden of Eden appear in the design of the tabernacle and, later, the temple.[1] Both the entrance to the Garden of Eden and the tabernacle faced east (Genesis 3:24; Exodus 38:13–18). The cherubim angels, signs of God's immediate presence, guarded the entrance to the Garden (Genesis 3:24) and were carved into the entrance of the temple (1 Kings 6:23–28). All parts of the temple's architecture—walls, pillars, furniture, and curtains—were filled with palm trees, lions, pomegranates, animals, and flowers (1 Kings 7:13–26,36; 2 Chronicles 3:5–7), vividly calling to mind the original Garden of God. The tabernacle was the initial reestablishment of God's habitation on earth (Deuteronomy 12:4).

The actual throne room of the sanctuary was the holy of holies. This was the one place in the world where God's "name dwelled," where his Shekinah glory-cloud resided. It was the one place that heaven and earth touched. But the holy of holies was separated from the rest of the tabernacle by a thick curtain or barrier on which cherubim were embroidered

(Exodus 26:1). The people could not go in. Only the high priest himself could go into the holy of holies once a year, and even then he had to put incense on the fire to create enough smoke so that he would not see anything that would kill him (Leviticus 16:1–34; see verse 13). In the holy of holies was the Ark of the Covenant, a wooden box, overlaid with gold, containing the tablets of the Ten Commandments. Over the top of the ark, between two carved angels, was a slab of pure gold called the "mercy seat." There, on Yom Kippur, the Day of Atonement, the high priest offered a blood sacrifice for the sins of the people. And God only spoke over the mercy seat (Exodus 25:10–22).

The imagery could not be clearer. The Ten Commandments demanded obedience, an obedience and a holiness of which no human being was capable. The only way to have fellowship with God, to have him speak to us, was for atonement for sins to be made. Just as a sword of justice guarded the way back into the Garden, so the high priest had to go "under the sword" with a blood sacrifice, symbolically atoning for sin, paying the penalty in order to go even briefly into God's presence. At the conclusion of the tabernacle service, God blessed the people with his *shalom*, or peace (Numbers 6:24–27). And yet the glory of God's holiness remained behind the veil in the sanctuary where no sinner could enter. The tabernacle brought God nearer but still no one could see his glory and live.

When King David planned to build a permanent physical sanctuary, the temple, God sent a prophet to tell him that one of his descendants would build a permanent "house" in which God and his people would finally dwell together (2 Samuel 5:6–10, 7:1–16) forever. David's son Solomon did build the first temple, but he was not the son of David of whom the prophets spoke, for his temple was destroyed (1 Kings 11:11–13; 2 Kings 25:8–11). During the exile, Ezekiel also prophesied a new temple and a new David to build it (Ezekiel 37:24–28,40–43). He wrote that the Lord's glory would fill it (Ezekiel 48:35), and it would become so large that all the nations of the earth would enter it (Ezekiel 37:28).

However, the temple constructed after the exiles returned from Babylon did not fulfill the vision of the prophets either. When the new foundation was laid, the older people wept because it was far less splendid than Solomon's, not more (Ezra 3:12). The new temple was not the one that was prophesied (Haggai 2:1–8). That one would be built only when the Messiah, the new "David," came.

The New Testament picks up the thread of these prophecies. The gospel of John declared that Jesus Christ became flesh and (literally) *tabernacled* among us, and we beheld his glory (John 1:14). In the same way, the book of Hebrews tells us that Jesus *is* "the radiance of God's glory and the exact representation of his being" (Hebrews 1:3). Jesus does not merely have God's glory or bring it—he *is* God's glory. He reveals and brings God's power and beauty. When Jesus was throwing the money changers out of the temple, he was asked what gave him the right to do such a thing. He replied:

> "Destroy this temple, and in three days I will raise it up." The Jews then said, "It has taken forty-six years to build this temple, and will you raise it up in three days?" But he was speaking about the temple of his body. When therefore he was raised from the dead, his disciples remembered that he had said this.
>
> **(John 2:19–21 ESV)**

It was no surprise that even Jesus's disciples had no idea what he was talking about. He was saying that when he rose from the dead, he would *be* the new temple, the place where one could meet God. Indeed, he was declaring, the older tabernacle and temples were pointing to him all along.

When Jesus said that his resurrected body is the true temple, he was saying something like this: "In all temples around the world, priests offer sacrifices and do rituals aiming to bridge the chasm you feel between yourself and God. But I am *the* sacrifice that ends all sacrifices. I am *the* priest who ends your need for priests. It was I who went under the sword (Genesis 3:24). I am the one who brings heaven to earth, because I am not just the bridge over the gap to God's glory. I *am* God's glory." No one, of course, had ever said anything like this before. The founders of other religions built many temples. But Jesus *is* the temple to end all temples.

In Matthew 27:51 we are told that the moment Jesus died, the veil of the temple was torn in two from top to bottom as if by two mighty hands from above. At his death Jesus dismantled the old temple, and at his resurrection he established the new one. Now when we unite with the risen Christ by faith, through the Holy Spirit, the Shekinah glory presence of God that had dwelled behind the veil, inaccessibly, is now available to us.

And what this means for the church is remarkable. It means that a Christian is not primarily a nice person who subscribes to certain beliefs and codes. Christianity is instead a radical regeneration of the heart and a reorientation of the life. We are regenerated when we believe (John 3:3), because now the same divine presence that once shook mountains, terrified people, and killed living things on contact lives in us. That means that we who believe in Jesus are now temples in which the Holy Spirit of God dwells (1 Corinthians 6:19; 2 Corinthians 6:16). It means that being a Christian gives us access to the presence of God through prayer. Moses's unrealized yearning to see the light of God's glory and face (Exodus 33:18) is now our privilege (John 1:14; 2 Corinthians 4:6).

It means that being a Christian makes us partners and participants with Christ in his work of spreading the healing and energizing kingdom power through the world. Because Jesus is the temple, we too are the final temple, now "living stones" in it (1 Peter 2:4–10). Because Jesus is the high priest, we are "priests" who can both draw near to God (Hebrews 4:14–16) and bring others to God (Hebrews 13). Because Jesus is a gate to heaven (John 1:51, 14:6) we are linked to heaven (Colossians 2:20; Philippians 3:20). Because Jesus is an anointed one (Luke 4:18), as was the temple, so we are anointed (1 John 2:20). All the lines and themes of the temple converge on Jesus—he is the sacrifice, the priest, the altar, the light, the bread, the blood of purification, the Shekinah glory. For all the promises of God become *yes* in Jesus (2 Corinthians 1:20).

When Jesus returns to earth, the new city of God will be a perfect cube (Revelation 2:16), as was the holy of holies (2 Chronicles 3:8). This eschatological, metaphorical language tells us that the entire world will be a giant holy of holies. The whole earth will be the Garden of Eden again. Why? Because we will finally be face to face with him—again, forever.

> I did not see a temple in the city, because the Lord God Almighty and the Lamb are its temple. The city does not need the sun or the moon to shine on it, for the glory of God gives it light, and the Lamb is its lamp.
>
> **(Revelation 21:22–23)**

Glory for the Individual

What are the implications of this stupendous reality, namely, that the risen Christ has brought heaven and earth together?

Moses first had an experience of the presence of God when he met the Lord in the burning bush (Exodus 3). It was a bush that burned but was not consumed because what looked like mere physical fire was really the glory of God. On Mount Sinai Moses again saw the glory and fire of God descend. He wanted to come near and look right into it. When God told him, "You cannot see my face" (Exodus 33:20), we learn what it was that Moses was after. He wasn't just seeking some sight of dazzling brightness. In Hebrew idiom, to "see someone's face" was to have intimate fellowship with them.

In Eden God "walked" with us (Genesis 3:8), a term that indicated friendship and love. Human beings were created for this fellowship with God as fish were made to live in water. God's loving presence was our ultimate fulfillment, but when humanity turned away from God, we lost the very thing we were made for. We were created to desire love and beauty and we still do, but apart from God we only find poor substitutes in which our hearts cannot finally rest. At some level Moses understood what Augustine so famously prayed to God: "Our hearts are restless until they find their rest in Thee."[2]

Here, then, is the ultimate paradox. The greatest disaster possible for human beings is to be "shut out from the presence of the Lord and from the glory of his might" (2 Thessalonians 1:9). And yet it is now fatal to us to have the very thing for which we were designed.

C. S. Lewis tries to get this across in his science fiction novel *Perelandra*, where the narrator comes into contact with an "eldil" from Mars, a being of absolute goodness. And to his disappointment, the narrator finds the experience tremendously threatening. He suddenly realizes that, while he flattered himself that he was a good person, he actually does not "like 'goodness' so much as I had supposed."

> This is a very terrible experience. As long as what you are afraid of is something evil, you may still hope that the good may come to your rescue. But suppose you struggle through to the good and find that is also dreadful? How if food itself turns out to be the very thing you can't eat, and home the very place you can't live, and your very comforter the person who makes you uncomfortable? Then, indeed, there is no rescue possible: the last card has been played. . . . I wanted it to go away. I wanted every possible distance, gulf, curtain, blanket, and barrier to be placed between it and me.[3]

Because of sin, the one thing that we most need—the presence and glory of God—becomes the one thing we most fear and avoid. That is, according to the Bible, the human condition.

In light of this Old Testament history, the language that the New Testament writers use to describe Christian experience is nothing short of astonishing. In 2 Corinthians Paul says:

> Now the Lord is the Spirit, and where the Spirit of the Lord is, there is freedom. And we all, who . . . contemplate the Lord's glory, are being transformed into his image with ever-increasing glory, which comes from the Lord, who is the Spirit. . . . For

God . . . made his light shine in our hearts to give us the light of
the knowledge of God's glory displayed in the face of Christ."

(2 Corinthians 3:16–18, 4:6)

While we still cannot see the Lord with our physical eyes as we will
when the kingdom comes in fullness (1 John 3:1-3), we have available a
partial but transforming faith-sight of his glory that comes through the
gospel (2 Corinthians 4:6). In prayer, through the Spirit that the risen
Christ has given us, when meditating on the Word, it is possible to get such
a sense on the heart of Jesus's beauty and glory that it reproduces his goodness, love, wisdom, joy, and peace in us.

The fire of God's glorious presence that Moses saw in the burning bush
and that will renew the world at the end of time has come into us, as signified by the tongues of flame over the head of every disciple on the day of
Pentecost (Acts 2:3). Every Christian is now a small burning bush, a new
creation, being made into Christ's image, as we behold his glory by faith.

Glory for the Community

Even though the Bible can speak of individual Christians as temples, filled
with God's Spirit (1 Corinthians 6:19), it also understands the church corporate to be a temple of God. "You also, like living stones, are being built
into a spiritual house [temple]" (1 Peter 2:5). The present progressive tense
shows that Christians as individual living stones are being built together
into a community around the presence of Christ. In the midst of the community are "the powers of the coming age" (Hebrews 6:5), a phrase that
speaks not only to heaven come to earth but to the future brought into
the present. The glory of God coming to earth does not only produce radically changed individuals, but a whole new kind of human community—
the church. Paul writes: "But our citizenship is in heaven" (Philippians
3:19–20).

The word translated as "citizenship" is *politeuma*, a word that is better translated as "commonwealth" or "colony." It means a politically organized body with both laws and loyalties that govern the behavior of its citizens. Literally it tells Christians that their politics—the way they conduct themselves in society—is to be based on the life of "heaven." Philippi was a Roman colony (Acts 16:22), and that word does not have a positive sound to modern people. Yet at that time it was a very coveted status. It meant all the people within it were considered Roman citizens. Their legal privileges—as well as their laws and obligations—were the same as if they lived in Rome itself.[4]

It meant that the church is an alternate society, not simply a collection of individuals who are forgiven. It is a "holy [distinct, set apart] nation" (1 Peter 2:9), a counterculture, a new society in which the world can see what family dynamics, business practices, race relations, and all of life can look like when the Spirit begins to heal all the effects of sin: psychological, social, and physical. In this sense the church must follow God's standards and directives and laws rather than the world's, and it shows the world what a new humanity should be.

Colonies of Heaven

What does a "heavenly commonwealth" look like on earth? It is always incomplete, a work in progress, yet there are also glimpses of glory, of "treasure in jars of clay" (2 Corinthians 4:7).

Pastor Jeremy Treat visited Kibera, an extremely poor area of Nairobi, Kenya. He walked into it following a stream of open sewage that flowed right by shelters made of pieces of wood and dried mud. He saw many children playing in the mud right by the sewage with no clothes on. He went by a twelve-year-old girl who his guides said was a prostitute. As he was feeling overwhelmed, he heard the first sounds of his destination. As the noise grew in volume, he recognized it as human voices. Finally he came to a building, "little more than a shack," and inside there was a church service. About seventy people were singing "at the top of their lungs, praising God in Swahili," arms raised in worship. "Tears. Smiles. Prayer. Praise." What could have possibly given people living in that darkness such hope and even joy? Treat wrote, "In that impoverished slum, I knew that the kingdom had come . . . not yet . . . in the fullness of God's future promise, but it was there in the midst of the most horrific suffering and brokenness I've seen."[5]

He saw that the transforming power was both individual and corporate. "God's reign was breaking in and transforming the lives of real people. These people had nothing, yet they knew that in Christ they had everything." And yet the people were not simply achieving a tranquil inner psychological state. "God's love was poured out on them and it flowed outward through them." They were not content to leave their community in its disempowered, miserable state. "Throughout the day, I heard stories of how these people loved and served others in the community." He concluded, "What I saw in that little shack was a glimpse of the same power that will one day renew all of creation."[6]

In the late 1940s Francis and Edith Schaeffer were Christian missionaries sent to Europe to promote American-style fundamentalist religion.[7] In Europe Francis had a crisis of faith, partly triggered by the lack of love he saw among conservative defenders of the faith in his church circles. After a season of doubt, he emerged recommitted to orthodox Christian doctrine but intent on creating a community that was in itself a powerful sign of the kingdom—a community that would demonstrate the reality of the Christian God. In 1955 they set up the ministry called L'Abri ("The Shelter") outside a small village in the Alps of Switzerland. It began simply with their oldest daughter, a student at the University of Lausanne, bringing students home on the weekends for eating, walks, and discussion.

The Schaeffers came in contact with something that had not yet become prevalent in the U.S. Increasing numbers of European students had lost faith, not merely in the church but in any belief in universal truth claims. They were struggling with "the fallout of the postmodern shift" before anyone had a word for it. They had new kinds of problems—how to find meaning, how to find a basis for moral values and justice and a stable identity, and how to deal with the shame that they seemed to feel nonetheless. The Schaeffers' work "was an extended and multifaceted effort to help a generation" of these young, alienated skeptics.[8]

They began simply by taking young people into their home as guests, providing the warmest and richest hospitality. They focused attention on the young people's concerns, whatever their background. They listened intently and did not push their own theology or agenda, although they continually expressed confidence that Christianity had the greatest resources for the various aspects of the human dilemma. The Schaeffers did not begin with a curriculum in which they set the agenda; instead they let the students' concerns drive the conversations. They engaged with the works and art and culture in which the students were immersed and provided Christian teaching that gave what they called "honest answers to honest questions."

For the next twenty years, hundreds and then thousands of young people came through L'Abri, which expanded to several chalets. During that time a large number of the most unlikely young adults were converted to Christianity. When asked about the factors that led them to faith, they pointed to the uniqueness of the community.

It was unique because it balanced both truth and love. In virtually all other communities one seemed privileged over the other, they said. Either there was an inclusive acceptance coupled with a relativistic view of things, or there was an orthodoxy paired with exclusive attitudes toward the "wrong kinds of people." But L'Abri did not fall into either category. It exhibited a spiritual reality that could not be accounted for—unless the message of Christianity at the heart of the community was actually true.

Even Frank Schaeffer, who has since rejected his family's Christian beliefs, gives strong testimony to this reality. For example, the Schaeffers taught the traditional Christian sex ethic, and yet when unwed mothers came to L'Abri, there was nonetheless a loving welcome.

> Our "single mothers" were sometimes accompanied by Mom, or another worker, to the hospital in Aigle for the delivery. Sin was

sin; but since we were all sinners who had fallen very short of the glory of God, there was no stigma attached to the pregnancy. Nor was there a stigma attached to . . . mental illness.[9]

The Schaeffers' decades-long hospitality was financially and emotionally expensive for them, and all guests and workers saw it. Francis wrote: "In about the first three years of L'Abri all our wedding presents were wiped out. Our sheets were torn. Holes were burned in our rugs. . . . Drugs came to our place. People vomited in our rooms."[10] Again, son Frank gives testimony to how compelling this was:

> I saw my parents' compassion was consistent . . . not advocating compassion that someone else would carry out with tax dollars, or at arm's length, but rather they opened their home. The result was that those gathered around our table represented a cross-section of humanity and intellectual ability, from mental patients to Oxford students and all points of need in between. My mother and father marshalled arguments in favor of God . . . but no words were as convincing as their willingness to lay material possessions, privacy, and time on the line, sometimes at personal risk and always with the understanding that if they were being taken advantage of, that was fine, too.[11]

See how different these "colonies of heaven" can be. One was a chalet in the beautiful Alps, touching the lives of many of the brightest young European minds, and the other a shack in the sewage and mud, touching the poorest of the poor in Africa. How radically different, and yet the same. The world's wisdom would set up a college in Europe and a social service agency in Nairobi. But both would be merely dispensers of products, not revolutionary new communities that changed lives from the inside out. Both the chalet and the shack were "pilot plants," communities of the King, changed by the presence of Christ, exhibiting the beauty of human societies reordered around his glory and love rather than around our glory and power. In both can be seen a glimpse of the same "powers of the age to come" that will one day renew all of creation.

Glory for the World

In Psalm 72 the psalmist speaks of a king who rules "to the ends of the earth" (verse 8) "as long as the sun . . . [and] moon" (verse 5). This king "will take pity on the weak and the needy. . . . He will rescue them from oppression and violence" (verses 13–14). And when this happens it will be said: "Praise be to the Lord God . . . may the whole earth be filled with his glory" (verses 18–19). Under the Messianic King, God's glory manifests itself when the widow, the orphan, the immigrant, and the poor are finally treated justly and liberated from the forces that oppress them. By contrast, in the world's cultures, people are dedicated to "making a name for themselves" (cf. Genesis 11:4). That is, they live for their own glory, not God's, and when that happens the result is conflict and exploitation. But when God's glory fills the whole earth, there will be perfect peace, harmony, and justice.

If in the Bible the glory of God is so tightly connected to righteousness and justice, and if through the resurrection we now have been given the heavenly and future world-renewing glory of God—what does that mean for our work in the world now?

Geerhardus Vos, in *The Kingdom of God and the Church*, writes that since the resurrection of Christ, "the kingdom-forces . . . are at work" but not only inside the walls of the church. He argues that since the purpose of the kingdom is to renew the entire world, it is "intended to pervade . . . the whole of human life."[12] By this he does not mean any kind of theocratic take-over by the church. Rather, he says that when Christians make the love of their neighbor and the glory of God the highest aims in their work, then in the fields of "science . . . art . . . the state . . . [and] commerce and industry" more just and right relationships will be established. People will not advance at one another's expense, by living for their own glory. Rather people will flourish through inter-dependence and love. And when Christians work under the "controlling influence of the principle of the divine glory" rather than of our own, "there we can truly say that the kingdom of God has become manifest."[13]

Vos again warns that this must not lead to a triumphalist effort to somehow rid human culture of all its impurities. Pointing to the various parables, he says: "Our Lord desires to make plain that . . . a complete separation between the evil and the good cannot be effected until the end of the world. During the present age the kingdom must partake of . . . limitations and imperfections" out in the world, and yet we can also see real progress against evil and injustice.[14] Christians have and will continue to be "salt and light" in the world. Christians' ability to manifest the kingdom of God in these spheres is limited yet real.

If the death and resurrection of Jesus "only" secured my individual forgiveness of sins and opened the way for me to go to heaven when I die, that would be a wonderful truth. But incredibly, it means even more. Michael Horton speaks of growing up in fundamentalist Christian circles that missed the very idea of the kingdom of God and did not see the renewal of the whole world as the purpose of the resurrection. He wrote: "When I was growing up, salvation was [merely] 'going to heaven when I die.' Of course, we believed in the resurrection of the body and life everlasting, but it was a little confusing: Are we saved by [Jesus's] death or by [his] resurrection?"

When we focus only on the cross, we may see Christianity as only bringing forgiveness and peace to individuals. But when Horton came to understand the meaning of the resurrection, he said:

> It was liberating to learn that Christ was the beginning (first-fruits) of the new creation; that, united to him [by faith] . . . everything that happened to him has happened, is happening, and will happen to me; and that my salvation is wrapped up in the redemption of a people—the Israel of God—and a place, the renewed creation where righteousness dwells. It makes a big difference in our daily living whether we think *It's all going to burn* or

whether we think *The whole creation longs to be liberated from its bondage and share in the freedom of the children of God.*

(Romans 8:21)[15]

Jesus, the Stairway of God

When Jesus saw Nathanael approaching, he said of him, "Here truly is an Israelite in whom there is no deceit." "How do you know me?" Nathanael asked. Jesus answered, "I saw you while you were still under the fig tree before Philip called you." Then Nathanael declared, "Rabbi, you are the Son of God; you are the king of Israel." Jesus said, "You believe because I told you I saw you under the fig tree? You will see greater things than that. Very truly I tell you, you will see heaven open, and the angels of God ascending and descending on the Son of Man."

(John 1:47–51)

In the book of Genesis, Jacob deceived his aged, blind father, Isaac, into granting him the blessing due to the firstborn, his brother Esau. When Esau discovered the ruse, he wanted to kill Jacob. So Jacob fled into the wilderness. Now homeless and friendless, he was in despair. He lay down to sleep with his head on a stone for a pillow (Genesis 28:11). And he had a dream. In the dream there was a giant stairway, reaching all the way from earth to heaven, and on it there were angels. In the Bible angels represented the immediate, glorious presence of God. As we have seen, the glory and presence of God is not something that sinful human beings could enter. When Isaiah saw the holy God high and lifted up, he said, to paraphrase, "I'm falling apart" (Isaiah 6:1–6).[16] Jacob was a liar and a cheat who had never repented for all his wrongdoings. Yet here was a stairway for him, a connection between heaven and earth. Why would God come with his presence into Jacob's life? How *could* God come with his presence into Jacob's life? How could heaven be open to Jacob?

The answer came centuries later. Philip was a disciple of Jesus and he went to his friend Nathanael saying that he had found the Messiah "Jesus of Nazareth (verse 45). "Nazareth!" Nathanael scoffs, and he asks how anyone great could come from such a backwater place like Nazareth.

But he went along with Philip to see Jesus. And when they met, Jesus said "I saw you under the fig tree." We have no idea what happened there, but Nathanael did, and he was shocked that Jesus knew about it. He guessed that Jesus had some supernatural powers, like a magician, and said, "You are the king of Israel."

And Jesus replied, in effect, "You think that's something? I solemnly and truly tell you, you will see greater things than that. You will see heaven open and the angels of God ascending and descending on *me*."

There may never have been a more remarkable claim. Many ancient legends spoke of an axis mundi—some thing that connected heaven and earth and through which a pilgrim could pass, because of his strivings and efforts, into the divine realm. If Jesus had said, "I can show you the gate to heaven. I can show you the connection between heaven and earth," that would have been a claim to be a prophet, like the founders of other great religions. But he is not saying this. He is saying, "*I* am the axis mundi. Heaven and earth intersect on *me*. It's my living and dying and rising that will bring the Spirit of glory into the world and into your life."

"A cleft has been opened in the pitiless walls of the world," C. S. Lewis wrote, by "our great Captain."[17] He has blown a hole through the impenetrable barrier between us and God. So for all of us Jacobs, all of us who have apparently ruined our lives, people with just stones for pillows—for us there is infinite hope. Even we can have the glory and power of God in our lives.

CHAPTER 4

SUBVERSIVE HOPE

> But God chose the foolish things of the world to shame the wise; God chose the weak things of the world to shame the strong. God chose the lowly things of this world and the despised things—and the things that are not—to nullify the things that are, so that no one may boast before him. It is because of him that you are in Christ Jesus, who has become for us wisdom from God—that is, our righteousness, holiness and redemption. Therefore, as it is written: "Let the one who boasts boast in the Lord."
>
> —1 CORINTHIANS 1:27–31

The Subversiveness of the Kingdom

When Jesus rose from the dead, he brought the future kingdom of God into the present and he brought heaven to earth. We enter this kingdom now through repentance and faith in Jesus, and through the new birth by the Holy Spirit (John 3:3,5). Then we are literally "transferred" out of the kingdom of this world into "the kingdom of his dear Son" (Colossians 1:13 ESV). That is much more than merely adopting new beliefs and ethical practices. Entering a kingdom means to come under a new set of allegiances, to grow in new loves, and to submit to new guiding values for your life. Then hearts, families, relationships, communities, and fields of human culture are healed and rewoven as they are redirected toward the glory of God and come under the authority of Jesus the King, through his Word and Spirit (Psalm 72; Colossians 1:16–20; Ephesians 1:9–10).

This summarizes what we have seen so far. But we have not yet looked specifically at how the unique message and values of the kingdom contrast with the kingdom of this world and how they remake our lives, slowly but surely.

In Jesus's day the message of the kingdom contradicted all the world's categories. In our time the Christian faith is seen as something traditional rather than radical and disruptive. Nothing could be further from the truth. Properly understood, the message of God's kingdom will subvert the dominant beliefs of our own culture. The main reason for this misunderstanding is that the Bible is seen as a series of stories about how we can save ourselves through moral living. It is not seen for what it is—a single, coherent story about how Jesus Christ saves the world through the Great Reversal. We will trace out that story throughout the next two chapters.

The Upside-Down Kingdom

The world's expectation was for a Messiah to come once. Instead Jesus announces a Messiah who comes twice, and that means something completely unlooked for—a Messiah who comes twice comes the first time in weakness, not strength. That is why the two-stage kingdom is, from the world's point of view, the "upside-down" kingdom. This King comes in a way that reverses the values of the world. He comes in weakness and service, not strength and force, to die as a ransom for us.

There are three massive implications. First, it means that we enter the kingdom through this same upside-down pattern. Unlike in other religions, we do not achieve salvation by summoning up our strength to live a virtuous life. We receive salvation through the weakness of repentance. Second, it means that we also live and grow and serve in this kingdom not by taking power but, following Jesus, by giving up power in order to forgive, sacrifice, and serve. Finally, we see the whole world differently. We do not overly value the competent, confident, and successful. We do not bow and cater to the wealthy, brilliant, and able (James 2:1–7). Rather, we lift up those at the margins.

Not only does this structure challenge the dominant culture in which we live, but it reshapes our lives from the ground up. The first way it does that is by giving us a key to understanding how the entire Bible fits together.

Scholars have pointed to many themes that run through every part of the Scripture and through all stages in the history of God's relationship to humanity. The concepts that recur are those of kingdom and covenant, of worship and sanctuary, of rest and Sabbath, of exile and return, and others that could be named. But threading through them all is the theme of the Great Reversal. Biblical scholar G. K. Beale calls this "God's ironic overturning of human wisdom."[1] In dramatic irony, narrated events are reversed, turned in a direction opposite to where we would have expected them to head. So, argues Beale, God deals with human beings in two different but similarly ironic ways.

There is *retributive reversal*, in which the desired successes of sinful living end up being curses. The freedom and reward sin appears to offer become slavery and curse. Sin has a boomerang effect, so that those who betray will be betrayed, those who lie will be lied to, those who live by the sword will die by the sword. Second, there is *redemptive reversal*, in which God chooses the weak over the powerful, the foolish over the wise, in order to save the world. And then God saves *through* the weakness, not despite it. "The faithful appear to be cursed, but as they persevere in faith, they are really in the midst of being blessed."[2]

The remarkable message of the Bible, then, is: "Everyone is ultimately caught in the matrix of one of these two . . . patterns of living."[3] The good things of this world seen as blessings (beauty, power, comfort, success, recognition) but received without God become curses. They will drive you and consume you. And so the most just thing God can do to those who reject him is to give them up to what they want (Romans 1: 21–25). However, the hard things of this world seen as curses (weakness, deprivation, loss, and rejection) but received with faith in God will be turned into blessings (2 Corinthians 4:16–17, 12:10). Every person lives within one of these matrices; each one of us is traveling along one trajectory or the other.

In God's economy the high will be brought low and the low lifted up. As Hannah sings: "The bows of the mighty are broken, but the feeble bind on strength" (1 Samuel 2:4 ESV). Those who seek to ascend to power will find they are only descending; those who descend in humility will find they have ascended, "for all those who exalt themselves will be humbled, and those who humble themselves will be exalted" (Luke 14:11; cf. Luke 14:7–10).

We can summarize it this way. *There are the good things of this world, the hard things of this world, and the best things of this world—God's love, glory, holiness, beauty. The Bible's teaching is that the road to the best things is not through the good things but usually through the hard things, as Jesus himself shows us in Philippians 2:5–11.* There is no message more contrary to the way the world understands life or more subversive to its values.

Not only does the Great Reversal challenge the world's thought categories, but it is the most practical guide to real life. These reversal patterns have been deeply embedded into the fabric of the world by its Creator and Redeemer. To be blind to them will make you temporarily arrogant like Job's friends, who were sure that anyone having a bad life must be a bad person. But this shallow smugness will be temporary, because suffering in life is inevitable, and when it comes upon you, your simplistic worldview will cause you to collapse into despair or cynicism. But if you see that God is the God of the Great Reversal—the God who brings life out of death, resurrection after crucifixion, the God who makes the last to be first and the first to be last—you will be able to take heart and be of good courage. If we remember this, we can face anything.

In the rest of this chapter, I will trace out this crucial biblical storyline through the Old Testament, and then I will proceed in the next chapter to look at Jesus himself, its ultimate embodiment and fulfillment.

The Boys Nobody Chose

In Genesis, we read about cultures in which there were two "iron laws."[4] One was that the worth of a woman was in her beauty and fertility, in how many children she bore in order to furnish the tribe with workers and soldiers. The other was the law of primogeniture, giving the oldest son nearly all the estate and wealth of the family. But in the pages of Genesis, you see God overturning the world's values. In every generation God works not with the son who has the greater cultural power and status but with the younger son. It's Abel over Cain, Isaac over Ishmael, Jacob over Esau, Joseph and Judah over Reuben, Ephraim over Manasseh. Later, we see God choosing Moses over Aaron and David over his older brothers.

And not only were all of these figures younger sons, which was remarkable in itself, but they were also flawed men, a fact the biblical texts do nothing to hide. Jacob was a man who, damaged by his father's favoritism toward Esau, became a dishonest schemer. Moses had some sort of speech impediment. Later in the Bible, God chooses deliverers like Gideon, Jephthah, and Samson, whose lives are littered with the wreckage of foolish decisions and evil actions. The repeated choice of such weak men in each generation cannot be a coincidence. God does it to better display his power to transform the most unpromising lives.

The Women Nobody Wanted

Another perennial feature of our world, whether ancient or modern, has been that the beautiful and fertile women receive favor, power, privilege, and of course the attention of the most powerful men. This pattern is so persistent that even in our more egalitarian societies, women's bodies and appearances are still used as a measure of their worth. Women who rightfully protest against others imposing such a standard on them find themselves struggling not to do it to themselves. That is how deeply ingrained it is in human life and culture.

But here again we see God turning the world's tables upside down long before Jesus did it in the temple. In the Old Testament we see God working through the spent and aged Sarah rather than the young Hagar, with the plain Leah over the beautiful Rachel, with Hannah and Samson's mother, the barren women.

God also worked through Tamar, Rahab, Ruth, and Bathsheba. Each one was an outsider by the social standards of the time. Tamar tricked her father-in-law into a sexual encounter. Rahab was a prostitute, Ruth a pagan of a despised race, and Bathsheba the wife of another man, forced into an adulterous affair with King David. Here again we see persons who, in the eyes of the cultural elites, were morally, racially, and socially marginal. Yet each woman is included in the genealogy of Jesus (Matthew 1:1–7) because they were all Jesus's foremothers. The salvation of the world came through them. God takes the people who the world consigns to the margins and brings them into the center.

The People Whom Everyone Despised

In Revelation 7 we are told that in the end God will have saved a great multitude from "every nation, tribe, people, and language" (Revelation 7:9) and, we could add, every social class. God is not biased against any race or class, and many of those who receive faith and whom God uses are wealthy. Abraham, Job, and Joseph of Arimathea are just three. Nevertheless, God puts special emphasis on honoring and using people and groups on the outside of worldly hierarchies of power.

In Deuteronomy 7 God says to Israel:

> The Lord your God has chosen you out of all the peoples on the face of the earth to be his people, his treasured possession. The Lord did not set his affection on you and choose you because you

were more numerous than other peoples, for you were the fewest
of all peoples. But it was because the Lord loved you and kept the
oath he swore to your ancestors that he brought you out with a
mighty hand and redeemed you from the land of slavery, from
the power of Pharaoh king of Egypt.

(Deuteronomy 7:6–8)

God knows everything, and he certainly knew that the Egyptians,
and then the Assyrians, Babylonians, Persians, Greeks, and the Romans,
would ascend to military, economic, and cultural power over the world.
Would not any of those have been better messengers through which God
could have sent his salvation into the world? Why didn't he reveal himself
to them? Why instead did he reveal himself to Israel, a small and backwater
nation? In this remarkable passage God tells the Israelites that he chose
them not in spite of their powerlessness but *because* of it.

Not only does he initially choose a small, powerless nation of slaves to
bring his salvation to the world, but he repeatedly brings strength out of
their weakness, as we have seen in the lives of the judges, such as Jephthah,
Gideon, and Samson, to whom the people turned when their helpless condition drove them to reliance upon the Lord. When the prophet Habakkuk
asked God to renew Israel's society, which had fallen into corruption and
injustice (Habakkuk 1:1–4), God replied that he was going to allow Israel to
become even weaker in order to bring it to new strength (Habakkuk
1:5–11).

And indeed terrible things happened to Israel. Babylon sacked Jerusalem and killed great numbers. Others were taken in exile to Babylon in
order to eradicate the cultural identity of the remaining Jews. Within two
generations, it was thought, the Israelites would lose their distinctive religious and national identity and become Babylonians. In short, Israel faced
complete extermination. The exiles seemed resigned to their fate when
they asked, "How can we sing the songs of the Lord while in a foreign land?"
(Psalm 137:4) And yet that is exactly what they learned to do. In exile the
Israelites finally confronted their own evil and sin (Daniel 9:4–14). They

also learned to do something crucial for the future of God's redemptive plan: they learned to sing the Lord's song in a foreign land, to maintain their faith and grow as a religious minority in a highly pluralistic society through synagogue worship. Not only did this ensure the long-term survival of Israel over the centuries while more powerful nations and national groups were going extinct but, as many have pointed out, the synagogue became one of the main models for the Christian church.

Again we see that the way up is down, that the way to strength is through weakness, and that God has a plan and walks with us in the midst of our suffering, fragility, and helplessness.

The Storyline Nobody Wants to Be In

We want the storyline of our lives to go from strength to strength, from success to success, and end happily ever after. But throughout the Bible we see something completely different—a persistent narrative pattern of life through death or of triumph through weakness that reveals how God works in history and in our lives.

In the story of Naaman, the Syrian general with leprosy (2 Kings 5:1–19), the kings of Syria and of Israel and Naaman himself were clueless about how God's salvation and blessing comes while the servants and slaves showed wisdom. In the story of Jonah we see the prophet of the Lord running from God and creating a crisis for the sailors, and yet these supposedly profane pagan men showed more wisdom, compassion, and moral fiber than Jonah (Jonah 1:1–17). Jonah himself became able to follow God's call only after he experienced an almost literal death (in the great fish) and resurrection.

Joseph saved Egypt and his family, but only after he went through a kind of death, the "death" of slavery and imprisonment and despair (see Genesis 27–50). Samson was a man of great physical strength but also, to put it mildly, of great emotional immaturity. Only after his foolishness and pride resulted in his being blinded and imprisoned did his faith finally come to maturity. It was only out of this experience of weakness that he was able to finally become truly strong to accomplish his greatest triumph over his people's enemies (see Judges 13–16).

Ruth had little social power, like nearly all women in ancient times. A Moabitess, she loved and followed her mother-in-law, Naomi, back into Israel, where she was socially defenseless as both a widow and a member of a despised race. She did this to help Naomi, though she knew she was vulnerable to being abused (Ruth 2:8–10). Yet through this willing "death" Ruth not only protected Naomi but was chosen by God to be a mother of King David and of Jesus himself.

The account of David and Goliath may be the most well-known story from the Old Testament that shows us how this narrative of reversal plays out. The Philistines' army had a champion, Goliath, who challenged an Israelite warrior to one-on-one combat. The nation of the man who lost the contest would be considered conquered and under the power of the country of the man who won. David was not a top soldier—he wasn't a soldier at all. He was a boy too young to fight in the army. But he won, not in spite of his smallness and weakness but because of it. His slight stature led the giant to lower all his defenses and made him vulnerable to a small but lethal stone from David's sling. "God . . . caused strength to come from his youthful weakness in order to conquer the strong giant."[5] To drive the point home, God says to Samuel the prophet, who at the moment was judging "king material" by physical appearance, that "the Lord sees not as man sees: man looks on the outward appearance, but the Lord looks on the heart" (1 Samuel 16:7 ESV).

The pattern is clear and pervasive. The author of the letter to the Hebrews, looking back on all the figures in the history of Israel, sums all the stories up this way.

> And what more shall I say? I do not have time to tell about Gideon, Barak, Samson and Jephthah, about David and Samuel and the prophets, who through faith conquered kingdoms, administered justice, and gained what was promised; who shut the

mouths of lions, quenched the fury of the flames, and escaped the edge of the sword; whose weakness was turned to strength.... Women received back their dead, raised to life again. There were others who were tortured, refusing to be released, so that they might gain an even better resurrection.

(Hebrews 11:32–35)

"Whose weakness was turned to strength." To whom is he referring? Virtually every major figure in the Bible. Gideon was the least in his father's family and his family the poorest in their tribe (Judges 6:15). Jephthah was an outcast and the son of a prostitute (Judges 11:1–33). Women such as the poor widow of Zarephath (1 Kings 17:17–24) and the wealthy woman of Shunem (2 Kings 4:17–37) were drawn out of the depths of despair when each "received their dead [sons] back by resurrection." In case after case God chooses the weak and then saves not just despite but through their weakness.

Biblical writers not only give us narrative accounts that follow this plotline but often speak directly about it. Isaiah tells us that God loves to reverse the world's order, bringing up the poor and bringing down the powerful (Isaiah 29:19–21). Psalm 8 says

> *Out of the mouth of babies and infants,*
> *you have established strength because of your foes,*
> *to still the enemy and the avenger.*

(Psalm 8:2, ESV)

God's deliverance and salvation will triumph over his enemies through "babies and infants"—the weak, not the strong. In this psalm David perceives the Great Reversal at work in history even though he cannot see clearly its climax in *the* death and *the* resurrection of God the Son himself, where Jesus "established strength" through his humiliation and crucifixion in order to dispatch once and for all our great enemy, death (Hebrews 2:9,14; cf. 1 Corinthians 15:26).

The Gospel People Do Not Want to Hear

When Mary hears from an angel that she will give birth to the Messiah, she exclaims: "He has brought down rulers from their thrones but has lifted up the humble. He has filled the hungry with good things but has sent the rich away empty" (Luke 1:52–53). This is not a categorical statement that God casts down every king and promotes every poor person without exception. But Mary looked back through the whole of the Hebrew Scriptures and, by the inspiration of the Holy Spirit, she saw herself as part of this plotline. Likewise James also looks back through the Old Testament and concludes: "Has not God chosen those who are poor in the eyes of the world to be rich in faith and to inherit the kingdom he promises to those who love him?" (James 2:5).

God in the end will save people from every class. Nevertheless the message of the gospel of grace does not appeal to the privileged and powerful. Our instinct is to always take credit for any success in life. We believe we have achieved our position only through hard work and moral fiber. We have earned everything we have. Any religion that appeals naturally to the competent, confident, and successful will support that self-understanding. The message that will make sense to human beings is "Pull yourself together! Summon up the blood! Be disciplined, moral, good. Earn your blessing and God will give it to you."

A message that will not make sense to them and that will threaten their self-image at its core is this: "You are a lost sinner. You have done many wrongs, but even the good things you've done you've largely done for self-interested motives. All your strivings, even religious ones, have been ways to get control of God, putting him in a position so that (you think) he will have to serve your interests. Everything you have is a gift from God, and you are not loving him and living wholly for him as you should. If you repent, you can be saved, but only through his sheer, undeserved grace."

That, of course, is the gospel of the New Testament, based on what the entire sweep of the Old Testament teaches about the character of God and of human nature. And the more powerful, well off, and pulled together you are, the more offensive and unthinkable such a faith message is.

I have lived in New York City for over three decades. It is one of the greatest concentrations of competent, confident, and successful people on earth. Not surprisingly, the Christian faith is weak at the center, in Manhattan, where our family has lived. But in the boroughs, where the working class and the poor live, Christianity flourishes. That should not surprise us at all. Once I heard a social scientist, himself not a man of faith, say about New York City, "The secular elites say they are on the side of the poor, but ironically, the poor are on the side of faith and especially of born-again Christianity."

How fair and just—and how subversive—of God to work so often and constantly among the people whom the "good and the great" of the world reject.

CHAPTER 5

THE GREAT REVERSAL

> Christ Jesus who, though he was in the form of God, did not count equality with God a thing to be grasped, but emptied himself, by taking the form of a servant, being born in the likeness of men. And being found in human form, he humbled himself by becoming obedient to the point of death, even death on a cross. Therefore God has highly exalted him and bestowed on him the name that is above every name, so that at the name of Jesus every knee should bow, in heaven and on earth and under the earth, and every tongue confess that Jesus Christ is Lord, to the glory of God the Father.
>
> —PHILIPPIANS 2:5–11 (ESV)

We have seen the prevalent pattern of reversal in the Old Testament. In every generation God has worked with the women and men, the families and nations, that no one else wanted. And not only did he choose the unwanted and weak, but he saved them again and again *through* their failures, their helplessness, and their sufferings. Is God a romantic who roots for the underdog? Certainly God is a loving God, *but* there is more going on here than sentimentalism.

These Old Testament accounts are not just interesting stories but foretastes of and signposts toward God's final salvation in Jesus Christ. In Jesus we discover not just another unexpected turn, but the Great Reversal. There is no better exposition of this than Philippians 2. Verse 8 tells us that

Jesus died on the cross, and verse 9 begins "*Therefore* God exalted him . . ." God raised Jesus not just in spite of his death but because of it. He was rejected, condemned, tortured, executed, and *therefore* God raised and exalted him. The vindication of resurrection is both the reversal and the result of the condemnation of crucifixion. The darkness of Good Friday brings about the sunrise of Easter. This is how God works. This is the Great Reversal of history and the New Testament bears witness to it throughout.

The Gospel of Mark—to Serve, Not to Be Served

The book of Mark is a prime example.

The gospel opens with Mark quoting the famous Isaiah 40 prophecy that the Lord himself would someday come to his people. Then he makes the astonishing claim that Jesus's coming is the fulfillment of Isaiah's words (Mark 1:1–4). The all-powerful Lord of the universe has come to earth in Jesus Christ. In the first half of Mark's gospel, readers are led to expect that Jesus will shortly put forth his strength and destroy all opposition. Again and again, we see his supernatural power as he heals the sick, calms the storm, and feeds the multitude. Even the demons cry out and are helpless before him (Mark 1:24). It soon seemed as if all the evil forces that oppress us would be overturned by Jesus, the Messiah.

But in the second half of the book of Mark everything reverses. We see the Messiah being persecuted by enemies, forsaken by his friends and even by his Father on the cross (Mark 27:46). In the middle of all this Jesus tells his listeners that he is a King that came not to be served, but to serve (Mark 10:45).

But even in the first half of Mark, there are signs that Jesus is not acting as we think a Deliverer should act. Duke New Testament scholar Richard B. Hays points out, Jesus's campaign against evil "is waged in a mysterious way that no one could have expected, culminating in the cross."[1] He notes three ways the ministry of Jesus in the book of Mark is so strange and startling.

First, he writes, "[In the Gospel of Mark], God's ... invasion of the world has wrought an inversion: God has reversed the positions of insiders and outsiders." In Mark 3 the leaders of the people reject him, but the common people, in huge crowds, are "pushing forward to touch him" (Mark 3:9–10). The people who should be leading are "behind" and the people who should be behind are in front.

> Those who are in positions of authority and privilege reject Jesus and the message; even Jesus's own disciples [are continually shown to be] slow to understand his teaching. Others, however—people of low or despised position in the social world of first-century Jewish culture—receive the gospel gladly, for their need is great. The lepers, the demon-possessed, the woman with a hemorrhage (5:25–34), the Syrophoenician woman (7:24–30), the little children (10:13–16), blind Bartimaeus (10:46–52), the nameless woman who anoints Jesus at Bethany for burial (14:3–9), the Gentile centurion at the cross (15:39)—these are examples put forth by Mark of faithful response to Jesus. "Many who are the first will be the last, and the last will be first" (10:31). Those of us who are familiar with the story should not underestimate the shock of this inversion.[2]

Second, "Mark's gospel redefines the nature of power and the value of suffering." Jesus chooses the powerless over the powerful, but he does not, as revolutionaries do, merely get them to exchange places. The gospel *redefines* power. Hays writes: "Those who exercise power to dominate others, to kill and oppress, are shown not only as villains but also, surprisingly, as pawns of forces beyond their control." Herod (Mark 6:14–29) and Pilate (Mark 15:1–15) are case studies.

We see Jesus giving up his power as he becomes a vulnerable mortal and falls victim to a violent miscarriage of justice. But Jesus's apparent powerlessness is actually power used to serve others, rather than power used to control others. To sacrifice power in love is to exert the power of love to change things. This, then, is the true power of God: "The Son of Man did not come to be served but to serve, and to give his life as a ransom for many (Mark 10:45)." In no other way could sin and death have been defeated. Hays writes that power deferral and suffering become "meaningful and necessary in the mysterious working of God's will."[3]

Finally, Hays writes: "Mark's vision of the moral life is profoundly *ironic*."[4] Like Beale, Hays understands irony as statements or events that eventually are turned into the opposite way that they originally appear to be headed. Irony is always surprising because it shatters expectations.[5] Contrary to the popular view, God is not just a cosmic rule-keeper who smites the disobedient and showers blessings on the obedient. Hays argues that to recognize that God regularly works in unforeseen and counterintuitive ways undermines over confidence and leads toward humility and open-mindedness.[6]

The Gospel of Luke—the First Shall Be Last

The author Luke penned both the gospel of Luke and the book of Acts. In both books the main plotline is driven by reversal. In Luke, perhaps more than any other gospel, we see Jesus's love for outcasts. "The last will be first and the first will be last" (Luke 13:30).

Samaritans were seen by the Jews as racial inferiors and enemies, yet Jesus places Samaritans on the same spiritual level as the Jews (Luke 9:54; 17:16) or higher (Luke 10:25–37). Jesus's freedom from the racist tribalism so common in his time was explosive. A riot was touched off when he declared that God loved Gentiles as much as the Jews (Luke 4:55–27).

Tax collectors were despised as well. They were usually Jewish men who contracted with the Roman government to collect taxes from the populace and who, backed by imperial power, were able to extort enormous sums that largely went into their own pockets. They were rightly seen as collaborators, much like those in France who took positions of authority and profited from them under Nazi occupation. Yet in the gospel of Luke tax collectors were referenced six times, and always in a positive way. Tax collectors eagerly sought out the preaching and ministry of John the Baptist and Jesus (Luke 3:12, 5:27–30, 7:29,31, 15:1). Zacchaeus came to faith in Christ, and it was the nameless tax collector in Jesus's parable, not the religious leader, who "went home justified" because he understood the grace of God. "For all those who exalt themselves will be humbled, and those who humble themselves will be exalted" (Luke 18:9–14).

Jesus showed special concern for children, despite his followers' argument that they were not worth his time (Luke 18:15–17). He reached out to lepers, who were impoverished, sick, dying, and who lived on the margins of society. Yet Jesus reached out his hand and touched them, fulfilling their need for human contact and defying social prohibitions (Luke 5:12–16, 17:11–19).

Luke documented Jesus's affirmation of women. Luke mentions thirteen women not mentioned elsewhere. He includes the story of the widow of Nain (Luke 7:11–17) and the women who supported Jesus financially (Luke 8:1–3). He accepts the "sinful woman" who wipes his feet with her hair (Luke 7:36–50). Women are prominent in Luke's birth and resurrection narratives.

Finally, Luke showed us how deeply concerned Jesus was for the poor. Several times Jesus says that his gospel message is "good news to the poor" (Luke 4:18, 7:22). He exhorts his disciples not only to be radically generous to the poor (Luke 11:41; 12:33; 19:8) but to welcome them into their homes and families (Luke 14:13). Jesus declared that the sacrificial giving of the poor widow—two copper coins—was more valuable to God than the philanthropy of the wealthy (Luke 12:2–3).[7]

"So Shall the Son of Man Be Lifted Up"

Why does God repeatedly choose the less powerful people and then work his deliverances through their powerlessness and suffering? The stories are moving because everyone loves to see a forgotten woman or belittled man come from behind and win. And these accounts of Jesus's love for the poor, outcasts, lepers, and tax collectors are encouraging, because we modern people care about justice. But it is a grave mistake to think that these biblical accounts are there to merely inspire us. Rather, they are written down to *convert* us, to convert us to Christ (1 Corinthians 10:1–4,11). All these little reversals point us toward the Great Reversal, the death and resurrection of the Son of God.

Jesus Christ was a King who triumphantly entered his city (John 12:12–19), where his followers expected that he would be exalted and lifted up to the throne. Immediately after his triumphal entry, Jesus said that he would be "lifted up from the earth," but in order to die (John 12:32–33). Instead of a throne he would be lifted up on a cross. Another time Jesus spoke of being lifted up to die is in John 3:14–15, where he said:

> Just as Moses lifted up the snake in the wilderness, so the Son of Man must be lifted up, that everyone who believes may have eternal life in him.

Jesus was alluding to the strange incident that occurred during the wilderness wanderings of the Israelites before they reached their homeland recounted in Numbers 21. The Israelites had been turning away from God, and so the Lord sent into the camp poisonous snakes to bite people, and now some were dying. They repented and asked Moses to call to the Lord for their healing. God heard their prayer and directed Moses to put a bronze image of a poisonous snake on a pole, high in the middle of the camp. Anyone who had been bitten merely had to look at the image and he or she would live. The irony of the remedy was that people would be healed by looking on the very thing that had made them sick in the first place. The whole incident hinted that God would not just remove the curse of death but would somehow bring a blessing *through* the curse of death.

When Jesus said he would be lifted up on a cross *just as* the serpent was lifted up on a pole, he was referring to what Paul meant when he wrote in 2 Corinthians 5:21 that Jesus was "made . . . to be sin" and in Galatians 3:13

that Christ redeemed us "by becoming a curse for us." The "wages of sin"—the just curse and penalty for sin—is death (Romans 6:23). On the cross Jesus became, as it were, the very thing that was destroying us. He was treated as if he were sinful, and so he was cursed and put to death in our place. And now it is only as we in faith look at him on the cross—as we look at him becoming the sin that was killing us and taking the death that should have been ours—that we can be forgiven and healed. On the cross God turned the curse of death on sin into a blessing for us.

The Gospel and the Great Reversal

The Great Reversal, then, helps us understand the gospel itself. In an article outlining Saint Paul's presentation of the gospel, Cambridge scholar Simon Gathercole noted that many people traditionally locate the gospel wholly in the cross, presenting it as simply "Jesus died to forgive you for your sins." In that gospel presentation the resurrection is just a miraculous afterthought.[8] More recently there are those who, in an effort to avoid this, have said that the gospel is simply "Jesus is Lord." This can be as simplistic as the alternative, giving the impression that the gospel is only obeying Jesus's teaching. Certainly Christians do this, but this formulation obscures the fact that Jesus's salvation comes by sheer grace, apart from our moral efforts.[9]

After looking at a number of Pauline presentations of the gospel, Gathercole identified three recurring ideas. First, there was the good news of who Jesus *is* (Romans 1:3–4). He is the eternal Son of God, who humbled himself and also became a human being, the Messiah. Second, there is the good news of what Jesus *has done*—he died on the cross and rose from the dead (1 Corinthians 15:3–4). Finally, there is the good news of what he *brings*. When he rose from the dead he brought in the new creation and the power of the Spirit (Colossians 2:13–15; Ephesians 2:4–7). In summary, Gathercole says that the gospel is that, through the "death and resurrection" of "Jesus the Messiah . . . he atones for sin and brings new creation."[10]

Gathercole's survey shows us that the idea of the Great Reversal is at the heart of the gospel. The incarnation, death, and resurrection of Jesus is good news because of the wondrous love he showed in exchanging places with us. He came from heaven to earth that we might go from earth to heaven. He was rich and became poor so that through his poverty we might become rich (2 Corinthians 8:9). He became sin so that through his becoming sin we might become the righteousness of God in him (2 Corinthians 5:21). His curse is our blessing (Galatians 3:13–14). That is the gospel.

Foolishness and Weakness

Jesus's death and resurrection not only brings in salvation but also constitutes the ultimate refutation of the world's wisdom.

Let's do a thought experiment. Assemble some business and political consultants who have gone to all the best schools and have worked for the best companies and campaigns and whose clients have seen the most success. Bring them together and pose this question: "I have a goal. My long-term goal is to be the most influential and famous person who ever lived. Centuries from now I want to have whole civilizations built on my teachings, and I want to be at the center of the lives of hundreds of millions of people. What should I do to accomplish this?"

Assuming the world's greatest consultants took you seriously, what would they say? Would it be anything like this? "Be born in obscurity. Avoid ever getting involved in any of the powerful political or economic or academic networks. Be tragically killed in your early thirties, before you ever write a book." Of course they would not give that counsel. But that's how Jesus did it, and he makes foolish the wisdom of the world.

And consider how greatly he would have failed if he had followed the world's advice for becoming successful. What if he had come as a philosopher with a great intellectual system of thought? Then the only people helped by him would have been the intellectuals. What if he had led a powerful movement of moral teaching with himself as the living example? Then only the people strong, able, and accomplished enough to imitate him would have benefitted.

But across both history and the nations of the world, we have seen people from all classes and conditions finding peace and power in the gospel of Jesus. Poor people do not gather in homes to discuss Plato or Aristotle, but they do to study and talk about the message of Jesus, and their lives are changed by it. Jesus did not come and say, "I'm strong and brilliant. Now pull yourself together and you can be like me." Jesus Christ exchanged places with you. He came to live the life you should have lived and die the death you should have died so you could be reconciled to God, forgiven, and remade.

This is why the gospel message is good for everyone and its transforming power continues to grow across the face of the earth. It's not just for the moral, the strong, the brilliant. It doesn't matter who you are or what you've done.

This is why Paul wrote:

> Where is the wise person? Where is the teacher of the law? Where is the philosopher of this age? Has not God made foolish the wisdom of the world? For since in the wisdom of God the world through its wisdom did not know him, God was pleased through the foolishness of what was preached to save those who believe. Jews demand signs and Greeks look for wisdom, but we preach Christ crucified: a stumbling block to Jews and foolishness to Gentiles, but to those whom God has called, both Jews and Greeks, Christ the power of God and the wisdom of God. *For the foolishness of God is wiser than human wisdom, and the weakness of God is stronger than human strength.*
>
> **(1 Corinthians 1:20–25)**

In the view of the world, Jesus's death on the cross was a complete failure. "How," asked some people, "could he help the world without becoming a great philosopher and teacher? He needed to establish a school of thought!" "How," asked others, "could he help the world without becoming a great general and leader? He needed to set up an empire!" The crucified Messiah was foolishness to the Greeks and weakness to the Jews—but surely history has proven those first-century skeptics wrong. The Great Reversal is both *true* wisdom and *true* power, and it shows, ironically, that the world's understanding of greatness is a weakness which leads to continual wars and conflicts. And the world's understanding of wisdom—reason without God—is the most fruitless thing possible. So "the foolishness of God is wiser than human wisdom, and the weakness of God is stronger than human strength."

The founders of the other great world religions died peacefully, surrounded by their followers and the knowledge that their movement was growing. In contrast, Jesus died in disgrace, betrayed, denied, and abandoned by everyone, even his Father.

Other world religions teach salvation through ascent to God through good works, moral virtue, ritual observances, and transformation of consciousness. In contrast, Christianity is about salvation through God's descending to us. This is the great difference between Christianity and every other philosophical and religious system.

Take Up Your Cross, Give Up Your Glory

When Jesus calls us to take up our cross and follow him (Matthew 16:24), it means that to be saved and changed by his Great Reversal we must go through our own reversal. Just as he did not accomplish our salvation through the exertion of power but through voluntary loss, so we receive this salvation not by summoning up our strength to achieve moral perfection but by admitting our utter weakness, helplessness, and need. And just as his weakness and shame was the only way to real strength and glory, so our repentance and acknowledgment of guilt and sin is the only way to the highest confidence and honor, the knowledge that in Christ we are accepted and delighted in by the Lord of all.

There are some gifts that can't be accepted without admitting weakness.

Imagine an aging man whose hearing is failing but who is in denial about it. He usually complains that it is other people who are mumbling. But finally his wife gets him to go get his hearing tested. The clear verdict is that he needs hearing aids, but when he sees what they cost, he is taken aback. "We can't afford that," he says. But his wife counters and says, "Buy the best ones and consider it a gift from me." That sounds nice, but the man realizes that to accept this gift is to admit weakness. It would be like saying, "Thanks so much for this. Indeed I *am* an aging man who can't hear what people are telling me!" There is no way to receive some gifts without admitting your need.[11]

The gospel is the ultimate gift that requires such a radical admission.

This humility and willingness to give up control of your life is impossible to produce without God's help. But I have seen that help come to people as they look on the beauty of what Jesus has done for them. The greatest glory is to give away your glory for someone else. There is nothing more beautiful than someone giving up their beauty to save someone else.

> He had no beauty or majesty to attract us to him,
> nothing in his appearance that we should desire him.
> He was despised and rejected by mankind,
> a man of suffering, and familiar with pain.
> Like one from whom people hide their faces
> he was despised, and we held him in low esteem.
> Surely he took up our pain
> and bore our suffering,
> yet we considered him punished by God,
> stricken by him, and afflicted.
> But he was pierced for our transgressions,
> he was crushed for our iniquities;

the punishment that brought us peace was on him,
and by his wounds we are healed.

(Isaiah 53:2–5)

John Calvin expressed the beautiful paradox of Jesus's Great Reversal like this:

> He was sold, to buy us back; captive, to deliver us; condemned, to absolve us; he was made a curse for our blessing, sin offering for our righteousness; marred that we may be made fair; he died for our life; so that by him fury is made gentle, wrath appeased, darkness turned into light, fear reassured, despisal despised, debt canceled, labor lightened, sadness made merry, misfortune made fortunate, difficulty easy, disorder ordered, division united, ignominy ennobled, rebellion subjected, intimidation intimidated, ambush uncovered, assaults assailed, force forced back, combat combated, war warred against, vengeance avenged, torment tormented, damnation damned, the abyss sunk into the abyss, hell transfixed, death dead, mortality made immortal. In short, mercy has swallowed up all misery, and goodness all misfortune.[12]

CHAPTER 6

PERSONAL HOPE: 1

＊

The resurrection of Jesus Christ actually happened, but this is not a historical fact like all others. Whether I do or don't believe that Julius Caesar crossed the Rubicon in 49 AD, it doesn't change my life. Belief in the historicity of the resurrection, however, can change you wholly—but not through intellectual assent alone. It is only by meeting the risen Lord personally and uniting with him by faith that we are changed. Only then can we truly experience the powerful "hope to which he has called you" (Ephesians 1:18). The New Testament gives us five case studies of people who met Jesus after his resurrection. Four of them are in the last two chapters of the gospel of John and the last, the conversion of Paul, is in Acts 9. Together these chapters tell us what it is like to meet the risen Christ personally.

Mary Meets Jesus

Now Mary stood outside the tomb crying. . . . She turned around and saw Jesus standing there, but she did not realize that it was Jesus. He asked her, "Woman, why are you crying? Who is it you are looking for?" Thinking he was the gardener, she said, "Sir, if you have carried him away, tell me where you have put him, and I will get him." Jesus said to her, "Mary." She turned toward him and cried out in Aramaic, "Rabboni!" (which means "Teacher"). Jesus said, "Do not hold on to me, for I have not yet ascended to the Father. Go instead to my brothers and tell them, 'I am ascending to my Father and your Father, to my God and your God.'" Mary Magdalene went to the disciples with the news: "I have seen the Lord!" And she told them that he had said these things to her.[1]

(John 20:11,14–18)

When the risen Jesus approached her, Mary saw him but did "not realize that it was Jesus" (verse 14). This is not surprising. We've already seen how the disciples on the road to Emmaus did not recognize him at first. Christ's resurrection body was the body he had before, yet now it was wholly transformed and perfected, and so people who had known Jesus could not immediately identify him when they saw him raised from the dead.

But there was probably more to the inability of Mary to recognize Jesus than that. In her mind she had a narrative through which she was interpreting everything. "'They have taken my Lord away,' she said, 'and I don't know where they have put him.'" (John 20:13) Because of this narrative she failed to recognize the angels and even Jesus himself. Jesus and his salvation did not fit her expectations, which functioned like a filter or screen, making it impossible to see him right in front of her. Although she was looking right at him, she couldn't see him.

In this, Mary represents the entire human race. Acts 13:27 tells us, "The people of Jerusalem and their rulers did not recognize Jesus, yet in condemning him they fulfilled the words of the prophets." We must not conclude that the residents of Jerusalem were unusually spiritually blind, so that if Jesus had gone to Rome or to some other place the people there would have realized he was Son of God and Savior. No, the problem is one shared by the entire human race.

"No one seeks for God," Paul wrote in Romans 3:10, meaning *not* that no one seeks for the divine and transcendent or for spirituality in general, but that no human being seeks the true God. We seek spirituality, but the human heart always wants a God who fits our desires, a God we can control, who doesn't challenge our self-assessments and narratives. Whatever Mary's idea was of Jesus at that moment, the figure standing before her did not fit it. The message of the Bible is that God never fits human categories and conceptions of what he should be.

There would be no hope for us if God waited for us to make the first move. We would be lost if he stood apart from us, tapping his foot impatiently, waiting for us to figure out for ourselves who and where he is. Unless he calls us by name, we would never come to him.

And that is exactly what he does with Mary. He begins with questions—"Why are you crying? Who is it you are looking for?" He does not approach like a sergeant seeking submission but like a counselor seeking insight. Mary may have spent the rest of her life thinking about the double meaning in his question "Who are you looking for?" It's as if Jesus was saying, "Mary, you love me, but your understanding of me is still far too small."

Finally Jesus breaks through to her heart. Notice the order. We do not hear her call him "Teacher!" followed by his "Mary!" Instead we hear him call "Mary!" followed by her amazement—"Teacher!" Christian salvation is never our attainment, a prize after a long struggle while God waits for us. No, he comes to us and wakes us out of sleep. It is always a gift of grace.

My heart owns none before Thee,
For Thy rich grace I thirst;
This knowing, if I love Thee,
Thou must have loved me first.[2]

We also learn that Christian faith means intimate, personal communion. As soon as Mary cries "Rabboni [Teacher]!" Jesus says to Mary, "Do not hold on to me" (verse 17). At first glance that is a strange statement. Some have thought he was saying, "Don't touch me; I'm too holy," as when God spoke to Moses out of the bush and told him not to come any closer (Exodus 3:5). But this does not explain why Jesus invited Thomas to touch him later in the chapter (John 20:27) and why he let other women who met him clasp his feet (Matthew 28:9).

Things become clearer when we realize that the term translated "hold on to me" is a word that means to cling very tightly, even to pinch. It is more than likely that when Mary realized it was Jesus, she embraced him with all her physical and emotional strength. This is not surprising. Luke 8:2 tells us that Jesus had freed Mary from "seven demons." He had delivered her from spiritual and emotional torment. When he died she had thought she had lost him forever, and now she was thunderstruck to learn he was alive. Of course she would have hugged him with all her might. Jesus, however, says:

> "Do not hold on to me, for I have not yet ascended to the Father. Go instead to my brothers and tell them, 'I am ascending to my Father and your Father, to my God and your God.'" Mary Magdalene went to the disciples with the news: "I have seen the Lord!" And she told them that he had said these things to her.
>
> **(John 20:17–18)**

What he is saying to Mary could be paraphrased like this:[3] "Mary, I know why you are clinging so tightly to me. You were grieving over the loss of our relationship, and now you are thinking that you will grab me and never let yourself be parted from me. But you don't understand. When I ascend to the Father and sit at his right hand and send the Spirit, then everyone in the world who believes in me will be able to have personal intimacy with me. Through the Spirit I will be able to come to you, to commune with you in love, to have my presence within you. Let me go to the Father, and you—and all who seek it—will have a fellowship with me beyond anything you can imagine."

Intimacy with the risen Lord is one of the gifts given to believers in the resurrection. There is an infinite distance between knowing *about* God and knowing God. To know God personally is eternal life (John 17:3). This is no abstraction. It takes the form of a genuine, give-and-take, speak-and-listen relationship with the Lord through worship, the Word, and prayer. And because Jesus is not a dead teacher but a risen, living Savior, we can have such a relationship.

Very practical questions can be asked about this intimacy. When you pray, do you feel like you are really making contact? Do you sense his presence in your prayer? Do you find that sometimes—not always and not even usually, but often—as you pray, thoughts about his wisdom, his mercy, and his goodness become big and clear and comforting and delightful? Do you find that sometimes as you pray, the burdens ease? These are all available to Christians who have this unmatched blessing—knowing the risen Lord.

There's a bit of a paradox in what Jesus is saying to Mary. He has to go away in order to come closer to her than he has ever been. All this has been laid out in detail in John chapters 14 through 16. There he told his disciples he was leaving them and sending them the Spirit (John 14:17,28) and yet that when the Spirit came to them, he would be coming to them (John 14:17–18). He said that the Spirit would "glorify" him to them (John 16:14) so they would be able to see his beauty and greatness in a way they could not have done while he was on earth. Paul declares that when we by faith contemplate Jesus in the gospel, in the power of the Spirit, his glory shines into our hearts and transforms us (2 Corinthians 3:7–4:6). Jesus is saying, "When I ascend to the right hand of the Father, I will send the Holy Spirit, and the Holy Spirit will make me real to you. He will show you my glory."

This is a statement of unsurpassable encouragement to us today. We might be tempted to think that it would have been so much better to have actually been there—to have, like the first disciples, actually heard his voice and touched his hand. But Jesus is saying that we can have a view of his glory and an intimacy with him better than any of his followers had when he was on earth, greater than if Jesus had actually held us in his arms and kissed us.

Despite Mary's failure to recognize Jesus, her passion for loving fellowship with him was a sign that she understood God's grace. Mary's life had been a ruin, and when Jesus brought her out, she must have thought in her heart or maybe said with her lips, "Me? I used to walk this street, crying out, half naked, out of my mind. I can't be a child of God." But Jesus had shown her that yes, she could be a child of God by grace alone. That is what made her who she was.

To the degree you understand your need for grace, to that degree faith explodes in your life in the form of love. Galatians 5:6: "Neither circumcision nor uncircumcision has any value. The only thing that counts is faith expressing itself through love."

John Meets Jesus

There was another person present at the resurrection in John 20. The text calls him "the other disciple, the one Jesus loved" (John 20:2). Tradition understands this figure to be John himself, one of the twelve apostles and the author of the gospel.[4]

> So Peter and the other disciple started for the tomb. Both were running, but the other disciple outran Peter and reached the tomb first. He bent over and looked in at the strips of linen lying there but did not go in. Then Simon Peter came along behind him and went straight into the tomb. He saw the strips of linen lying there, as well as the cloth that had been wrapped around Jesus's head. The cloth was still lying in its place, separate from the linen. Finally the other disciple, who had reached the tomb first, also went inside. He saw and believed.
>
> **(John 20:3–8)**

Unlike Mary, John and Peter go into the empty tomb and begin to look around. They look carefully at the grave clothes and their reasoning powers go into high gear. That is not so clear in the English translation. When verse 1 tells us Mary *saw* that the stone at the tomb's mouth had been rolled away, the most typical Greek word for sight is used—*blepei*. But the Greek word used to describe how Peter and John looked at the tomb's contents is the word *theōreō*, which means to reason, theorize, and ponder. In other words, they were not merely glancing. They began "theorizing" about the condition of the grave clothes—they began to posit hypotheses in their minds that could account for what they saw. This is the same reasoning process that a scientist uses in seeking a working hypothesis to explain a phenomenon.

What were they looking at? First they saw the grave clothes *lying*, a Greek word that means to be arranged in an orderly way. The clothes had not been torn to shreds, nor were they in an unraveled heap. They also saw that the head cloth was not thrown aside nor on a pile with the rest but it was in another place, neatly folded. Why did these sights provoke them into reasoning and deduction? Dead bodies in those days were not dressed in street clothes for funerals. They were wrapped tightly around with long strips of cloth—today we might think they looked like mummies. That is why when Lazarus was resuscitated, Jesus said, "Take off the grave clothes and let him go." (John 11:44). Lazarus could not have ripped the grave clothes off of himself without help.

And that's why what John and Peter saw made no sense to them. Why would the grave clothes be lying there neatly folded? If enemies had stolen the body, why would they remove the grave clothes at all, since the body would have begun to decay (cf. John 11:39)? But if friends had stolen the body, why would they have shown such disrespect by disrobing him and carrying him out naked? If Jesus had just revived himself, why wouldn't the grave clothes have been ripped and shredded? Further, how could a seriously wounded, barely alive man been able to take them off at all, and, even if he had done it, why would he have calmly and neatly folded them up?

In their minds, slowly but surely, every nonsupernatural explanation for what had happened was being eliminated. As Arthur Conan Doyle said through the mouth of his character Sherlock Holmes, "When you have eliminated the impossible, whatever remains, however improbable, must be the truth."[5]

The text tells us that John was able to come to this improbable conclusion before either Peter or Mary, namely, that Jesus had been raised from the dead. It says that "He saw and believed" (verse 8), and in the gospel of John, the word *belief* is not merely intellectual assent but it is heart faith that brings salvation.

So faith is more than intellectual reasoning and assent. It is more than looking at the evidence and working it all out, but it is not less than that. Faith includes the mind—how else will it be an act of the entire person? John, the thinker, becomes the very first person to believe that Jesus was raised from the dead. He was open to the evidence, he worked it out rationally, but he did not keep things on the intellectual plane. He did not just conclude that Jesus had risen. He was willing to base his life on it.

The story is told of a famous tightrope walker who showed his skill and dexterity to a crowd, by walking over a high space on a rope again and again.[6] He walked out to the middle and ate his lunch, he went over on a bicycle, and he took a wheelbarrow across again. The audience could not have been more impressed. He asked the crowd if they believed that he could safely carry two hundred pounds of weights across the rope in the wheelbarrow. No one had any doubts—they all believed that he could do it. Then he asked for a volunteer. None was forthcoming. The evidence was quite strong. They believed a fact about the acrobat, but they would not entrust their lives to him.

John reasoned his way to a rational belief that Jesus had risen from the dead. But then, as it were, he got into the wheelbarrow. It is noteworthy that John came to genuine, saving faith without having actually seen the risen Jesus. Most of the other disciples required an actual, literal sight of him, but as we will see, Jesus insists that people can receive transforming faith without such an experience. Here's John, who is a model for us. He reasoned and then he believed, without having literally seen the risen body of Christ. So can we.

Thomas Meets Jesus

Now Thomas (also known as Didymus), one of the Twelve, was not with the disciples when Jesus came. So the other disciples told him, "We have seen the Lord!" But he said to them, "Unless I see the nail marks in his hands and put my finger where the nails were, and put my hand into his side, I will not believe." A week later his disciples were in the house again, and Thomas was with them. Though the doors were locked, Jesus came and stood among them and said, "Peace be with you!" Then he said to Thomas, "Put your finger here; see my hands. Reach out your hand and put it into my side. Stop doubting and believe." Thomas said to him, "My Lord and my God!" Then Jesus told him, "Because you have seen me, you have believed; blessed are those who have not seen and yet have believed."

(John 20:24–29)

The gospels do not tell us much about Thomas. In John 11:16 he shows loyalty to Jesus, though with a resigned and fatalistic attitude ("Let us also go [to Bethany] that we may die with him.") In John 14:5, after Jesus speaks about going to his Father's house and preparing rooms for his disciples, Thomas shows he doesn't understand what Jesus has been saying at all. From these brief glimpses we conclude that Thomas was a "a loyal but somewhat unimaginative person who will act only on what he is [absolutely] sure of."[7] His absence from the other disciples after the death of Jesus (verse 24) is not surprising. One commentator surmised that "the death of Jesus was such an overwhelming reality that he must get alone to try to come to terms with it. So when Jesus comes to the disciples on the Easter evening, Thomas is not there."[8] When he hears others say that they have seen Jesus, he is not impressed.

Rather than accepting his friends' testimony, Thomas laid down conditions for his belief, insisting that, unless he could put his fingers right into the places on Jesus's hands that the nails had pierced, and unless he could put his hand into Jesus's side where the spear had been thrust, he would not believe. He knew that no one who had received such wounds could have survived. And so if he was able to see and actually touch a living body that had received these wounds, then he might be able to believe that he was seeing not an impostor or a ghost but Christ himself.

Thomas is the most famous doubter of ancient times, and as such, he can almost serve as a stand-in for today's secular skeptics. Many doubt the resurrection as Thomas did, on the basis of temperament as much as reason. It's likely that Thomas would have come up as a "sensing" person on tests like Myers-Briggs. Sensing temperaments pay more attention to physical reality, facts, and hard evidence, and Thomas has millions of such "descendants" today. Many others today have a philosophical objection to the doctrine of the resurrection. "Dead people simply can*not* come back to life," they say. As we have seen in chapter 1, Thomas and all other Jews of that day would have had a similar objection, though it would have been stated a little differently: "An individual dead person in the middle of history cannot come back to life." There is one more way that Thomas might represent modern doubters well. Obviously he admired and loved Jesus— he had been a disciple. But it's likely that for that very reason Thomas was afraid to get his hopes up. The other disciples say, "He is alive!" and Thomas may be saying: "Don't get my hopes up. It's too painful."

All these reasons and motives create barriers to belief for modern people today. You might have a worldview that says it can't happen, a temperament that tends to be skeptical or even cynical, or a heart fearful of disappointment.

But despite all this, the passage shows Thomas moving from the deepest doubt among the disciples to the highest profession of faith anywhere in the gospel. He finally cries "My Lord and my God!" (verse 28), an astonishing thing for a Jewish man to say to any human being. This incident is considered to be the climax of the gospel of John. The biggest doubter became the greatest believer. And it happened in the following steps.

First, Thomas received the testimony of the apostles. In that sense

Thomas was in the same spot that we are today. He listened to the reports of eyewitnesses who had seen Jesus. Thomas's eyewitness accounts were from people who were then alive, while you and I have them written down in the New Testament. One good way for contemporary people to take this step is, besides reading the gospel accounts themselves, to consult N. T. Wright's *The Resurrection of the Son of God* and Richard Bauckham's *Jesus and the Eyewitnesses*.[9] Bauckham proves that the gospels do not have the marks of fictional oral tradition but rather those of eyewitness testimony.

So first Thomas had the same eyewitness evidence that we can have today. Second, however, Thomas had to be brought to see that Jesus did not merely rise from the dead but that he rose from the dead *for him*.

When Jesus next appeared in the midst of his disciples, he turned directly to the doubter and, stretching out his hands, said: "Put your finger here—reach out your hands! Here's my side—put your hand in it!" Thomas responded immediately: "My Lord and my God!" What brought him so decisively to faith? Despite the offer, there is no indication in the text that Thomas actually did what he had asked to do—namely, put his hands into Jesus's wounds. So then what overcame his doubts? Leon Morris writes:

> It is possible that it was the *words* of Jesus more than anything that brought conviction, for they showed that Jesus [had been] perfectly aware of what Thomas had laid down as his demands. How did he arrive at this knowledge unless he [had been with Thomas], unseen?[10]

Morris's argument is this. How did Jesus know about all Thomas's demands? Did one of the disciples know where Jesus was staying and run to him saying, "Let me tell you what Thomas said!" Of course not. Jesus knew everything because he was always walking, unseen, right next to Thomas. He had heard Thomas's refusal to believe his friends. He saw the cynicism and fear in Thomas's heart. And yet he came to him as requested.

Jesus was saying to Thomas, "I know all your doubts, all your fears, all your broken promises, and all your flaws. I've seen you to the bottom, but I still love you and I'm still here for you." Thomas was humbled by Jesus's grace and suddenly the wounds took on new meaning. He originally wanted to see the wounds as evidence of Jesus's power. Now he saw them for what they really were—evidence of Jesus's love, his sacrificial love for him. Jesus was saying, in effect, "The wounds are not simply evidence that I am alive. They are proof that I died for you, that your debt was fully paid, and that the power of death over you is broken."

As a simple miracle, the resurrection is spectacular and the evidence for it is formidable. But it is when we look at it not as a mere display of supernatural power but as the climax of the story of our salvation, as the final defeat of our two greatest enemies, sin and death, that the resurrection becomes the most compelling. That is what happened to Thomas.

Did Thomas Get Special Treatment?

Finally Jesus says, "Because you have seen me, you have believed; blessed are those who have not seen and yet have believed" (verse 29). Jesus is saying, essentially, that we don't need to see him with our physical eyes in order to come to full, life-changing resurrection faith. That is true, as we have seen in the case of John. Then why did Jesus show himself to Thomas at all? Why did he get special treatment?

We must remember that Thomas was an apostle, and those first apostles were sent out to be the original teachers and evangelists. One of the marks of an apostle was that they were trained personally by Jesus and were eyewitnesses to his resurrection. And so Thomas *does* require special treatment. What Jesus is doing here is insuring his qualification as an apostle.

And, while Jesus says we need not have the same eyewitness experience as Thomas in order to believe, we need to make the same discovery that Thomas made. We need to see Jesus patiently at work in our lives to bring us to himself.

In C. S. Lewis's children's fairy tale *The Horse and His Boy*, the main character, Shasta, is trying to escape from a foreign land and get home to Narnia. On his journey, however, everything seems to go wrong. He keeps running into wild lions that threaten him in various ways. At one point in his journey he finds himself in a fog and senses a presence guiding him through it. There is a voice that begins a conversation with him. Shasta speaks about his journey and says, "Don't you think it was bad luck to meet so many lions?"

> "There was only one lion," said the Voice.
>
> "What on earth do you mean?" . . .
>
> "I was the lion." And as Shasta gaped . . . the Voice continued. "I was the lion who forced you to join with Aravis. I was the cat who comforted you among the houses of the dead. I was the lion who drove the jackals from you while you slept. I was the lion who gave the horses the new strength of fear for the last mile so that you should reach King Lune in time. And I was the lion you do not remember who pushed the boat in which you lay, a child near death, so that it came to shore where a man sat, wakeful at midnight, to receive you."[11]

In this story C. S. Lewis is remembering his own journey to faith from being an atheist. As you draw nearer to faith, you realize that the God you are coming to believe in is never passive. Jesus is alive, he is risen, and he is actively seeking you. Like Thomas, you may come, in amazement, to see that he was walking right beside you all the time.

CHAPTER 7

PERSONAL HOPE: 2

✳

Peter Meets Jesus

Peter met the risen Jesus many times. He was with the rest of the disciples—once without Thomas and once with him—when Jesus appeared to them (John 20:19–29). Jesus also appeared to Peter alone (Luke 24:34; 1 Corinthians 15:5). And there may have been other encounters: "[Jesus] presented himself to them and gave many convincing proofs that he was alive. He appeared to them over a period of forty days and spoke about the kingdom of God" (Acts 1:3). But John 21 tells of a remarkable conversation between Peter and the risen Christ.

Seven of the disciples—Peter, Thomas, Nathanael, James, and John, and two other unnamed disciples (John 21: 2)—were fishing through the night on the Sea of Galilee but had caught nothing. While they were still out on the water, Jesus appeared on the shore.

> Early in the morning, Jesus stood on the shore, but the disciples did not realize that it was Jesus. He called out to them, "Friends, haven't you any fish?" "No," they answered. He said, "Throw your net on the right side of the boat and you will find some." When they did, they were unable to haul the net in because of the large

number of fish. Then the disciple whom Jesus loved said to Peter, "It is the Lord!" As soon as Simon Peter heard him say, "It is the Lord," he wrapped his outer garment around him (for he had taken it off) and jumped into the water. The other disciples followed in the boat, towing the net full of fish, for they were not far from shore, about a hundred yards. When they landed, they saw a fire of burning coals there with fish on it, and some bread.

(John 21:4–9)

Luke 5 recounts another episode of the disciples' fishing that is both similar to and different from this one. In both cases the disciples were in a boat fishing, had worked all night, and had caught nothing. In both cases Jesus told them to throw their nets back into the water one more time, and each time the result was an enormous, miraculous catch of fish. But in Luke 5, Peter responded by saying, "Go away from me, Lord; I am a sinful man!" (verse 8). Here in John 21 he does the very opposite. He jumps into the water and struggles to shore, trying to get as close to Jesus as possible as fast as he can.

The claims of Jesus Christ, if they are truly heard for what they are, never evoke moderate response. Jesus claimed to be the Lord God of the universe, who had come to earth to give himself for us so that we could live for him. That is a call for total allegiance. You will have to either run away screaming in anger and fear or run toward him with joy and love and fall down at his feet and say, "I am yours." Nothing in the middle makes any sense. Unless you are running away from him or running toward him, you actually don't really know who he is. Peter has done both. Because of the instruction that he has received from the risen Jesus, Peter now knows enough about the gospel of grace to realize he has nothing to fear from Jesus's divine presence. But there is a great deal of unfinished business between Peter and his Savior.

Jesus Confronts Peter

After a meal with his disciples, Jesus took Peter for a walk on the beach.

> Jesus said to Simon Peter, "Simon son of John, do you love me more than these?" "Yes, Lord," he said, "you know that I love you." Jesus said, "Feed my lambs." Again Jesus said, "Simon son of John, do you love me?" He answered, "Yes, Lord, you know that I love you." Jesus said, "Take care of my sheep." The third time he said to him, "Simon son of John, do you love me?"
>
> **(John 21:15–17)**

To understand what Jesus is doing, we must remember the magnitude of Peter's failure. Peter had loudly insisted that, while the others might abandon Jesus, he *never* would, even if it meant prison or death (John 13:37; Matthew 26:33–35). Yet after Jesus was arrested and the other disciples fled, Peter was publicly asked three times if he was one of Jesus's disciples (Luke 22:54–62; Mark 14:66–71). He had three opportunities to identify himself with his Lord, and yet he denied him every time. Perhaps one denial could have been chalked up to a momentary lapse, a temporary weakness. But there's no excuse for three.

And the third time he denied Jesus, Peter called down curses (Mark 14:71). Peter was in a panic. He wanted to prove that he was not Christ's disciple lest he be arrested as well. And the best way to prove to the onlookers that he was no follower of Jesus was to call down a curse on Jesus.[1] In that shame and honor culture, loyalty was everything, and no real disciple would ever do such a thing to his teacher. Peter did it to save himself, but as the rooster crowed the terrible truth must have dawned on him. He *was* no true disciple of Christ.

Think of someone to whom you owe everything, and imagine abandoning him or her to die in order to save your own skin. How could anyone forgive himself for something like that? Was there any way back for Peter? Yes, and Jesus shows it to him and to us.

To begin, Jesus made Peter painfully retrace his steps. He brought Peter to a fire (John 21:9), and Peter had denied Christ three times around a fire (Luke 22:54–62). Also, Jesus asked Peter three times if he loved him. Three times—the same number of times he had denied him. It will be obvious to anyone who has read the gospels and seen Jesus's character that this was no effort to humiliate. Jesus wanted Peter to see himself, to understand himself. And that became clear when Jesus asked Peter, "Do you [still say you] love me *more than these*?" (verse 15). Jesus is going back not just to Peter's behavior but to the underlying flaw in Peter's heart that led to the failures. Jesus is not twisting the knife—rather, he is using a knife, like a surgeon, to get down to what is causing Peter's problem.

Peter's problem was what Yale theologian Miroslav Volf calls a "false identity."

In his book *Exclusion and Embrace*, Volf recounts the biblical story of Cain and Abel. He asks: why did Cain kill his younger brother? His answer is that Cain's identity was "constructed . . . in relation to Abel. . . . He was great in relation to Abel." Cain got his sense of worth from being superior to his brother. However, when Abel began to surpass him, Cain had to deny that reality, because his self-esteem was fully dependent on the certainty that he was better than Abel. "Cain either had to readjust radically his identity, or eliminate Abel." The murder, argues Volf, did not stem from some irrepressible violent urge. Rather it was the result of the cold logic of "a perverted self in order to maintain its own false identity." The facts of Abel's character and life threatened Cain's self-image, and therefore his heart reasoned: "Abel cannot continue to be."[2]

Like Cain, Peter's identity was based on the assumption of his superiority to his fellow disciples. Peter told Jesus that he was the most passionate and faithful of all. He was not basing his identity on Jesus's great love for him but on his great love for Jesus. That meant that while Jesus was Peter's teacher, Peter was being his own savior.

Any identity based on our superior performance over others will produce at least two results—fragility and hostility. First there will be a deep insecurity and an inability to see yourself. Peter, despite Jesus's direct warning to him about his coming failure (Matthew 26:34; Mark 14:30; Luke 22:34), had no sense of his danger. Why not? Because if you base your very self-worth on being brave, and if you look into your heart and see cowardice, you will *have* to screen it out and deny it, or you won't have a self left. And that is true of any identity not rooted in Jesus's unmerited love—whether a traditional one, based on family approval, or a Western one, based on individual achievement. Any such identity is fragile and radically apprehensive and leads to denial and a lack of self-awareness.

The second result is hostility toward those who are different. If you get your identity from being the most passionate follower of Jesus, then you will have to be angry or even violent toward someone who opposes your Lord. When Jesus was arrested, Peter was the only disciple who did violence. He got out a sword and cut off someone's ear. There was Peter, claiming to be the greatest and most faithful follower of Christ, doing the very opposite of what Christ was doing. Jesus was dying for his enemies, saying, "Father, forgive them." But because Peter, like Cain, based his identity on his performance, on being more enlightened and better than these infidels, he had to attack the people Jesus was seeking to save. When a false identity is endangered, the result is always hostility.

The stories of Cain and Peter hit uncomfortably close to home for American believers today. We live in a country that is coming to terms with the issue of race. The arguments are fierce over whether the United States has made progress against racism or not. While there may be debate over specifics, Christians, of all people, should know how deeply rooted racism is in humanity's sin nature. Modern philosophy and anthropology talk about creating an identity through "othering." When we "other" a group or people, we treat them as alien and strange, and we stress what we see as their weaknesses and evils in an effort to prove to ourselves and others how superior we are by contrast. A classic biblical example is the man in Jesus's parable who prays at the temple: "God, I thank you that I am not like *other* people—robbers, evildoers, adulterers—or even like this tax collector" (Luke 18:11).

Here is a man quite literally "othering." He is using not the category of race but that of morality and politics. Tax collectors were Roman collaborators in an occupied country. He creates a positive identity as noble, good, and true by contrasting himself with—and showing contempt for—others. As many contemporary thinkers have pointed out, when you create an identity by despising other groups, it makes you dependent in many ways on them. Ironically, the "other" becomes part of who you are. You *need* for them to stay in their place and to fit your stereotypes of them. And if something threatens your one-dimensional, negative view of them, it shakes your very foundations. This is what brought Cain to kill Abel, and why Peter responded violently as well. Their false identity was shaken, and rather than change it and give it another foundation, they lashed out at the people who were endangering it.

While the man in Luke 18 is not "othering" people of a different race as a way to build up his own identity, we know how often this has been done in world and U.S. history. According to Bryan Stevenson's Equal Justice Initiative, 4,400 racial lynchings occurred in the U.S. between Reconstruction and World War II—an average of more than one a week for over seventy-five years.[3] These violent outbursts against "the other" are the terrible and tragic out-workings of the pattern established by Cain. If your race and culture, or your moral performance, or your politics, or anything but the love of God is the foundational source of your self-worth, when people threaten that positive self-image, you will not be able to listen to them or learn from them. You will strike at them.

Jesus Restores Peter

Peter was hurt because Jesus asked him the third time, "Do you love me?" He said, "Lord, you know all things; you know that I love you." Jesus said, "Feed my sheep. Very truly I tell you, when you were younger you dressed yourself and went where you wanted; but when you are old you will stretch out your hands, and someone else will dress you and lead you where you do not want to go." Jesus said this to indicate the kind of death by which Peter would glorify God. Then he said to him, "Follow me!"

(John 21:17–19)

Peter had built his self-worth on being more faithful to Jesus than all others. When Jesus says, "Do you love me *more* than these?" Peter responds simply, "Lord—I just love you." He is beginning to reject the old identity. Then Jesus asks about his love three times—one for each of Peter's denials. How does he respond?

Let's notice what Peter does *not* do. He makes no excuses. There is no defensiveness or blame shifting. He does not say, "Well, yes, I failed to love you, but you have to understand that . . ." Nor does he point to any great deeds on his part to prove how much he *does* loves Jesus. He does not say, "Yes, I denied you—that was terrible. But remember all other ways I served you." That would have been to return to the old false identity. But neither does he grovel. He doesn't talk about how unworthy he is, beating himself up in an effort to atone for his own sins. No, he simply says, "Lord, I love you." That is to say, "I know I denied you three times. But I still want a love relationship with you. No excuses. I know I failed."

Peter is showing us what Paul in 2 Corinthians 7:10 calls "godly sorrow" and true repentance rather than "worldly sorrow." The former heals, restores, and changes us permanently; the latter, while often accompanied by intense emotion, is a passing thing. Worldly sorrow is a form of self-pity, in which grieving persons are upset about the painful effects of the sin in their lives, about their shame before others, and especially about the damage to their self-image, which is still based on being good, virtuous people. In worldly sorrow you are sorry for the consequences of the sin, for your sake. In true repentance you are sorry for the sin itself, for how it has wronged and grieved your Creator and Redeemer. In self-centered sorrow, you never come to hate the sin itself, and so when the consequences recede, the sin will roar back, as powerful within you as ever. True repentance is fueled by grief for hurting the one we love, and that intensified love of Christ makes the sin appear hateful, and so it begins to lose its power over you.

So Peter repents. And Jesus's response is nothing less than shocking. Every time Peter responds to Jesus in loving, humble repentance, Jesus in turn says to "feed" or "take care" of Jesus's sheep—his people. Peter is being called not to a probationary status. He's being called to leadership.

How could such failures and weaknesses be a path to greatness and leadership? It would be impossible within the framework of Peter's old identity. It also makes little sense in the world, where leaders must be competent, confident, and successful. In the world your confidence and inner peace grow in direct proportion to your achievements. The better you do, the better, the more love-worthy a person you feel you are. But Jesus is inviting Peter into a completely different kind of identity, one that can say with Paul, "When I am weak—*then* I am strong" (2 Corinthians 12:10).

It is not an identity based on achievement but on free grace. How could Jesus offer Peter such affirmation? Why doesn't he demand that Peter work off his debt in some way?

Peter may have called curses down on Jesus to save himself—but Jesus actually bore and took the curses that Peter and you and I deserve in order to save us. "Christ redeemed us from the curse of the law by becoming a curse for us" (Galatians 3:13). A Christian identity is based ultimately on a realization of the magnitude of God's unchanging love for us. We know this dynamic, that the more we admire someone, the more their admiration for us satisfies and fulfills us. "The praise of the praiseworthy is above all rewards."[4] So the knowledge of God's perfect love for us and delight in us in Jesus can and will eventually transform us like nothing else.

Jesus is saying something like this to Peter: "Your identity was based so much on your own bravery and wisdom and goodness that my love for you seemed nothing more than wages that you earned. But now you've seen your sin—and turned to me—now your failure, plunged into my grace and forgiveness, will make you a leader. For who can speak into people's lives better than someone who finally knows their own heart? Who can lead better than someone who is humbled by the grace of God and yet at the same time is affirmed by my free, gracious love?"

The default mode of the human heart is to believe that it is *strength* that connects you to God, but the gospel says that it is *weakness* that connects you to God. Only to the degree that you see you are weak are you strong.

Paul Meets Jesus

> As he neared Damascus on his journey, suddenly a light from heaven flashed around him. He fell to the ground and heard a voice say to him, "Saul, Saul, why do you persecute me? "Who are you, Lord?" Saul asked. "I am Jesus, whom you are persecuting," he replied. "Now get up and go into the city, and you will be told what you must do." The men traveling with Saul stood there speechless; they heard the sound but did not see anyone. Saul got up from the ground, but when he opened his eyes he could see nothing. So they led him by the hand into Damascus. For three days he was blind, and did not eat or drink anything.
>
> (Acts 9:3–9)

For our last case study of resurrection faith, we go to the book of Acts, to the conversion of Saint Paul.

Before we look at his case, a word of warning is in order. Paul's conversion story is dramatic. There's a visible light and an audible voice from heaven. He was literally knocked to the ground. And some people say, "Now *that's* what I'm talking about! If God wants to come into my life, that's what it's going to have to look like." Fortunately, however, we have the rest of the book of Acts. In Acts 8 we read of the conversion of an African finance minister, who came to faith through a simple Bible study with Philip, reading the book of Isaiah (Acts 8:30–36). In Acts 16 we read about the prominent businesswoman, Lydia, who heard Paul talk about the gospel of Jesus Christ in a women's prayer group. All we hear is that "the Lord opened her heart to respond to Paul's message" (Acts 16:13–14). That's all. No miracles, no lights, no vision—just conversation.

The most well-known modern-day illustration of this truth is in the contrast between Billy Graham and his wife, Ruth Bell Graham. In 1934 the evangelist Mordecai Ham came to Charlotte, North Carolina, to preach for eleven weeks, morning and evening, in a sawdust-floor "tabernacle" put up hurriedly on the edge of town. While the revival meetings and the attending crowds were big news in the city, the sixteen-year-old Billy Graham "did not want anything to do with anyone called an evangelist."[5] He told friends and family he would not go and hear him. But a friend who had attended told him that this preacher was a "fighter" who preached like no one he'd ever heard. Intrigued, the young Billy slipped into the back and listened. He was shocked by the speaker's directness. Though the Graham family had attended Methodist and Presbyterian churches, "I had never heard a sermon on Hell."[6] He also spoke about sin in such a convicting way that Billy completely revised his self-understanding. Finally, after attending many evening meetings, Billy Graham made what he called "the 180-Degree Turn" and was converted.[7]

By contrast, Ruth Bell had been raised by Presbyterian missionaries in China. She could not remember a time in which she did not believe. Throughout her years as a child, she was receiving one Christian belief after the other, and she always embraced in faith what she could know and understand at the time. At some point she knew enough of the gospel to put her faith in it, but she could not remember exactly when that occurred. "I have had 'crisis' experiences but my salvation did not happen to be one of them, for I cannot remember the time when I did not love and trust Him. In fact my earliest recollections are of deep love and gratitude that He should love me enough to die for me."[8]

When Luke, the author of Acts, recorded these case studies of conversion, he was inviting us to look at what was common to them all. They were not all dramatic. They did not all follow some fixed set of steps. In every case the *how* of conversion was different, but the *what*—the result—was the same. Each person was changed from the inside out. And so we should read Paul's story not to learn how Jesus reveals himself to every person, but to learn about the profound life changes that always occur after he does.

A God We Don't Make Up

Paul thought he knew what God was like—and what he wasn't like. Paul knew, for example, that God could not become a human being, so all these claims about Jesus being the Lord could not be true. Paul had also heard Stephen's final speech (recorded in Acts 6–7), where he declared that the temple and the priesthood and the sacrificial system were all going to be made obsolete by Jesus. For Paul this was unthinkable. "That would make whole books of the Bible irrelevant," he must have thought, "and God would never do that." No, God was a God who favored highly religious, moral, and disciplined men like Paul, those who followed all the rules and regulations to the letter.

Paul, like all the rest of us, believed in a God who supported the person he already was and wanted to be, and who despised all the people he despised. Some want a divinity who smites the immoral and irreligious, while others want a Spirit of love who embraces all and judges no one, and still others want to believe in a universe without any God at all. Our beliefs or nonbeliefs about God are driven as much (or more) by our personal wants and needs than by reason. Aldous Huxley, the prominent atheist, said candidly: "I had motives for not wanting the world to have a meaning. . . . The philosopher who finds no meaning in the world is not concerned exclusively with a problem in pure metaphysics. He is also concerned to prove that there is no valid reason why he personally should not do as he wants to do."[9] We should not, however, pick on atheists. There are many more people who believe in God than who do not, and we must remember

Paul's startling claim that none of us without the intervention and aid of the Holy Spirit ever seek the real God of the Bible (Romans 3:10–12). We create for ourselves a customized deity, as Paul did.

Certainly a God whom you create can sometimes be a comfort, just as a dress or suit that is tailored to your body is comfortable. But such a God cannot challenge you when you need to be challenged and can never change you. Think about people who are deeply unsure of their own worth, people who struggle with feelings of inadequacy. What's going to turn them into people with poise, without debilitating self-doubts? 1 John 3:20 says: "If our hearts condemn us, we know that God is greater than our hearts." But that assumes you have a God who is *there*, who is real and can tell you things you don't want to believe. How can your God overcome the deep conviction of your heart that you're worthless, if he is just a creation, an extension of your heart's desires?

The biblical God is a God we modern people today would never invent—a God who is holy, who cannot just overlook sin and guilt (Exodus 6:7), who is a consuming fire (Deuteronomy 4:24; Hebrews 12:29). It is because he is so holy and just that it was necessary for Jesus Christ to take the curse we deserve so we could receive the blessing he deserves (Galatians 3:10–14). It is only this Savior, with his nail prints and wounds still visible, who can come in and say to believers, "You feel condemned? You're not! You feel worthless? You're not!" It is only this God, one who is not a product of your wishful thinking, who can profoundly reprogram your self-understanding and make you something new.

Your heart's deepest need is for a God who is not just the product of your heart's wants and needs.

As a modern man, C. S. Lewis knew that the God he was meeting in the Bible could not be something he was making up. He wrote:

> Reality, in fact, is usually something you could not have guessed.
> That is one of the reasons I believe Christianity. It is a religion
> you could not have guessed. If it offered us just the kind of

universe we had always expected, I should feel we were making it up. But, in fact, it is not the sort of thing anyone would have made up. It has just that queer twist about it that real things have. So let us leave behind all these boys' philosophies—these over simple answers. The problem is not simple and the answer is not going to be simple either.[10]

This is where conversion starts. You may have believed in God all your life, but you get converted only when you start to realize you're dealing with a God who is not the way you want him to be. He is the way he is. There are some scary things about him, some disturbing things about him, some things you have trouble accepting. Well, now you are on the right track. Until you are wrestling with a God like that, you have a one-dimensional God you created, not the Lord of heaven and earth who created you. And unless you have a God who tells you things you don't want to be true, you'll never be changed when he tells you things that are too good to be true, like that he forgives you, that you're going to be resurrected, or that he's going to adopt you.

So an "untame," living and real God is the first requirement for the great life change of conversion. You are approaching such a God when you start to realize it doesn't matter so much what you think of him as what he thinks of you (Galatians 4:9).

A Bible That Fits Together

When Paul asked, "Lord, who are you?" the answer to his question overthrew his entire way of thinking: "I am Jesus."

Paul had reasons to believe that Christianity couldn't be true. He knew the Bible taught that there is only one God, yet these Christians were worshipping this man as if he were God. Also, the Bible said the Messiah would be a descendant of David who "will strike the earth with the rod of his mouth" and gather the people and defeat all their enemies (Isaiah 11:1–16). But Jesus was crucified and never came to power, so he could not possibly be the Messiah. And the Bible said that anyone who is executed for a crime and hung on a tree is cursed (Deuteronomy 21:22–23). Jesus did not merely die; he died a shameful death as a criminal. Clearly God was rejecting and abandoning Jesus, not confirming him as King. No wonder Paul concluded that the Bible condemned the teachings of Christianity.

But then on the Damascus road Paul was confronted with the irrefutable fact that Jesus had risen. Just three days later he began to preach from the Bible in the synagogues "that Jesus is the Son of God" (Acts 9:20). He had begun to rethink the entire Bible in light of the fact of the resurrection. By using the rest of Paul's writings as a guide, we can retrace trains of thought that must have begun in his mind during those three dark days.

His train of thought must have gone something like this. Since Jesus was cursed and rejected by God—but then raised and vindicated by God—then he must have died and been cursed for *somebody else*. Could it be that he was absorbing the law's curse on sin for us—in our place (Galatians 3:10–13)? Isaiah did indeed speak of the Messiah as a figure of strength who would judge the world, but he also wrote about a strange suffering Servant figure who was "pierced for our transgressions" and "crushed for our iniquities" (Isaiah 53:5). Could the Servant and the messianic King be the same person (Romans 10:16–17)? And what about all those animal sacrifices every day in the temple? The blood of animals could not atone for human sin. Could it be, then, that the entire sacrificial system was just a pointer—that pointed toward an ultimate Passover lamb, a man who takes away sin (1 Corinthians 5:7)? And what about the promise to Abraham that through one of his descendants all the nations of the earth would be blessed (Genesis 12:3)? Could it be that this was the way that would happen (Galatians 3:14)—through Jesus?

Paul had seen the Bible as a series of laws and moral stories that told you how to live so you could merit God's blessing. But when he grasped the stubborn fact of the resurrection of Jesus, he began to reread the Bible within a Christ-centered framework, and everything looked different. The

Bible is not a series of Aesop's fables telling us how to live a good life. Instead it is a single coherent history—a wonderful true story—about the ways God was bringing salvation into the world—ways that all climaxed in Jesus Christ.

Once Paul began to look at everything in the light of Jesus resurrected and vindicated by God, the Bible fit together and everything in the world and in his life looked different.[11] Certainly he had not worked out all the implications of this in three days. Nor had he figured out all the answers to his original objections to Christianity. But once he realized Jesus was risen, he knew there had to be answers to all those objections. So he believed in Christ, began to preach, and proceeded to work out the details as he went along.

We should proceed in the same way. Think of all the objections to Christianity regarding repressive sexuality or the record of the church's injustices. Do any of these things, if true, mean Jesus could not have risen from the dead? That's the first and foremost question to ask. Have we looked at the evidence for the resurrection thoroughly? All our objections actually hang on this issue. If he did not rise from the dead, who cares what the Bible says about sex or about the history of the church? But if he *did* rise from the dead, then Christianity and its gospel is true, and while we don't yet have solutions to all those other objections, we can move forward knowing that answers to those questions exist.

If you are looking at Christianity, start by looking at Jesus's life as it is shown to us in the gospels, and especially at the resurrection. Don't begin, as modern people do, by asking yourself if Christianity fits who you are. If the resurrection happened, then there is a God who created you for himself and ultimately, yes, Christianity fits you whether you can see it now or not. If he's real and risen, then just like Paul, even though he had none of the answers to any of his questions, you'll have to say, "What would you have me do, Lord?"

A Relationship of Law and Love

When Paul asks, "Who are you, Lord?" Jesus says twice that he is the one "whom you are persecuting." How could this blinding figure from heaven be someone Paul was harming? Why did Jesus say not, "Why are you persecuting *them*" rather than "Saul, Saul, why do you persecute *me*?" (verse 4).

In these first words Paul heard from Jesus there was an insight so profound that it shaped all the rest of Paul's life, ministry, and theology. Paul learned that to be a Christian meant far more than merely adopting another set of beliefs and practices in the hope that God would favor him and answer our prayers. The words point to a relationship infinitely deeper and richer than that. Jesus Christ was claiming such an intimate *union* with his people that what happened to them happened to him and therefore—by implication—what is true of him is also true of them.

In the letters of Paul alone Christians are described as being "in Christ" or "in the Lord" or "in him" over 160 times. In Romans 6:1–4, Paul says that we died and were "buried with him." In Ephesians 2:6 he says that when Jesus Christ was raised from the dead and was seated at the right hand of God, "God raised us up with Christ and seated us with him in the heavenly realms in Christ Jesus." Paul is not talking about something that will happen, because he uses the past tense. Christians are so united to Christ that when he died, rose, and ascended to heaven, so did we. And this union has two important aspects.

First, we are united to him legally. In God's eyes, we are as free from sin's penalty as if we had died on the cross ourselves. We are "justified by faith" (Romans 3:28) and are seen as perfectly righteous in Christ though, in ourselves, we are flawed and sinful (Philippians 3:9). And after his death Jesus was raised to a place of honor such that if you believe in him, God treats you as if you had accomplished everything Jesus accomplished. He rewards you as if you were as great as Jesus.

But this union is not just legal—it is also vital and spiritual. God the Spirit himself comes into us, as he did when Paul was converted (Acts 9:17).

We become partakers in God's divine nature (2 Peter 1:4) and therefore we are as united to him as a hand is united by the nervous systems to the head. And so Jesus can say of his people: "When you touch them—you touch me."

The idea of a union that is legal and yet also vital and personal is not unfamiliar to us. Martin Luther famously says that when we put saving faith in Christ, our faith "unites the soul to Christ just as a bride is united with her bridegroom." A marriage is a relationship based on both law and love. He points out that a husband who marries a wife assumes her debts and the wife in turn now shares in his wealth, so our sin and death fall on him and his righteousness and glory are given to us (2 Corinthians 5:21). Therefore, Luther concludes, "by the wedding ring of faith . . . the soul that trusts Christ . . . is free from all sins, secure against death and hell, and given eternal righteousness, life, and salvation."[12] Here we see the way the legal and vital connect and strengthen each other. The more we are assured of our legal acceptance, the more free our hearts are from fear and shame and the more they are drawn to our Savior in joyful love, the more we experience his love shed abroad on our hearts by the Spirit (Romans 5:5).

To understand the legal aspect of our relationship, consider the little diagnostic that pastor David Martyn Lloyd-Jones used to understand where a person was spiritually. He would say: "Let me ask you a question. Are you a Christian?" The person would often say, "Well, I'm trying to be." If they said that, he knew they didn't understand the first principle of what it meant to be a Christian. Christianity is a status and a union, like being adopted or being married, not a reward you get on the basis of your achievement. You are either married or you are not—you are either a Christian or you are not.

To understand the vital aspect of our relationship, consider the questions used by leaders during the Great Awakening in Britain, spearheaded by John and Charles Wesley. In the eighteenth century virtually everyone in the country was a churchgoer, but the preachers of the Great Awakening challenged their audiences with a question: Were they converted?[13] Were they spiritually alive or did they just live according to ethical principles? Did they have a living relationship with God? The preachers of the

Great Awakening organized their followers into societies that met in homes. "The object of the societies was primarily to provide a fellowship in which [their] new spiritual life and experience could be safeguarded and developed."[14] In one of the manuals written for leaders of societies, the following kinds of questions were to be asked every week:[15]

How real has God been to your heart this week? How clear and vivid is your assurance and certainty of God's forgiveness and fatherly love?

Are you having any particular seasons of delight in God? Do you really sense his presence in your life, sense him giving you his love?

Have you been finding Scripture to be alive and active?

Are you finding certain biblical promises extremely precious and encouraging? Which ones?

Are you finding that God is challenging you or calling you to something through the Word? In what ways?

Have you been freed to see and admit more of the ways you sin against God and others? But with that increasing sense of your own sinfulness, is God's grace also becoming more glorious, moving, and comforting?

The questions helped distinguish between believing in a remote God and having a living relationship with a living God. In such a relationship, based on Christ's grace, there is actual interchange of knowledge and love, and so God will challenge, comfort, summon, teach, and lead you.

Because Jesus was raised from the dead, we can be justified legally

(Romans 4:25) and regenerated vitally (Romans 8:10–11)—in short, we can be converted and live a converted life.

We Meet Jesus

We cannot get God's hope for times of fear without personally meeting the risen Lord. We have reviewed five accounts of how that can happen. Looking back on them, we can see that they vary greatly, and that is a final lesson for us.

Jesus takes different approaches with different hearts and temperaments. There is no template, there are no five steps to becoming a Christian that are required of everyone. Some have said that Mary was a feeler, John a thinker, and Thomas a pragmatist. These are oversimplifications, but Jesus recognized temperamental differences and met each person at their point of need. He comes right to Mary and Thomas and speaks to them personally, but he leaves John and Peter alone to think and figure things out for themselves. He gives everyone what they need when they need it. You therefore must not compare your pathway to Christ to those of others, saying, "My coming to faith wasn't like theirs. Am I really converted?" He knocked Paul flat with a rebuke but gently spoke Mary's name.

What Jesus is telling us all is this: "I know you individually. Your path is going to be your own. It's not necessarily going to be like that of the person next to you. I want you to follow not them but *me*." Near the very end of the gospel of John, Peter points to another disciple and asks the Lord what will eventually happen to him. Jesus refuses to answer, saying, "What is that to you? You must follow me." (John 21:22). So don't compare yourself to others. Fix your eyes on Jesus and run on the path he has uniquely set out for you (Hebrews 12: 1–2).

CHAPTER 8

HOPE FOR YOU

As for you, you were dead in your transgressions and sins. . . . But because of his great love for us, God, who is rich in mercy, made us alive with Christ even when we were dead in transgressions—it is by grace you have been saved. And God raised us up with Christ and seated us with him in the heavenly realms in Christ Jesus, in order that in the coming ages he might show the incomparable riches of his grace, expressed in his kindness to us in Christ Jesus.

—EPHESIANS 2:1,4–7

W e have seen that the resurrection of Christ offers matchless resources for hope and confidence in the face of fear. In the final chapters I will look at specific fears and the particular ways this hope enables us to face them. We fear suffering, death, and the future. We experience fear in times of social unrest and upheaval. The thing the resurrection overcomes, however, is the fear that we will not be sufficient to face all the others. The resurrection does not promise that all the circumstances of life will go smoothly, but it does give us hope that *we* can be turned into the kind of people who can handle whatever comes.

Risen with Christ

In Ephesians 2 Paul claims not only that we will *be* resurrected bodily at the end of time but that we have already *been* resurrected spiritually the moment we believed in Christ as our risen Savior and Lord. In fact, Paul adds, we have already spiritually ascended into the heavens. "God raised us up with Christ and seated us with him in the heavenly realms in Christ Jesus" (Ephesians 2:4–6).

This statement shows how profound the changes are when anyone becomes a Christian. It is not a matter of turning over a new leaf and working harder at living a good life. It is not just membership in a new religious society. Rather, it is to be taken from one realm into another realm. It is to be united to him in the Holy Spirit and the powers of the age to come, such that "by the new birth, by our regeneration, we are joined to the Lord Jesus Christ, and we become sharers and participators in His life and in all the blessings that come from him."[1]

Specifically, Christians have been made alive spiritually though they were dead. Imagine you are in a room full of people and you go to the podium to speak. There is a microphone there, so you lean forward a bit and speak normally, thinking that the mic will carry your voice to the far reaches of the room. But nothing happens. The mic is not switched on and so you say it is "dead." But if someone throws the switch, now the microphone is alive to you and your voice. In the same way, our spiritual resurrection makes us "alive unto God" (Romans 6:11). We were dead to God, but now the Spirit makes us able to hear the truth about God.[2]

This spiritual resurrection comes about when we believe that Jesus Christ died and rose for our salvation. But on the basis of that objective truth, a principle of future, heavenly life is put into us and that affects us subjectively. We begin to experience foretastes of our final future state—a freedom to change and be like Christ, a sense of God's reality, glory, and love in our hearts, and a new, loving solidarity with brothers and sisters in Christ.

Spiritual resurrection means that we are, in a sense, living in heaven while still on earth, living in the future while still being in the present.

> Because we are with Christ [in the heavenly realms] . . . we are already enjoying something of the life of heaven even now. The apostle [Paul] talks about partaking of the first-fruits; he talks about having a foretaste. The great harvest has not yet come, but the first-fruits are available. . . . The glimpses of glory! . . . We should have the occasional glimpse. We should occasionally have heard something of the music; we should have some sensation of the life that [will be] lived there.[3]

The hymn writer Isaac Watts put it like this:

> *The hill of Zion yields*
> *a thousand sacred sweets*
> Before *we reach the heavenly fields*
> *And walk the golden streets.*[4]

In the rest of this chapter I will consider some of these forestates, these "sacred sweets" that we have by virtue of Christ's resurrection.

Resurrection and Experience

The founding professor of Princeton Theological Seminary, Archibald Alexander, gave years of thought to understanding the relationship between what has been called the Christian's great "Objectivities"—the doctrine to be believed, the sacraments of baptism and the Lord's Supper to be administered, and the ethical practices to be followed—and the subjectivities of spiritual encounter. His *Thoughts on Religious Experience* (1844) provides an important illustration:

There are two kinds of religious knowledge which, though intimately connected as cause and effect, may nevertheless be distinguished. These are the knowledge of the truth as it is revealed in the Holy Scriptures; and the *impression* which that truth makes . . . when rightly apprehended.

The first may be compared to the [raised] inscription or image on a seal, the other to the impression made by the seal on the wax. When that impression is clearly and distinctly made, we can understand, by contemplating it, the true inscription on the seal more satisfactorily, than by a direct view of the seal itself. Thus it is found that nothing tends more to confirm and elucidate the truths contained in the Word, than an inward experience of their efficacy on the heart.[5]

Christianity is a faith based on belief in historical realities and truths, but it is also a spiritual union with Christ through the resurrection. So holding to sound doctrine is absolutely essential and yet insufficient at the same time. We are to examine whether the truth is shaping the habitual affections of our hearts and the practices of our will and character. In Ephesians 1 again we see this link between truth and experience via the Spirit and resurrection. Paul prays for his readers

that the eyes of your heart may be enlightened in order that you may know the hope to which he has called you, the riches of his glorious inheritance in his holy people, and his incomparably great power for us who believe. That power is the same as the mighty strength he exerted when he raised Christ from the dead and seated him at his right hand in the heavenly realms, far above all rule and authority, power and dominion, and every name that is invoked, not only in the present age but also in the one to come.

(Ephesians 1:18–21)

At first sight the prayer raises questions. Surely Paul's readers already knew intellectually that they have a future hope and glorious inheritance awaiting them, so for what was he praying? The phrase the "eyes of your heart" is a clue to the answer. Paul wanted his friends to move beyond mere mental assent. He wanted the truths they held in their minds to fill them with joy, love, confidence, peace, comfort and power. This was possible because Christians are united to the one who currently rules over both the present age and the age to come at the same time (verse 21), so he can bring the powers of the end-time into our hearts and lives now.

In Ephesians 3 Paul prayed the same thing. He asked that God would "strengthen you with power through his Spirit in your inner being, so that Christ may dwell in your hearts through faith. And I pray that you, being rooted and established in love, may have power, together with all the Lord's holy people, to grasp how wide and long and high and deep is the love of Christ, and to know this love that surpasses knowledge—that you may be filled to the measure of all the fullness of God" (Ephesians 3:16–19). Again, we know Christians already have Christ dwelling in them (Ephesians 2:22) and already have come to fullness in him (Colossians 2:9–10). While these things were objectively true of his readers, Paul asks the Spirit to make these truths so spiritually real and affecting to the heart that they change how they live every day. These are prayers, then, for experience based on what we have been given through Christ's resurrection.[6]

Perhaps no Christian thinker emphasized the presence of the future in Christian experience as much as did the seventeenth-century British theologian John Owen. Owen pointed to the teaching of 1 Corinthians 13:12 and 1 John 3:2–3, that the greatest blessing of the coming age was the "Beatific Vision," seeing Christ face to face with our physical eyes. But he also noted how 2 Corinthians spoke of seeing the glory of Christ now. This meant that some small but wonderful portion of that ultimate joy must be available to us. "Owen turns repeatedly to the concept of beholding the glory of God by faith now . . . [in] anticipation and consummation of the beatific vision [in heaven.]"[7] We walk by faith, not sight (2 Corinthians 5:7), yet: "We all, who with unveiled faces contemplate the Lord's glory, are being transformed into his image with ever-increasing glory, which comes from the Lord, who is the Spirit" (2 Corinthians 3:18) and "For God, who said, 'Let light shine out of darkness,' made his light shine in our hearts to give us the light of the knowledge of God's glory displayed in the face of Christ" (2 Corinthians 4:6).

These verses teach us, Owen argued, that there are two ways of beholding the glory of Jesus—one is by faith now, the other is by direct sight in eternity. Therefore, we must not merely believe in the doctrines of Christ's person, offices, and work but we must learn how to contemplate the glory of each of them, to get a sense in the heart of their beauty, greatness, and wonder. This happens now through the work of the Spirit, and even though the experience falls infinitely short of the eventual vision, we nevertheless will find ourselves changed into the image of his glory as we gradually come to love him above all other things.[8]

Owen supplies important pieces of guidance for beholding Christ's glory now. First, we see his glory as we meditate on the wisdom of the gospel itself, the Great Reversal. Owen pointed to the apostle John, who said the disciples beheld Jesus's glory when he was on earth. Owen asked:

> They "beheld his glory" (John 1:14). And we may inquire what was this glory of Christ which they so saw . . . ? It was not the glory of his outward condition, as we behold the glory of a king . . . for he walked in the condition of a man of low degree. . . . It was not with respect to the outward form of the flesh which he was made . . . for he had in that neither form nor comeliness that he should be desired [Isaiah 52:14; 53:2–3]. . . . It was not . . . the eternal essential glory of his divine nature that is intended, for this no man can see in this world, and what we shall attain in a view thereof hereafter we know not. . . . It was his glory, as he was "full of grace and truth." They saw the glory of his person . . . in the administration of grace and truth [the gospel]. . . . This was that glory the Baptist saw when he said . . . "Behold the Lamb of

God, which takes away the sin of the world" (John 1:29ff). . . . His glory being confined absolutely to the gospel alone."[9]

Since this "faith-sight" of Jesus is not a literal, physical vision of his resurrected body, how can we be sure we are really seeing *him* and not letting our imaginations fashion a Jesus of our own liking and making? Owen answered that we can have confidence if we are careful to center our meditations on what the Bible says about Jesus. "The glory of our Lord Jesus Christ which is revealed in Scripture . . . [is] . . . the principal object of our faith, love, delight, and admiration. . . . The only true guide in this [is not] fancy and imagination [but] Scripture revelation."[10]

Owen occasionally tried to express the inexpressible and describe the beholding of Christ's glory. His words fall short. Nevertheless "there is in true believers a [real] foresight and foretaste of this glorious condition."[11] Sometimes the ideas of the biblical text burst the banks of the intellect, as it were, and become like a light to see or like food to eat. The truths become as sweet and strengthening as a feast. The mind is engaged deeply, because you can often see all sorts of things in a particular verse or word that you never saw before, but the effect goes to the heart and soul, not just to the head. Owen admitted that these times of sweetness and light are only episodic and mild, yet they are life-changing for all that. The "high" experiences we may seek, Owen admitted, were few and far between.

> There enters sometimes by the Word and Spirit, into their hearts such a sense of the uncreated glory of God, shining forth in Christ, as affects and satiates the souls with ineffable joy. . . . These enjoyments, indeed, are rare, and for the most part of short continuance. But it is from our own sloth and darkness that we do not enjoy more visits of this grace, and that the dawnings of glory do not more shine on our souls.[12]

Resurrection and Change

Christian experience is not an end in itself, a way to have exciting emotions. The purpose of God's salvation is that we be "conformed to the image of his Son" (Romans 8:29). How does concrete, long-lasting change actually happen? In Ephesians and Colossians Paul spoke of a two-stage process that leads to permanent life change.

> Put off your old self, which is being corrupted by its deceitful desires; to be made new in the attitude of your minds; and . . . put on the new self, created to be like God in true righteousness and holiness.
>
> **(Ephesians 4:22–24)**

> Since, then, you have been raised with Christ, set your hearts on things above, where Christ is, seated at the right hand of God. Set your minds on things above, not on earthly things. For you died, and your life is now hidden with Christ in God. When Christ, who is your life, appears, then you also will appear with him in glory. Put to death, therefore, whatever belongs to your earthly nature: sexual immorality, impurity, lust, evil desires and greed, which is idolatry.
>
> **(Colossians 3:1–5)**

I know very little about cars, but in one of my rare forays into automotive research I learned about an internal combustion engine that requires only two strokes—one up (compression stroke) and one down (the combustion stroke)—to complete its power cycle, which turns the crankshaft and moves the car forward.

In Ephesians Paul is also speaking of two "strokes"— "putting off the old self" and "putting on the new self"—that lead to righteousness and holiness of character. In Colossians, speaking of the same process, he uses somewhat different terms. Christians are to "put to death" the old nature and are to "set your heart on things above" where "your life is hidden with Christ in God." In both passages, Paul was writing about discarding or killing something and enlivening or strengthening something.

We can't help but notice that, once again, this dynamic for change is modeled on the Great Reversal. As there could be no salvation without Jesus's death and resurrection, so that salvation cannot transform us and work itself all through our lives without a constant practice of death and resurrection.

First, there is what we will call the downward "killing the sin" stroke. In both Ephesians and Colossians the things that are being killed off are *epithumia*, inordinate, enslaving desires (translated as "deceitful desires" in Ephesians 4:22 and as "evil desires . . . idolatry" in Colossians 3:5). Colossians 3:2 says human beings always set their hearts on earthly things. We rest in them, build our lives on them, and look to them rather than to God for our identity, meaning, salvation, and love. That makes them idols, things we *have* to have in order to receive life joyfully. Idols always master us, creating inordinate, hard-to-control desires of fear, anger, drivenness, and addiction. We *have* to have our idols in order to have an identity or self-worth or meaning, and so we will overwork, exploit, lie, harm, and abuse others and even ourselves to get what our hearts have been set on. The downward stroke is an effort to cast those idols out of our lives, to pull our hearts off of them, to weaken or eliminate their hold on us.

Second, there is what we will call the upward "setting the heart" stroke. This is to raise the mind and heart toward "things above" and, in particular, to Jesus himself. The heart's desire to have some ultimate source of love and meaning cannot be erased or eliminated—it is how we were created. So an ultimate love cannot be displaced—it can only be *re*placed with a more powerful one.[13] It is only as you inflame the heart with love for Christ through meditation on him as he is revealed in the Word and gospel that you can get freedom from enslaving idols.

These two strokes are continuous and inseparable—they involve each other. You can't remove the heart's inordinate affections for power, approval, comfort, and control from one object without showing the heart a greater, more desirable and beautiful object—Jesus himself. Only then will your sin lose its attractive power, and only then will you begin to be free. On the other hand, without the assurance and knowledge of our acceptance in Christ, the admission of our sin will be too traumatic. If our self-worth is based on being a good person rather than on Christ, then we will, like Peter, not be able to admit our flaws or sins.[14] The more we know Christ's love, the easier it will be to confess our sin, and the more we confess our sin, the more precious and wonderful the grace of Jesus will become.

Mistakes About Growth and Change

When people first hear of this growth process described by Paul, they often jump to mistaken conclusions.

The first common mistake is to think of killing sin as "just saying no" to wrong behavior or as merely repenting and asking forgiveness for our sins. Of course, Christians should do both those things, but they are not the heart of what this growth process has in view. The downward stroke bears not only on behavior but even more on the habits of the heart and the patterns of your mind and emotions that make you prone to sin. That means identifying background attitudes of self-pity or bitterness or self-indulgence or anxiety that set you up for your particular sinful behaviors. Some of us sin by being cowardly and not speaking out when we should. Others of us sin by being harsh and speaking too quickly and rashly.

Everyone has something about which they say, "If I get *this* then I'll know my life counts and that I'm worthy of love." Those for whom "this" is power don't mind offending people to get it, but those for whom "this" is approval would not dare do such a thing. Whatever we set our hearts on as a substitute for Jesus and his salvation will determine how we feel and how we act. To kill off the inordinate desires that flow from our idols is not merely to repent of sins we have done. It is to identify and weaken the sinful roots and structures of our heart so our particular heart sin patterns won't keep reasserting themselves.

A second mistake is much like the first one. We think "setting the heart" is just working hard to live as we should. That again puts all the emphasis on behavior rather than dealing with the heart. Certainly the rest of Colossians 3 speaks of practicing love and patience and self-control and forgiveness. But that is not what Paul meant when he spoke of "setting the mind on things above." This is setting the heart's *affections*—the deepest desires of the heart—on Jesus (cf. Colossians 3:1 and 2). It is, as John Owen argued, to meditate on the gloriousness of who Jesus is and what he has done until he begins to attract and incline your heart toward himself. Only then will your heart no longer be fixed on other things. Your goal is to replace your idols in the deepest recesses of your heart with Jesus Christ, the one who is altogether lovely.[15]

That sounds esoteric, but we can begin very practically. Consider the little phrase Paul uses in verse 4, namely, that Christ is "your life." Use that as a tool for self-analysis. When you are downcast, or tempted, or angry, or frightened, ask yourself, "Have I made something else 'my life'? That is, have I put something in the center of my life that doesn't belong there?" To "set your heart on things above," look at the thing and say, "You are not my life. Only Christ is my life. You're a good thing but I don't need you to have life and joy. Christ is my life and joy."

When you do that, you're shooting an antidote right into the heart of your negative emotions. It is an antidote that says, "I am his beloved child, in whom he is well pleased. What else do I really want?" That antidote goes in and it lessens the fear, despair, or anger—as well as making you less likely to fall into sin.

The last mistake people make about this process is that they think it means making yourself feel guilty, beating yourself up about how bad you are, in order to shame yourself into better behavior. Nothing could be further from the truth.

We are already raised and seated in the heavenly places. As we have seen, all that language is to say that we are as loved and forgiven, as accepted and sure of salvation as if we had already died and were literally seated in heaven. There is now no condemnation for us (Romans 8:1). All the condemnation we deserve fell into the heart of Christ. He absorbed it, he paid it, and now he is risen and serves as our mediator and intercessor before the throne of the universe (Hebrews 7:25; 1 John 2:1–3). All this is behind the statement that "your life is now hidden with God in Christ" (Colossians 3:3). That is the basis for the dying to sin and living unto righteousness that begins changing us now and will deliver us without stain or blemish on the last day.

Putting sin to death does indeed involve repentance, but there's a repentance that frees us and another kind of "worldly sorrow" that makes us worse (2 Corinthians 7:10). This latter kind of sorrow over sin arises strictly out of the fear of punishment. The focus is on what our action is going to do for us. Our alarm and grief are basically forms of self-pity. We may grovel and confess, but our motivation is to escape pain and to try to impress God, others, and ourselves that we don't deserve to be punished too much. In all this we are more upset about sin's consequences than about the sin itself. That means once the consequences are gone, the sin will be as entangled in your affections as it ever was. You will not change.

There's another kind of repentance and sorrow for sin that Paul calls "godly" and that leads to genuine change and cleansing (2 Corinthians 7:10). It says, "God will never cast me off. Look what he did so that he would never have to condemn me. Look what it cost my Savior to secure this grace for me! How could I turn away from this kind of love and beauty for this other thing?" This is painful conviction of sin, but it is not mixed with a slavish fear. You know he will never forsake you (Hebrews 13:5). This frees you to focus not so much on yourself but rather on how your sin grieves your loving Savior. That kind of sorrow makes you hate not yourself but the sin that dishonors him. And that genuinely weakens the sin's hold over you. "If he loved me the way he did," you say to your heart, "how can I have anything more to do with this evil?" Now you are on the road to lasting change.

Resurrection and Practice

In 1988 two ordained Christian ministers ran for the presidency of the United States. One, Jesse Jackson, ran as a liberal candidate and the other, Pat Robertson, ran as a conservative candidate. Both cited the Bible as the basis for their positions as they "championed widely divergent visions of Christian morality." While there was no Christian minister running for president in 1992, Republicans pointed to the Bible to support their "family values" platform while the Democrats and Bill Clinton talked about a "new covenant" and their platform for racial and economic justice.[16] Richard B. Hays of Duke University opened his classic *The Moral Vision of the New Testament* with the example of the 1988 election. He pointed out that each candidate did have some warrant for his claims. Each party was working for some things that were supported by the Bible's ethical teaching, but each party was also ignoring important elements of the Bible. Hays concluded that neither party was really doing full justice to all that the Bible calls human beings to do. The ethics of the New Testament are "far more nuanced than a simple conservative/liberal polarity would suggest." Hays warned that Americans in particular have "uncritically accepted the categories of popular U.S. discourse . . . without subjecting them to sustained critical scrutiny in light of a close reading of the Bible."[17]

Hays's example warns us that we can read the Bible selectively and have our opinions hijacked by the political trends of the moment. How can we avoid that? Again—we can turn to the resurrection. We have been talking about how the resurrection provides us with the resources of inward heart change and experience. But the resurrection also provides us with a framework for Christian ethical practice.

Hays lays down some principles for finding Christian ethical principles in the Bible. First, he says, we must read our moral ideas out of the entire Bible, and not just our favorite part of it. Second, he says that the Bible gives us moral guidance not only in the form of "rules"—direct commandments or prohibitions of specific behaviors—but also through "principles" and "paradigms."[18] An example of a rule is the prohibition of divorce except in the case of adultery (Matthew 19:9) or irremediable desertion (1 Corinthians 7:15). Examples of principles are Jesus's two great commandments of loving God supremely and loving your neighbor as yourself (Mark 12:28–31). Unlike a rule, a principle requires wisdom and reasoning for its application. You know if you have committed adultery or not. It is more difficult to discern if you have been loving or not.

Examples of moral paradigms are the parable of the Good Samaritan (Luke 10:29–37) and the lessons Paul draws from the behavior of Israel in the wilderness (1 Corinthians 10:1–11:1). The character of God himself is paradigmatic. Psalm 145 tells us that God loves all he has made (verse 9), he is near to anyone who is brokenhearted (verse 14), and he feeds every living thing (verse 16), yet he will judge and punish the wicked (verse 20). God's behavior includes remarkable compassion with unflinching declarations of justice. Does the character of God serve as a paradigm for us? It certainly does. "Be holy for I am holy." (1 Peter 1:16; cf. Matthew 5:48) When God came to earth in Jesus Christ, his character became visible to us in the life of a human being. In the end, he saved us through death and resurrection, which become a master paradigm for our lives.

The Ethics of the Great Reversal

Hays believes that all the ethical rules, paradigms, and principles are brought together in what he calls central, biblical "focal images," and the final two he names—"the cross and the new creation"—are what we have been calling the Great Reversal. Hays writes:

> Jesus's death on the cross is the [ultimate] paradigm for faithfulness to God in this world. . . . Jesus's death is . . . an act of self-giving love. . . . The New Testament writers consistently employ the pattern of the cross precisely to call those who possess power and privilege to surrender it for the sake of the weak. . . . *The new*

creation . . . [is] the power of the resurrection in the midst of a not-yet-redeemed world. . . . In the present time, the new creation already appears, but only proleptically.[19]

All the moral rules, principles, and paradigms are aspects of this central biblical theme—the Great Reversal, the deep pattern of God's salvation in which he saves through the death of rejection, weakness, and sacrifice, and yet through this death he raises us up, rescuing us from our sins and making us into something great.

How do the cross and resurrection bring the moral guidance of the Bible into sharp focus?

First, the Great Reversal helps us see obedience to moral *rules* in a gospel light, not as a means to save ourselves, but as a way to imitate, delight, and resemble the one who saved us through his death and resurrection. We come to see, for example, that every act of obedience to God is a "death" followed by a resurrection. Elisabeth Elliot wrote that whenever two wills cross, "somebody has to die. Life requires countless 'little' deaths—occasions when we are given the chance to say no to self and yes to God."[20] She meant that every time we obey God and give up the right to self-determination, we are dying to control over our own life. But, she adds, "We are not meant to die merely in order to be dead. God would not want that. . . . *We die in order to live.*" She goes on:

> A seed falls into the dark earth and dies. Out of its death comes multiplied life. As Saint Francis prayed, "It is in giving that we receive, it is in pardoning that we are pardoned, it is in dying that we are born to eternal life." It takes faith to believe this. . . . A failure of faith here leads certainly to resentment and then to depression. The destruction will go on and on.[21]

It is crucial that we read the Bible's moral rules, as Elliot does, through the focal image of the Great Reversal. If we think of the moral rules as ways of going from strength to strength in order to earn our salvation, we will be crushed to see how often obedience does not work that way. We must be convinced that it is Jesus's death and resurrection that has already earned our salvation, and that now obedience is the way to be conformed into the image of the one we love. If we don't grasp this, as Elliot says, we will fall into despair. We must instead see every act of obedience as a little death that leads us to new life—new self-understanding, new levels of trust in God, new growth in love, patience, humility, and self-control. And, most of all, new intimacy and communion with God.

Second, Hays argues that the Great Reversal gives content and definition to the Bible's moral *principles.*

Many people would say that the principle of *love* is the main ethical directive to Christians. And certainly Jesus himself says that all the moral rules, all God's law, boils down to love of God and love of neighbor (Mark 12: 28–31). But Hays says that the term *love* has become debased in popular discourse, so that the "loving" thing to do is simply not to displease or make any demands of people. He relates, as an example, that he has been told that pressing Christians to the standard of radical financial generosity, one of the moral principles of the New Testament, is "unloving."[22] The problem is that if we remove the concept of love from the focal idea of Jesus's cross and resurrection, we empty it of any content. It becomes whatever we say it is.

Others, Hays writes, would say that *liberation* is the basic moral theme of the Bible, but the problems here are similar. In popular parlance liberation now has an almost completely political meaning, and those who appeal to the Bible in their efforts to liberate people from various political injustices often lose touch with "the New Testament's emphasis on the power of God as the sole ground of hope and freedom."[23] Secular conservatism fights for the liberation of the individual from state power while progressivism fights for the liberation of oppressed groups through state power. It is easy for Christians who talk about liberation to be more influenced by one of these political views than by the Bible. Liberation understood in light of the Great Reversal looks very different from either ideology.

In short, without the Great Reversal as the lens through which to understand them, the terms *love* and *liberation* will end up stamping Christians with the world's understanding of morality rather than the Bible's.

Finally, the Great Reversal keeps the cross and resurrection together as a comprehensive whole. *Cross* alone as an isolated paradigm could lead to an attitude of asceticism or even masochism and pessimism, while *resurrection* alone could lead to triumphalism, what Luther called "a theology of glory." Either cross or resurrection abstracted from the other encourages simplistic narratives but, as Hays argues, the biblical image is of the Great Reversal:

> [It] imparts to Christians . . . [an] odd capacity for simultaneous joy amidst suffering and [yet] impatience with things as they are. . . . In Christ we know that the powers of the old age are doomed, and the new creation is already appearing. Yet . . . all attempts to assert the unqualified presence of the kingdom of God stand under the judgment of [this] reservation: not before the time, not yet. Thus [the new creation] pronounces judgment upon our complacency as well as upon our presumptuous despair.[24]

He goes on to say, as does Elisabeth Elliot, that when we love others sacrificially, we do so in the power of the resurrection, knowing that there may and can be redemption and healing through the presence of the Holy Spirit. Yet he warns against a kind of prosperity gospel that always assumes success as a result of our sacrifice. "The death of Jesus carries with it the promise of the resurrection, but [that] power . . . is in God's hands, not ours. Our actions are therefore to be judged not by their calculable efficiency in producing desirable results but by their correspondence to Jesus's example."[25] The Great Reversal prevents us from wrecking our ship either on naive optimism or on hopeless pessimism.

So the Great Reversal gathers together and focuses all the Bible's many moral directives. It keeps us from falling into moralism or relativism, quietism or triumphalism. It also keeps us from a private, individualistic focus only on our own moral renovation. Our goal is the future of the resurrection—the creation of a new humanity. And this will come about not with clashing swords but through deeds of sacrificial service, the mark of the upside-down dynamic of cross and resurrection. We secure true freedom and the good of others through the sacrifice of our own freedoms and goods.

The death and resurrection of Jesus are the basis not only for Christian moral practice, but also for the inward spiritual growth that will enable us to carry out our mission in the world.[26]

CHAPTER 9

HOPE FOR RELATIONSHIPS

> But when you give a banquet, invite the poor, the crippled, the lame, the blind, and you will be blessed. Although they cannot repay you, you will be repaid at the resurrection of the righteous.
>
> —LUKE 14:13–14

The death of George Floyd at the hands of the Minneapolis police on May 25, 2020, touched off protests around the world against racial injustice. It is estimated that over fifteen million people in the U.S. had participated in these protests by early July, making them easily the largest such demonstration in the country's history.

It also touched off an intense conversation over the issue of race. It was immediately clear that we have no common vocabulary with which to conduct a discussion. At the time of my writing there has not been a national conversation. Instead many speakers of sharply different views angrily assert their position to the world and then denounce and dismiss one another.

Before the demonstrations about race took center stage, the #MeToo movement was challenging American culture about the treatment of women by powerful men. Those concerns are not as much in the public eye as I write these words, but that is a temporary situation. The bigger reality is that in Western culture there is tremendous unrest and dissatisfaction regarding all social relationships—between the economic classes, the races and nationalities, and the sexes.

In the death and resurrection of Jesus, Christians have the resources for a transformation of social relationships that can be a powerful sign to the watching world. In the next two chapters I will explore what such a community of changed relationships would look like.

The Resurrection and Race

The book of Galatians focuses on the difficulty of getting Jews and Gentiles to live together as equals in the church. The racial divisions were deep and there was great suspicion, disrespect, and mistrust on both sides. Paul addressed it in two ways.

In Galatians 2 Paul confronted Peter. Jews had always refused to eat with Gentiles, who were seen as spiritually unclean. Now Peter had fallen back into his pre-Christian ways, refusing to eat with Gentile fellow believers. Because eating together was symbolic of friendship and equal regard, Peter's action was raising his racial identity above the common identity he shared with Gentile believers in Christ. His behavior "racialized" the Gentiles. That is, he was ignoring who they were in Christ and instead was focusing on their racial and ethnic difference.

Paul's first response to this error came in Galatians 2:11–16, where he declared that Peter's behavior denied the gospel of justification by faith alone. Peter had to remember, Paul argued, that *he* had not been made acceptable before God by morality but only because of Christ's righteousness. How, then, could race make someone more acceptable?[1] "God did not enter into fellowship with you on the basis of your cultural pedigree," Paul is saying to Peter, "so how can you have fellowship with people only on the basis of theirs?"

Then, near the end of the epistle, Paul addressed the issue of race relations in a different way. He made a statement that many scholars believe is a summary of the argument of the whole letter: "Neither circumcision nor uncircumcision means anything; what counts is the new creation" (Galatians 6:15). "Circumcision and uncircumcision" is a metaphor for the racial and ethnic differences that had been troubling the church. When Paul says such distinctions mean nothing, he is not speaking absolutely. Elsewhere he expresses a love for and pride in his Jewish heritage (cf. Romans 9:1–5). What Paul means is that racial and cultural distinctions, though wonderful goods, are nothing in comparison with the new creation.

As we have discussed before, the new creation is the renewed world wiped clean of all death, suffering and tears, sin and shame (Isaiah 25:7–8), brought forward into the present. In his commentary on Galatians, Herman Ridderbos writes of the term *new creation* in verse 15:

> *New* includes everything that has been given in and through Christ—the new reality of the kingdom of God. Through Christ this new thing is not merely future-eschatological (Rev. 21:1–5, 3:12 and Mark 14:25) but is already present, is already *in* man. This new creation is first of all a gift, but it brings its task with it. This . . . then, is the one thing that counts.[2]

Through the resurrection of Christ, we now have the new creation, but as Ridderbos says it "brings its task with it." We must live in light of the resurrection and the future world, a future world in which racial differences—circumcision and uncircumcision—no longer create tension, hate, or violence. In a vivid expression of racial equality before God, the Lord will say on that final day: "Blessed be Egypt my people, Assyria my handiwork, and Israel my inheritance" (Isaiah 19:25). Isaiah 60:11–12 says of the city of God at the end of time that "people may bring you the wealth of the nations—their kings led in triumphal procession."[3] The image here is of each nation's unique cultural riches, splendors, and glories being brought into the new creation. And Revelation 21:24,26 makes it clear that these "kings of the earth" are doing it voluntarily, out of a desire to worship and give glory to God.[4]

These visions of the final age show that our racial and cultural distinctions are part of God's good creation and so important that they will be carried over into the new creation, not eradicated but purified of all the sinful distortions, just as our bodies with their distinctions will be brought in and purified of all weakness and decay. The people of God in the new world will not be homogenous but will consist of "every nation, tribe, people and language" (Revelation 7:9). They will be *a single* people (Revelation 5:9) still marked by these differences. Yet these differences will only make our unity greater and the new humanity more beautiful in all its glory.

Bearing Witness on Race

"In Christ Jesus . . . there is neither Jew nor Gentile" (Galatians 3:26–28). In Galatians Paul urges Christians to live in the light of the resurrection—not to mention the doctrine of justification—in such a way that the world's high barriers and prejudices between races and peoples are removed. There are two ways to do that.

Larry Hurtado, in his study of early Christianity, argued that Paul's efforts had a good degree of success. He observed that early Christianity broke the normal tight bond between a person's ethnicity and his or her religion. Before the coming of Christianity, one was "born to one's gods," because every people, city, place, craft guild, and large estate had its own gods. Religion was a mere extension of culture. If you were born in a particular place or into a particular people, worshipping those gods was one of the ways you were part of that community.

But Christians believed that there was only one God and everyone should worship him regardless of their race, ethnicity, class, nationality, or vocation, or of any other human status. The radical implication was that your faith in God was not merely independent of your ethnicity—it was more fundamental to who you were than your ethnicity. It gave you a bond with all other Christians that was deeper than any you had with your own race. This created the first multiracial, multiethnic faith community. Hurtado wrote:

[Christians'] . . . ethnic, social, and gender distinctions are to be regarded as relativized radically, [for] all believers of whatever ethnic, sexual, or social class are now "one in Christ Jesus." But . . . Paul did not treat these distinctions as actually effaced. So for example . . . he persisted in referring to himself proudly as a member of his ancestral people, a "Hebrew" and an "Israelite" . . . but he also insisted that "in Christ" . . . these distinctions were no longer to be regarded as *defining* believers in the ways that they had functioned before.[5]

Christianity did not destroy your national identity by taking you out into the desert into a new exclusive community to live apart from the rest of the world. Nor did it give you a detailed set of rules on how to dress and eat, whom to associate with and avoid—rules that removed you completely from your culture. No, if you were Jewish or Greek or Asian and you became a Christian, you remained Jewish, Greek, or Asian, and positively so. Yet your most fundamental identity now lay elsewhere, and it gave you a critical distance from your own culture that enabled you to better assess its strengths and weaknesses. It also gave you deep bonds with Christians from other cultures and races, people who could give you insights to which you would never otherwise have had access.

Modern-day Christians must admit that that these extraordinary resources for racial understanding, healing, and unity are largely going untapped. The new self (Ephesians 4:22–23) that is rooted in Christ's love and work rather in than our race, culture, and achievements is something that must be *put on*. Only then can it overcome the natural "hostility" between races (Ephesians 2:14). Paul would not be exhorting believers to put on the new self or to overcome racial hostility if this happened automatically to Christians. You can be a believing Christian and *not* put off your old identity with its idolatrous desires, including the natural human inclination to make an idol of our culture, in order to feel superior to others.

What if I, an older white male, find myself listening to a young African American sister in Christ who is telling me about the difficulty of her life in a white-dominated society? How shall I respond? There is an instinct within me to respond the way my parents and grandparents and most of the people I grew up around would have responded. They would be polite and pleasant outwardly and say nothing negative, but inwardly they would dismiss her concerns. They would say, "Sure, there's still prejudice out there but nothing like it was in the past. It's a free country, and if you work hard you'll prosper and you will be fine." So I could just smile and hope the uncomfortable conversation will be over soon.

Or I can remember that my old self, because of its idolatries, tends to be self-justifying and blind to many of the very things she is telling me. And I can remember my new self, that I am a Christian first and a white man second and that I must treat this sister in Christ as an equal and as a person through whom God is speaking to me. That doesn't mean I can't use my critical faculties to discuss and even debate. But even an imperfectly, partially assumed new Christian self, rooted in Christ's love and grace, enables a person to be less defensive and quick to repent. It produces an openness and humility that make such conversations and learning possible. With all the shouting and anger so prevalent around these issues, I don't know of a better way forward than for millions of Christians to put on their new selves and to start to listen.

Another way for Christians to be salt and light regarding race in our polarized culture is by continuing to multiply multiethnic churches. The New Testament church was wonderfully multiethnic and this, as we have noted, was a radical phenomenon. Today, as our Western societies become increasingly multiethnic in population, that does not mean that people of different races and cultures are really mixing. Studies show that even in neighborhoods that are very multiethnic in population, different groups largely congregate in homogeneous gatherings and associations and institutions. Multiethnic churches, in which leadership and community are diverse and working together in close contact, can be a testimony to the surrounding community of how Christ can unite us.

We must not be too rigid about this. There are plenty of human communities and whole regions in the world that are monoethnic. Not every local neighborhood is ethnically diverse, and so not every Christian church can be multiethnic. But in a globalized, mobile world, more and more places are becoming diverse, and that is true especially of urban and metro areas. In a world so polarized by race and tribe and class, there is no greater witness to the power of the gospel and the reality of the new creation than when believers do the hard work of establishing multiethnic churches. This is of course a huge subject and not at all an easy task, but there are good resources for congregations that want to bear witness to the power of the gospel in this way.[6]

The Resurrection and Class

In Luke 14 Jesus was at a banquet and "noticed how the guests picked the places of honor at the table" (verse 7). In that culture the closer you sat to the host, the greater the public display of your importance, as well as the more important your conversation partners. This was an ancient version of networking, in which the purpose of your dinner appointments and party-going was to cultivate relationships that helped you climb the social ladder. You associated with people who could open doors for you, and who in turn expected favors from you and access to *your* network of contacts. The goal, as sociologist Pierre Bourdieu might say, was the mutual enhancement of one's social, cultural, economic, and "symbolic" (status and prestige) capital.[7]

But Jesus told his disciples that if they were invited to such a feast, they should "*not* take the place of honor" but choose a seat lower down or farther from the people with greater honor and prestige. This was a startling thing to say. His listeners would have wondered what was the point of going at all then? The whole dinner party system—a major social institution in that culture—was designed to help you meet people of a higher social status for whom you could perform mutually beneficial favors.

Jesus instead points to the divine principle of reversal. He says his followers should remember that "All those who exalt themselves will be humbled, and those who humble themselves will be exalted" (Luke 14:11). Jesus is not saying that his disciples should just try to *look* humble so that they will get credit for being virtuous. Rather, he is telling them not to play the game at all, not to use hospitality and social gatherings like that.

Jesus then directs his followers to do something even more countercultural, even more disruptive to the social status quo:

> Then Jesus said to his host, "When you give a luncheon or dinner, do not invite your friends, your brothers or sisters, your relatives, or your rich neighbors; if you do, they may invite you back and so you will be repaid. But when you give a banquet, invite the poor, the crippled, the lame, the blind, and you will be blessed. Although they cannot repay you, you will be repaid at the resurrection of the righteous."
>
> **(Luke 14:12–14)**

Here we see Jesus breaking completely free from the transactional, self-interested model for social relationships on which the world had been based for centuries, right down to the present day. Without this conclusion, Jesus's counsel to not seek the more honored seats could have been read as a subtle way to fit into the world's model. The idea would have been to "Act very humble and never look like you are social climbing—and that is the very best way *to* social climb."

But in verses 12–14 Jesus told Christians to actively befriend and serve people who could never open doors for you or invite you to their villas or bring you more clients and business. And the reason Christians live in such a radically different way is—the resurrection! "Although they cannot repay you, you will be repaid at the resurrection of the righteous." The glory and richness and bliss and love of the final resurrection and renewed world will infinitely, innumerable times over, more than recompense you for any sacrifices for righteousness in this life.

We must not miss the implications of this. Jesus is sharply criticizing a major feature of Roman culture, and he is forbidding his disciples to be part of its systemic injustice. Biblical scholar Joel B. Green writes:

> Central to the political stability of the Empire was the ethics of reciprocity, a gift-and-obligation system that tied every person, from the emperor in Rome to the child in the most distance province, into an intricate web of social relations. . . . Gifts, by unwritten definition, were never "free," but were given and received with either explicit or implicit strings attached.

Green explains that people of means would never invite the poor to a meal, because their presence would endanger the social status of the host, the others at the meal would feel their time wasted, and the poor themselves would be embarrassed because they could not reciprocate. But this systemically disadvantaged those at the lower end of the social order. They were forever excluded from the kinds of connections and resources that would help them advance. Jesus not only critiques the injustice of the existing system, he directs that his followers create a new social institution, one that lifts up people rather than pushing them down. Jesus "constructs a new vision of life."[8] Jesus calls on his disciples to invite the poor, the crippled, the lame, and the blind into their homes. That would bring Christians into direct relationships with people whom the culture had taught them to avoid and it would trigger significant generosity.

Jesus adds, in verse 14, that those who provide uncalculating generosity toward those of low status will experience "blessing" from God. But even here, Jesus does not tell people to give to others in order to get blessing. He is saying that only those who pour themselves out for others without any care for repayment—but merely as a joyful response to how God has already given them all things possible—will be blessed.[9]

The Resurrection and Wealth

In Luke 14 Jesus applied the Great Reversal to transform Christians' class relationships. Similarly, in 2 Corinthians, Paul applied the Great Reversal to believers' attitudes toward their own wealth.

> I am not commanding you, but I want to test the sincerity of your love by comparing it with the earnestness of others. For you know the grace of our Lord Jesus Christ, that though he was rich, yet for your sake he became poor, so that you through his poverty might become rich.
>
> **(2 Corinthians 8:8–9)**

Notice that Paul did *not* give his readers a "rule" or command. He had one available—the biblical rule of the "tithe"—10 percent of one's annual income—that should be set apart for charitable giving (Deuteronomy 12:5–6; Malachi 3:8–12; Matthew 23:23). But rather than a rule, he gave them what Hays would call a paradigm. Just as Jesus enriched us and the world through his poverty, so we, out of fullness of love and joy, imitate him. The effect of a paradigm is greater than that of a rule.

First of all, the rule doesn't deal with the underlying reason for our lack of generosity. We keep our money for ourselves out of pride or fear, but the gospel—the Great Reversal—reminds us that we have all genuine riches, the only inheritance that cannot fade or be stolen, and all at infinite cost to Christ. This assures our hearts where there is anxiety and melts our hearts where there is arrogance. Second, the paradigm doesn't let us off the hook. What if we are so wealthy that a 10 percent tithe does not entail sacrifice on our part? Then we must give more, until our giving becomes the sacrifice that Jesus's self-giving was.

Jesus insisted we live our lives now not merely through rule keeping within the old creation but by seeking to live, as much as possible, according to the life we will live in the new creation, "the resurrection of the righteous" (Luke 14:14).[10] We are not to live according to the spirit of this age, one of honor scarcity, in which every relationship must be made to benefit our wealth or status. Instead we are to live in accordance with the new creation, despite the sacrifices and losses that may bring, remembering that at the first sight of Jesus in our new bodies with our new eyes we will be inundated with unimaginable joy and splendor (1 John 3:2–3; 2 Corinthians 3:16–18). Belief in the resurrection should be the end of the calculation in relationships. It should be the end of the constant, semiconscious inner monologue: "Do I like this person? Do they appreciate and thank me enough? Is this person worth my time?" And it should be the end of stinginess with our wealth and goods.

The Resurrection and Broken Relationships

The Great Reversal and the new creation transform how we handle conflict as well.

In 1 Corinthians 6:1–6, Paul addressed Christians who were going to court and lodging lawsuits against one another. He rebukes them, but his exhortation is not only based on Jesus's command to forgive one another (Matthew 18:35). Paul said "Do you not know that the Lord's people will judge the world? And if you are to judge the world, are you not competent to judge trivial cases?" (verse 2). Biblical scholar Gordon Fee writes:

> Here is a clear illustration of the "already but not yet" framework of Pauline theology. The future realities, which for Paul are as certain as the present itself, condition everything the church is and does in the present. . . . Here he is speaking of the *final* judgment on "the world" as a whole, the entire anti-God system of things that will come under God's judgment, in which God's people are in some way to be involved. . . . [He is] trying to shame

them for having lawsuits at all. Such matters are "trivial"; they add up to zero in light of the eschatological judgment. Such people are simply after the wrong things.[11]

Paul was not saying that lawsuits are never warranted or that justice is unimportant. But he argued that vengefulness, quickness to litigate, and self-interest are part of the spirit of this age. If instead Christians live in light of the future "resurrection of the righteous," which Jesus says will "recompense" for all, they would be famous for their willingness to reconcile, to mutually give up rights and forgive.

In Romans 2:1–10 Paul forbade Christians from "passing judgment on someone else." Again, his call to tolerance and graciousness to opponents is grounded in the future. He argues that God alone has both the sufficient knowledge and the moral right to determine what a person deserves. On "the day of God's wrath . . . God 'will repay each person according to what they have done'" (verses 5–6). To live in light of that great day when perfect justice will be done and all things will be put right is to live a life free from the need to pay people back or hold grudges.

Peter wrote: "When they hurled their insults at him, he did not retaliate; when he suffered, he made no threats. Instead, he entrusted himself to him who judges justly."(1 Peter 2:23) When Jesus was charged and condemned unfairly, Jesus did not explode in anger and pay them back with insults and counter-denunciations. Nor did he embark on lengthy speeches to vindicate himself and defend his reputation. During his trials he calmly and briefly witnessed to the truth (cf. John 18:23), but this was not because Jesus was some stoic who had learned emotional detachment. Rather, he "entrusted himself" to the true Judge. Because he knew that the Judge of the Universe accepted him, Jesus was not emotionally overthrown by what any human court said about him. And instead of trying to give the wrongdoers all that they deserved, he relied on God to do that rather than trying to mete out a punishment on them himself.

When Christians forgive others, we can look to Jesus in multiple ways. In the future, he will stand as the Judge of the world. So we can rest in the knowledge that whatever happens now, Jesus will square all accounts and put all things right in a way we could never do ourselves. And we also look to the past. It was *our* sins that put Jesus on the cross, yet he forgave willingly. So we should forgive those who sin against us and if we do, we will find that the forgiveness that can be excruciatingly hard, like a death, will eventually lead to a resurrection and to new freedom and peace. The resurrection, then, both past and present, is the key to forgiveness and to the reconciliation of broken relationships.

As a community, Christians must be a witness to the present world of the new creation by showing that we can, by the power of the Spirit, solve and heal our disputes.

The Resurrection and Sexual Relationships

A final social category to which the resurrection speaks is that of sexual relationships.

We have been looking at how the resurrection and the new creation have begun to shape our attitudes toward race and social relationships. The biblical teaching stresses racial equality and social justice and to the modern ear much of this will sound somewhat "liberal." But when we see how the resurrection shapes our understanding of sexuality, the results will seem to many observers to be "conservative." I began this section with a reminder of Richard Hays's point that today's church tends to adopt the categories of U.S. political discourse rather than to think in biblical categories. Despite contemporary sensibilities, there is no contradiction between what the Bible says about race and class and what the Bible says about sex. The Bible applies the inner logic of the Great Reversal equally to both.

In 1 Corinthians 6 Paul wrote: Do you not know that . . . neither the sexually immoral . . . nor the greedy . . . will inherit the kingdom of God? (1 Corinthians 6:9,10) Again, Paul calls the Corinthians to walk in the present in line with the future the kingdom of God (verse 9), not with the spirit of this world. As we saw in 1 Corinthians 6:1–6, he applied this first to how we handle personal disputes, but then turned to sexual relationships. Not only are the "greedy" and "swindlers" out of accord with the future new creation, but so are the "sexually immoral" (verse 9). In verses 12–20, he moves to a full discussion of sexual morality.

Christian teaching on sex is highly controversial in the West today. When Christian rules and behavioral codes are compared with the modern culture's mores about sex, they appear restrictive and unhealthy. People seldom explore the foundational logic behind the rules—what Hays calls principles, paradigms, and the worldview. That is what Paul did in this passage. Right in the middle of laying down rules about sexual behavior, he goes behind the rules and appeals to the resurrection of Jesus (1 Corinthians 6:14) and to our spiritual union with Christ through the first-fruits of the new creation (1 Corinthians 6:15,19).

In 1 Corinthians 6, Paul laid down a very clear behavioral rule for sex: "Flee porneia [sexual immorality]" (verse 18). The word *pornos* is usually translated as "sexual immorality" in modern translations, but that is too general and doesn't convey the sharp and clear meaning it had for Paul and the readers of the New Testament. The word meant any sexual intimacy outside an exclusive marriage relationship, not only adultery but premarital sex. "Porneia could be used to describe a whole array of improper sexual configurations: incest, prostitution, [premarital sex], homosexuality."[12]

The biblical condemnation of *porneia*, as Kyle Harper and Larry Hurtado both point out, was one of *the* distinctive marks of the early Christian church, as can be seen in Matthew 15:19; Mark 7:21; Acts 15:20; Romans 1:29; 1 Corinthians 6:9–10,18; Galatians 5:19; Ephesians 5:3–5; Colossians 3:5; 1 Thessalonians 4:3; 1 Timothy 1:10; and Hebrews 13:4.[13] Paul did not merely say, "It's a good idea to avoid *porneia* as much as you can." He says to *flee* it—stay free from it at all costs. In Acts 15, the Apostolic Council issued a very short list of moral imperatives by which all Christians—both Gentile and Jewish, in any cultural setting—must abide. One of them is the avoidance of *porneia* (Acts 15:20). The Christian sex ethic was understood by the apostles to be a nonnegotiable part of orthodoxy, one of the core beliefs of Christianity.[14] What Christians taught and practiced about sexuality was as much a necessary implication of the gospel and the resurrection as were care for the poor and the equality of the races. This makes it impossible to argue, as many try to do, that what the Bible says about caring for the poor is right but what it says about sex is outmoded and should be discarded. To get a clearer picture of this, see how Paul appeals to principles behind the rule of "no porneia." Paul wrote:

> The body, however, is not meant for sexual immorality but for the Lord, and the Lord for the body. By his power God raised the Lord from the dead, and he will raise us also.
>
> **(1 Corinthians 6:13–14)**

Here Paul confronts the Greco-Roman idea that the body is the relatively unimportant receptacle for the immortal soul. In that view sex was merely a physical appetite, nothing of major consequence—"no big deal." Against this Paul said that the resurrection of Jesus proves that the physical body is of greatest importance, that Jesus died to redeem not merely our souls but our bodies (Romans 8:23). Therefore our bodies *are* part of who we are, and they belong to the Lord, who died and rose to redeem them, and so we must honor our Savior with our bodies. That, of course, raises the question "Well then, how can we honor God with our bodies?" Paul went on:

> Do you not know that he who unites himself with a prostitute is one with her in body? For it is said, "The two will become one flesh."
>
> **(1 Corinthians 6:16)**

Paul was quoting Genesis 2:24, that when God brought Eve to Adam they became "one flesh." From earliest times Jewish and Christian commentators recognized that "one flesh" referred not just to sexual union. The term was a metonymy. The physical union of two persons' bodies pointed to the complete union of every aspect of their lives—spiritual, emotional, social, economic, legal. Sexual union was made by God to deepen and reflect the whole life union of marriage, and only the whole life union of marriage qualified you for sexual union.

When Paul told his male readers that every sex act, even with a prostitute, made them one flesh with their partner, he was not in some legalistic way declaring they had become automatically married. Rather, he was saying that when you have sex outside of marriage you are disastrously forgetting the whole purpose of sex. He was saying something like this:

> "The monstrosity of sexual intercourse outside marriage is that those who indulge in it are trying to isolate one kind of union (the sexual) from all the other kinds of union which were intended to go along with it and make up the total union. The Christian attitude does not mean that there is anything wrong about sexual pleasure, any more than about the pleasure of eating. It means that you must not isolate that pleasure and try to get it by itself [apart from the other things that go along with it], any more than you ought to try to get the pleasures of taste without swallowing and digesting, by chewing things and spitting them out again."[15]

The resurrection teaches us that the physical body is not an unimportant piece of meat—it matters. God has created us as integrated, embodied souls, so that what we do with our bodies affects us spiritually and wholly. Bodily union was created to both signify and strengthen a whole-life, permanent commitment, and covenant between spouses. Sex is a God-ordained way for two people to give up their independence and to say mutually to each other, "I belong completely and permanently to you." Commentator Anthony Thiselton writes about 1 Corinthians 6:12–18:

> Far from *devaluing* sex, *the very opposite comes about.* In this area Paul was far ahead of first-century cultural assumptions in perceiving the sexual act as one of intimacy and *self-commitment*

which involved the whole person; not the mere manipulation of
some "peripheral" function of the body. . . . In the context equally
of union with Christ and of physical union the issue becomes one
of fully "giving" oneself to the one to whom one belongs.[16]

Thiselton is right that Paul is giving sex a value far beyond anything
known in antiquity. It is not, as in ancient times and in the minds of many
today, merely a physical appetite and pleasure. Nor is it, as in modern culture, a kind of consumer good or a means for personal authenticity. It is a
unique mode of communication between two persons who are giving
themselves to each other in every aspect. But this high Christian valuation
of sex does not stop there.

Sex and Salvation

At the end of 1 Corinthians 6, Paul wrote:

> Do you not know that your bodies are members of Christ him-
> self? . . . Whoever is united with the Lord is one with him in
> spirit. . . . Flee from sexual immorality. . . . Do you not know that
> your bodies are temples of the Holy Spirit, who is in you, whom
> you have received from God?
>
> **(1 Corinthians 6:15,17,18,19)**

Paul has argued that sex must be a pointer to whole-life union with an
earthly spouse. Here Paul argues that it also is to be a pointer to our whole-
life union to Christ, our heavenly spouse. That is, our spiritual union with
Christ is to be a model for sexual unions between human beings. Let's notice three aspects of our spiritual union with Jesus, and its implications.

The initial step toward our union with Christ was his giving of himself.
"Christ loved the church and gave himself up for her" (Ephesians 5:25). The
Son of God became vulnerable to torment and death. He lost his glory, his

immortality, and his life for us. The second step toward our union is that we must respond by giving ourselves utterly and exclusively to him and no other god. Our union with him is a covenantal, binding, and exclusive one.

Finally, the wonder of our union is that it is not between two beings who are the same—as in two human beings or as in two divine persons in the Trinity. The miracle of our salvation is an intimate, personal union between two radically different beings—God and humanity. A seemingly unbridgeable chasm between the divine and the human has been spanned. The two most alienated beings have been joined.[17]

Now we are in a position to see that the Christian "rules" for sexuality which at first sight may appear restrictive are grounded in the very character of our salvation. Because we are saved into an exclusive, permanent, covenantal union, sex is only for those within marriage. Because our salvation brings a unity not of the same but of the deeply different, so marriage is to be the union of male and female. Secular thinking says sex is a way for the individual to get pleasure and personal satisfaction. Christianity says sex is a way to connect your life to the self-giving divine love that is at the heart of the universe and the meaning of history. Jesus literally died in order to enter into an eternal, binding union with us. We figuratively "die" when we repent and give up control of our lives and commit ourselves unconditionally to him. But these deaths have led to resurrection—spiritual now, bodily and cosmically later.

So Christian sexuality, seemingly restrictive, is based on a high and rich vision of what sex is and can be. And the sex ethic is shaped by the same master paradigm that shapes our stances toward race, the poor, and injustice—the Great Reversal in which Jesus Christ gave himself for us and saved us. He came to the greatest freedom, for himself and for us, through the giving up of his freedom. So in marriage we come into a freedom and love inaccessible to any who will not sacrifice their independence and make a whole-life commitment. Modern culture teaches us to only go into relationships that benefit us more than they cost, to have sex if it is pleasurable and fulfilling to us without entailing long-term commitments. This transactional understanding of relationships is based on a completely different understanding of human purpose and even of reality than the biblical account of a world created by a self-giving, loving God.

In *The Problem of Pain*, C. S. Lewis argues that when Jesus Christ went to the cross, he was doing what the Father, Son, and Holy Spirit had been doing inside the Trinity, in a sense, forever; each deferring to the other, each seeking not their own glory but the glory of others. There is an *other orientation* in the heart of God that is profound.

> For in self-giving, if anywhere, we touch a rhythm not only of all creation but of all being. For [Jesus] gives Himself in sacrifice; and that not only on Calvary. For when He was crucified He "did that in the wild weather of His outlying provinces which He had done at home in glory and gladness." From before the foundation of the world He surrenders begotten Deity back to begetting Deity in obedience.[18]

Lewis goes on to explain that the principle of "losing yourself to find yourself"—of giving up your independence to find the deepest love and freedom—runs through the creation from top to bottom. "For in self-giving if anywhere we touch the rhythm not only of all creation but of all being." He then says:

> From the highest to the lowest, self exists to be abdicated and, by that abdication, becomes the more truly self, to be thereupon yet the more abdicated, and so on forever. This is not a heavenly law which we can escape by remaining earthly, nor an earthly law which we can escape by being saved. What is outside the system of self-giving is not earth, nor nature, nor "ordinary life," but simply and solely hell.[19]

If the world was made by a God on the basis of that principle—of the Great Reversal—then we should not be surprised if the sexual relationships of the modern world so often are disappointing and exploitative. They are going against the "grain" of a universe created by the God who saves us through sacrifice and resurrection.

In many ways the modern sexual revolution is surprisingly retrograde. It is a return to the view that reigned in the Roman world, namely, that sex is basically a physical appetite and that it is unrealistic and unhealthy to confine it only to marriage. But from the #MeToo movement to the falling rate of sexual activity, marriage, and childbearing, it can be argued that the modern approach to sex is harming us as a society.

As a pastor working in Manhattan for almost three decades, I have seen hundreds of people who participated in the modern sexual revolution turn away from it and find greater wisdom, safety, and freedom in the Christian vision and practice of sexuality. That does not constitute a social movement because religion in general is still declining in Western societies. But I expect that despite this trend, each year many in our Western culture, out of exhaustion and frustration, will take a second look at the Christian understanding of sex that our society jettisoned so confidently in the name of fulfillment and freedom.

CHAPTER 10

HOPE FOR JUSTICE

But God has promised us a new heaven and a new earth, where justice
will rule.

—2 PETER 3:13, CEV

I n the previous chapter I looked at how the Bible connects the resurrection and new creation to specific social relationships of race, class and
wealth, and sex. However, in our day when the topic of justice is in the
foreground of innumerable cultural conversations, I want to show what the
Bible says more foundationally about what justice is, and how the resurrection helps us define and promote it.

The Resurrection and Justice

When Jesus rose from the dead, he came as the first installment of the
power of God, which will renew the world at the end of history. The Bible
tells us that, at that time, God will not just save individuals and discard the
world as if were an unimportant shell or chaff. Rather, "the creation itself
will be liberated from its bondage to decay and brought into the freedom
and glory of the children of God" (Romans 8:21). All the effects of sin—all
the decay—of the world will be healed. Not only will there be physical

liberation from disease, aging, and death, but there will be social liberation from the poverty, war, racism, and crime that infest our world now, as well as psychological liberation from the fear, guilt, shame, and despair that infect us now. All things will finally be mended, put fully right. We ourselves will be made new, but we will also receive a renewed world in which to live with Christ in our resurrected bodies. It will finally be, as Jonathan Edwards says, "a world of love." On earth, what often passes for love is a selfish, instrumental use of desirable persons to supply our selfish and envious needs for power and control. In the new creation we will know Jesus, the infinite fountain of love. We will love one another for his sake and for their sake. All relationships, then, will finally be right and just.[1] So 2 Peter 3:13 says that the new heavens and new earth will be filled with *dikaiosune*—justice.

The resurrection and new creation, then, have a major influence on the Christian's understanding of how to regard the various forms of decay that we see around us in creation now. One of the ways that nature "groans" under decay is in unjust relationships. Christians are not to be passive in the face of injustice. If all the repairing of the world was to happen in the future, then there is little for us to do but to live lives of personal morality and holiness and sit on our hands and wait. But, as we have learned throughout this book, the resurrection means that the liberating, repairing power of God is here now, through the risen Christ and his presence in our lives through the Holy Spirit. We have not been saved just to be safe, but saved in order to serve.[2]

The Great Reversal and Justice

If there is one thing clear from the Bible's treatment of the kingdom of God throughout, it is that it is a kingdom of justice. In Luke 4:18–19 Jesus tells us that the coming of the kingdom is to "proclaim good news to the poor" and to "set the oppressed free." Who are the poor to whom Jesus refers? Conservatives tend to read this text in strictly spiritual terms—it is only the *spiritually* poor or oppressed who are being addressed. But that does not fit well with the remarkable amount of attention Jesus gives to the outcasts and the poor, as we saw when looking at the gospel of Luke. Liberals, on the other hand, read Jesus's words as referring wholly to the socially and economically poor and oppressed—he came to put down the rich and lift up the poor in a revolution. But if Jesus came mainly as a political revolutionary to liberate the poor from economic poverty, it is hard to explain why he spent all his time preaching rather than mounting a military or political campaign.

The answer is this: Jesus's salvation comes to anyone—if they are willing to go through the spiritual poverty of repentance and faith. So the primary "poor" whom Jesus always saves are the "poor in spirit" (Matthew 5:3)—those who are willing to admit that they are spiritually bankrupt, that even their good deeds have been done for less-than-good reasons, and that they can be saved only through sheer, charitable, free grace. The rich who become spiritually poor in this way are saved, and the economically poor who will not humble themselves in this way are not saved.

So the paradigm of the Great Reversal requires that we be saved through spiritual poverty followed by spiritual riches in Christ. However, that experience opens believers' eyes to the needs of the economically weak and poor around us. The book of James, after reminding us that we are saved by grace, not by good works, then declares what kind of good works come naturally from a heart that knows it has been saved through sheer divine charity and grace. "Suppose a brother or sister is without clothes and daily food. If one of you . . . does nothing about their physical needs, what good is it? In the same way faith by itself, if it is not accompanied by action, is dead" (James 2:14–17). Jonathan Edwards drives home the point that anyone who has been truly saved through the Great Reversal—through admitting one's spiritual poverty—will inevitably have sympathy for the poor:

> Consider how much God hath done for us, . . . Christ loved and
> pitied us, when we were poor, and he laid out himself to help, and
> even did shed his own blood for us without grudging. He did not

think much to deny himself . . . to make us rich, and to clothe us with kingly robes, when we were naked; to feast us at his own table with dainties infinitely costly, when we were starving; to advance us from the dunghill, and set us among princes, and make us to inherit the throne of his glory, and so to give us the enjoyment of the greatest wealth and plenty to all eternity. . . . Considering all these things, what a poor business will it be, that those who hope to share these benefits, yet cannot give something for the relief of a poor neighbor without grudging! . . . What would have become of us, if Christ had been so saving of his blood, and loath to bestow it, as many men are of their money or goods?[3]

The paradigm of the Great Reversal leads us to personal faith but it does so in a way that orients us to love the poor and the weak, as Christ loved us.

The City of God and Justice

So Christians looking forward to the fullness of the kingdom—to the final resurrection and the new heavens and new earth—should be concerned to see justice done now. But how do we know what justice will look like in that final city of God? The few Bible passages that describe the new world (Isaiah 60,65–66; Revelation 21–22) give us breathtaking glimpses but few details. Is there anything within the Bible that gives us guidance about what God's future justice looks like?

Just before God gives the children of Israel the Ten Commandments for the second time near the end of Moses's life (Deuteronomy 5:1–21), Moses explained that the obedience of Israel to divine law is meant to be a witness to the world. He says:

See, I have taught you decrees and laws as the Lord my God commanded me, so that you may follow them in the land you are entering to take possession of it. Observe them carefully, for this will show your wisdom and understanding to the nations, who will hear about all these decrees and say, "Surely this great nation is a wise and understanding people." What other nation is so great as to have their gods near them the way the Lord our God is near us whenever we pray to him? And what other nation is so great as to have such righteous decrees and laws as this body of laws I am setting before you today?

(Deuteronomy 4:5–8)

One of God's purposes was that his people be a *corporate* witness to the nonbelieving world, to the "nations" around Israel. A law-obedient people was not just a cadre of moral individuals. They constituted a counterculture, an alternate human society, and that was because the Mosaic law was marked by two outstanding things. First, it created a wise and understanding people (verse 6), and second, it created a just society (verse 8). When the text speaks about the law as "righteous decrees," it translates both *mishpat* and *tzedeqah*, the two Hebrew words most often used in the Bible for justice.

Law-keeping Israel was to lead other societies to do self-critique. This is a remarkable claim, because "in the ancient world nations were accustomed to think that they had superior gods and . . . institutions. . . . The repeated 'this great nation' . . . specifically echo claims made for King Hammurabi, the great Babylonian lawgiver."[4] Yet here the Bible says that if the people obey the law, the surrounding nations, despite their assumptions of cultural superiority, will conclude that Israel has found the wisdom and justice that they had sought in their own laws but had been unable to realize. They will see that Israel's society is wise and just because the Lord is nearer to Israel than their gods are to them. And so the impact of law keeping—if it is carried out as it should be—would ultimately be evangelistic. Jerusalem, in particular, was to be an urban community revealing the wisdom and justice of God to the nations. It was to be attractional—"the joy of the whole earth" (Psalm 48:2).

So the city of Jerusalem, if its citizens obeyed God, was to be an evangelistic witness. The earthly Jerusalem, in its communal life together, was to be a pointer to the perfect peace and justice of the New Jerusalem, the city of God to be established on earth at the end of time (Revelation 21–22). Was that merely an Old Testament idea? Not at all. Jesus said to his disciples that they were to be "the light of the world" as a "city set on a hill." "Let your light shine before others, so that they may see your good works and give glory to your Father who is in heaven." (Matthew 5:14–15 ESV)

This is exactly the same call Moses gave to Israel in Deuteronomy 4. Christians are to be "a city." A city is not just a collection of individuals but a society. Jesus's call comes in the midst of the Sermon on the Mount, Jesus's reissuing of the Ten Commandments, in which he tells disciples how to live, how to care for the poor, how to be generous with their wealth, how to love their neighbors. If believers are a counterculture of justice and peace, they become an attractive witness to the world, a foretaste and glimpse of the New Jerusalem, when all of human life will be healed by the presence and Lordship of Christ.

Glimpses of the City

So both Moses and Jesus tell us that the life of the believing community must reflect the justice and peace of the final City of God. That means that Christians today, drawing from both the Old Testament and the New, must pursue biblical justice as an evangelistic witness.[5] Biblical justice is marked by at least the following four aspects.

1. JUSTICE IS EQUAL TREATMENT FOR ALL

The Mosaic law said: "You are to have the same law for the foreigner and the native-born" (Leviticus 24:22). This was a radical and unique standard, especially when compared with the laws of the surrounding cultures. There must be equal treatment regardless not only of race and nationality but also of class. For example, there are repeated prohibitions of bribery (cf. Isaiah 1:23). Bribery disadvantaged the poor and even the less wealthy. People with less money will not be treated the same as people with lots of money if bribery and kickbacks are a systemic feature of government, jurisprudence, or commerce.

Behind this emphasis on equality was the teaching of Genesis 1:27 that all human beings are made equally in the image of God. Other societies saw people of different races as almost different species. The Greeks and Romans considered barbarians to be subhuman or at least fit by their nature to be slaves. But the Bible says: "Rich and poor have this in common: The Lord is the Maker of them all" (Proverbs 22:2). The concept of the image of God lies behind the shocking teaching of Jesus in Matthew 5:22 that insulting others—calling them "fool" or "idiot"—is tantamount to murder, an assault on their dignity. James 3:9 says to curse people made in the image of God is a serious sin and speaks of the great evil of treating people differently on the basis of their wealth (James 2:1–7). Every individual on earth, regardless of race, class, gender, ability, and behavior, must be treated with equal fairness and respect.

2. JUSTICE IS RADICAL GENEROSITY

The Bible lays down the concept of private property in strong terms. The eighth commandment condemns as injustice any theft, and Exodus 21:16, Deuteronomy 24:7, and Leviticus 19:11 forbid kidnapping, which is the usurping of a human being's rights over his own person as well as his rightfully owned goods. On the other hand, God reminds his people that he is the owner of all things (Psalm 24:1, 115:16) and we are stewards of his possessions (1 Chronicles 29:14: "Everything comes from you, and we have given you only what comes from your hand."). We have *not* ultimately earned our wealth but have been given it as a gift. If we had we been born in another place and time, or in different social and physical conditions, all our hard work would have yielded little. "What do you have that you did not receive?" (1 Corinthians 4:7). And so our rights over our goods are not absolute. God calls those with more worldly goods to voluntarily share them with the poor and weaker of society.

Because the land and its produce were ultimately owned by God (Leviticus 25:23), property and wealth rights were not absolute. There was the gleaning principle. No one was allowed to gather in *all* of the produce of their field. They had to leave some of it for the poor to "glean" (Leviticus 19:9–10, 23:22). In other words, no owner could squeeze the highest possible profit from the land's production. Then there was the Sabbath year. Every seventh year all debts had to be forgiven and cleared. If a man or family had fallen deeply into debt, they worked as indentured servants in order to pay off what they owed. But in the sabbatical year all indentured servants were released and debts forgiven (Deuteronomy 15:1–18). These ordinances were unique among world cultures. They are incompatible with either strict socialism or laissez-faire capitalism. Craig Blomberg writes that therefore the Mosaic law "suggests a sharp critique of (1) statism that disregards the precious treasure of personal rootage, and (2) the untrammeled individualism which secures individuals at the expense of community."[6]

In the Sermon on the Mount, Jesus extends the biblical teaching on generosity by addressing the habits of the heart that keep us from sharing our goods with others. He speaks of money as an idol that we serve, thinking that net worth can bring us self-worth (Matthew 6:21,24). But he also recognizes that fear and anxiety can be the motivation behind a self-protective, ungenerous amassing of wealth (Matthew 6:25–34). He warns of how greed can distort the way we look at all of life (Matthew 6:22–23). Unlike many critics of the powerful classes, Jesus speaks to their hearts and shows them the way to change.

3. JUSTICE IS ADVOCACY FOR THOSE WITHOUT POWER

The Bible never says, "Speak up for the rich and powerful," for the simple reason that they don't need you to do this for them. On the other hand, the Bible *does* say: "Speak up for those who cannot speak for themselves, for the rights of all who are destitute. . . . Defend the rights of the poor and needy" (Proverbs 31:8–9). Jeremiah writes: "Rescue from the hand of the oppressor the one who has been robbed. Do no wrong or violence to the foreigner, the fatherless or the widow, and do not shed innocent blood in this place." (Jeremiah 22:3). Here Jeremiah singles out groups of people who can't protect themselves from mistreatment the way others can. Zechariah 7:9–10 lists four such groups that needed this special concern in ancient times: widows, the fatherless, immigrants, and the poor. Believers are to have strong concern to help them. Proverbs 22:22–23 says, "Don't take advantage of the poor just because you can," and Psalm 41:1 says "Blessed is the one who considers the poor."[7] The word *considers* means long, careful study and strategic planning.

In the Sermon on the Mount Jesus calls on his disciples to give to the poor, and he calls such giving "righteousness"—*dikaiosune*—justice (Matthew 6:1). In other places Jesus becomes an advocate when he calls out Pharisees for being "lovers of money" (Luke 16:14) and denounces the scribes for "devouring widow's houses" (Luke 20:47), that is, taking advantage of their precarious financial and legal situation.

4. JUSTICE IS CORPORATE AND INDIVIDUAL RESPONSIBILITY

Justice means giving people their due. For the oppressed and the poor, it means advocating for their rights as human beings made in the image of God. But it also means getting perpetrators of injustice to take responsibility for what they have done. This brings up the question of how injustice happens, and the Bible indicates that it happens both directly (individually) and indirectly (systemically and corporately).

Sometimes God holds families, groups, and nations corporately responsible for sins of other individuals even though they did not personally commit them. Daniel repented for the sins committed by his ancestors—refusing to listen to the prophets and disobeying their commands (Daniel 9:5–6)—even though there is no evidence that he personally did those things himself. In 2 Samuel 21 God held Israel responsible for the unjust violence that King Saul perpetrated on the Gibeonites, even though Saul had been dead for years. Some have argued that this corporate responsibility was unique to Israel, but in Amos 1–2, 1 Samuel 15:2, and Deuteronomy 23:3–8 God holds members of the current generation of a pagan nation responsible for the sins committed by their ancestors. Peter held that all present in Jerusalem at the time of Jesus's persecution were responsible for his death (Acts 2:14,23,36), even though only a small number of persons actually perpetrated it (verse 23). The implication is that they were responsible because the crucifixion would not have happened unless there was silence on the part of the majority and no protest against it.

The Bible also recognizes that there are socially institutionalized ways of life that favor the powerful and oppress a particular group, even though many people participating in and supporting the system are not deliberately or consciously intending to do harm. In chapter 9 we looked at the Roman patronage system that operated through dinner parties and hospitality (Luke 14). It systematically excluded the poor and helped the rich and connected get richer and more connected. Jesus refused to allow his disciples to participate in it at all. In the same way, Paul forbid Christians to participate in slavery based on kidnapping (1 Timothy 1:8–11), though it was an institution profitable for those within it.

Despite the reality of corporate responsibility and systemic evil, the Bible puts the greatest weight on individual responsibility. While we have seen that God can condemn groups for the sins of individuals (Joshua 7; Numbers 14), the Bible makes it clear that in human jurisprudence "parents are not to be put to death for their children, nor children put to death for their parents; each will die for their own sin" (Deuteronomy 24:16). Yes, our parents and families could teach and encourage us toward evil, but we can resist them and we are responsible to do so. Ezekiel 18 is a case study of what can happen if we put too much emphasis on corporate responsibility. The result is fatalism and irresponsibility.[8] Ezekiel counters that, in the end, we are fully responsible for all our sins, and our salvation before God lies in what we do as individuals.

So when it comes to responsibility for injustice, the Bible recognizes complexity. The reality of corporate sin does not swallow up individual moral responsibility, nor does individual responsibility disprove the reality of corporate evil. Biblical justice teaches me that I am responsible for my sins, yet I may be also complicit, responsible, and involved in other people's sins and injustices.

The Richness of Biblical Social Analysis

One of the most striking things about the biblical account of injustice is its richness of analysis. In modern individualistic Western society there has been strong bias toward the belief that we are wholly the product of our individual choices. If we are poor or well off, it is because of our own behavior. In this view there is no sin except voluntary, conscious, personal sin and therefore no guilt or responsibility for any other kind of evil. Western people, and especially white Americans, feel little responsibility for the impact of social systems—such as systematic racial exclusions on mortgages and homeownership in northern cities,[9] Jim Crow laws in the South, and slavery itself—as long as they have not individually and personally participated in them. Robert Bellah has written the classic description and critique of this view.[10]

But we cannot, as Marxist social theory has done, be just as reductionistic in the other direction, namely to insist that poverty and crime are never the result of individual moral choices but are always the product of social structures. This leads a socialist like the famous American lawyer Clarence Darrow to say that there is no difference in the moral condition of a murderer inside Cook County Jail and an upstanding citizen outside it, that social forces put each of them where they are and individual choices were completely determined by them.[11] As Charles Taylor said in a recent interview, nonreligious views of human nature reduce our behavior to some mechanical factor that can explain everything and that can be managed and controlled.[12] They tend to explain all human behavior either by evolution and neurochemistry or by culture and social construction or by some other mechanical factor.[13]

By contrast, the Bible says that we are made in the image of a triune God (Genesis 1:26–28) who is both one and three (Matthew 28:19), that we are both individual and communal beings. We are also both material and spiritual (2 Corinthians 5:1–10). We are not shaped only by our physiology, by our personal choices, or by social influences but also by spiritual forces, both good and evil, within us and surrounding us (Ephesians 6:10–13; Romans 7:14–25).

So are unjust conditions such as poverty produced by individual actions or by systemic, unjust social structures? The biblical answer is by both and yet much more than both. In Proverbs 10–12 we see a number of statements that indicate that a lack of personal responsibility can bring someone into poverty. So Proverbs 10:4 says, "Lazy hands make for poverty, but diligent hands bring wealth." Similar statements about irresponsibility causing poverty pepper these chapters (cf. Proverbs 12:27). But then Proverbs 13:23 says, "An unplowed field produces food for the poor, but injustice sweeps it away."[14] In short, the Bible does not reduce poverty and injustice either to individual actions and choices *or* to systemic social structures. It has both dimensions, but Scripture goes beyond that and speaks of injustice as caused by sin, by evil in the heart and in the world. We are not merely individual and social but also soul and body. Indeed, the term *world* (*kosmos*) in the New Testament has both a material reality (as in God loving the world of human beings, John 3:16) and a spiritual reality, an inevitable tendency to make counterfeit gods out of good created things (1 John 2:15–16). The biblical view of justice gives full weight to both personal responsibility and social structures while being based on a rich understanding of human life that goes well beyond the world's alternative views.

No wonder we are such complex beings and why no scientific account can fully account for who we are and how human life must be lived. And no wonder the resurrection is such good news, because it means healing for *all* of creation's decay and corruption (Romans 8:21)—from all the ruptured relationships—spiritually, socially, morally, psychologically, racially, economically, culturally, physically. All other views of justice reduce the problem to the social or the personal or the moral. But through Christ a new creation is coming (Isaiah 65:17–25).

Practical Justice

How, practically, can Christians do justice? How can the account of biblical justice given here help believers be "salt and light" in the world, a city on a hill?

First, Christians can be active agents for change while avoiding the political polarization and rancor that creates gridlock and blocks wholesome change. James Mumford in *Vexed: Ethics Beyond Political Tribes*[15] speaks of "ethical package deals" that today's political parties force on its members. If you have sympathies with some of the Democratic or Republican platforms, and try to support them, you will be under pressure to support *all* of the party line. As we have seen, biblical justice does not fit well into these categories. It often straddles them and mixes elements that in the secular world seem "conservative" and "liberal." Christians are not beholden to rigid, simplistic solutions. To change the system of failing schools in poor communities may require a confrontation with Democrats over rules for teachers' unions as well as with Republicans over the local-only tax policies that support the schools. While the Bible commands us to care for the poor and to welcome the immigrant, it does not dictate exactly how to do that. As we have seen, the principles of "general equity" that the Bible lays out need to be applied differently in diverse times and places. This requires wisdom and nuance, not doctrinaire political programs.

Second, Christians need to be willing to identify themselves as believers as they work with others for justice, though treating all their allies and partners as equals. One of the greatest weaknesses of our secular society is that we no longer have the moral sources to support our moral ideals, such as human rights and care for the poor. Christians' beliefs give us a strong motivation to make the sacrifices of money and power that are necessary to create a more humane and just society, but the secular world increasingly lacks such incentives. The most difficult question for secular workers for justice to answer is "I want relief for *my* need, but why ought I to sacrifice to meet the needs of these other people whom I don't even know?" When Christians identify as believers, without self-righteousness or superiority, and pay the personal costs of doing justice, they serve both their friends and their Lord. They bear witness to God's work in their lives, and they help the world see that there *are* moral sources sufficient to motivate and support the difficult work of doing justice.

Third, I propose for all the reasons above that Christians especially work for justice locally and on specific issues rather than enter into the broad "national conversations." In many places in the Western world our national political institutions are no longer functioning to forge laws through compromises that involve the greatest number of people and constituencies. Instead they have become transformed into "platforms" for individual leaders to speak to their bases and press their agendas rather than cooperate at all with other legislators and leaders.[16] In general, more will get done if Christians concentrate on an important local issue, like public schools, or the local criminal justice system, or racially segregated housing, or health-care disparities, or a host of other projects on which progress can be made.[17]

Resurrection Justice

The resurrection means that God has not at all given up on the world.[18] Christ's rising affirms the importance of actual material life. "[God] likes matter. He invented it," wrote C. S. Lewis.[19] But beyond that, it gives meaning to suffering and gives hope that through the suffering will come healing. The resurrection guarantees that this renewal is certain, and is also a call for Christians to work now against what is wrong and unjust. "For Christianity is a fighting religion. . . . It . . . thinks that a great many things have gone wrong with the world that God made and that God insists, and insists very loudly, on our putting them right again."[20] N. T. Wright puts it best when he writes:

> The message of the resurrection is that this world matters! That the injustices and pains of this present world must now be addressed with the news that healing, justice, and love have won. . . . If Easter means Jesus Christ is only raised in a spiritual sense—[then] it is only about me, and finding a new dimension in my personal spiritual life. But if Jesus Christ is truly risen from the dead, Christianity becomes good news for the whole world— news which warms our hearts *precisely because it isn't just about warming hearts.*
>
> Easter means that in a world where injustice, violence, and degradation are endemic, God is not prepared to tolerate such things—and that we will work and plan, with all the energy of God, to implement victory of Jesus over them all. Take away Easter and Karl Marx was probably right to accuse Christianity of ignoring problems of the material world. Take it away and Freud was probably right to say Christianity is wish fulfillment. Take it away and Nietzsche probably was right to say it was for wimps.[21]

But if Easter happened, it is the secular theories of Freud, Marx, and Nietzsche that will eventually find themselves in the ashbin of history.

CHAPTER 11

HOPE IN THE FACE
OF SUFFERING

*Therefore I will boast all the more gladly about my weaknesses, so that
Christ's power may rest on me. . . . For when I am weak, then I am strong.*

—2 CORINTHIANS 12:9–10

The Great Reversal is not just the way Christians are saved—it also can
be, in the words of Christopher Watkin, "a dynamic" that "opens out
onto a rhythm of life, an ethic, and a way of looking at and living in the
world."[1] When we use the resurrection as a way of "looking and living in
the world" it especially changes how we view and experience difficulties
and suffering in life.

The Sermon and the City

In the books of Exodus and Deuteronomy we see Moses going up onto the
mountain to meet with God and then coming down with the Ten Commandments, which created a nation that was to live in such a way that the
rest of the world could see the glory of God (Deuteronomy 4:5–8). And Jesus also went up onto a mountain to meet with God and pray (Luke 6:12)

and then came down, choosing his twelve disciples (Luke 6:13–16), and teaching the crowd, beginning with the Beatitudes (Luke 6:17–20). Jesus's goal was to lay the foundation for a new community, a "counter-culture."[2]

As we saw in the last chapter, Jesus's sermon creates a "city on a hill"—an alternate human society pointing toward the City of God that will fill the earth at the end of time. Christians are an alternate city in every city. John Stott says that a key theme in Jesus's sermon was "Do not be like them" (Matthew 6:8). Sometimes he draws a contrast between his disciples and religious people. So in Matthew 6:1–18 he critiques how religious people pray and give to the poor in a self-righteous way. At other places in the sermon he contrasts his disciples with the pagan Gentiles. Matthew 5:44–47 critiques how shame-and-honor cultures pursue revenge on enemies, and in Matthew 6 how they worry and obsess over material prosperity and possessions.

> With [Jesus] the new age had dawned and the rule of God had broken into history. "Repent," he cried, "for the kingdom of heaven is at hand." The Sermon . . . is the most complete delineation anywhere . . . of the Christian counter-culture. Here is a Christian value-system, ethical standard, religious devotion, attitude to money, [sexuality, power], life-style and network of relationship. . . . This Christian counter-culture is the life of the kingdom of God, a fully human life indeed but lived out under the divine rule.[3]

Students of the Sermon on the Mount know that there are two versions of it—one in Matthew and one in Luke. Scholars debate over the differences between them, but many point out that there are no contradictions and there is every reason to believe Jesus delivered this material more than once. For our purposes in this chapter, the version of the sermon in Luke addresses more directly how Christians are to face difficulties.

> And he lifted up his eyes on his disciples, and said: "Blessed are you who are poor, for yours is the kingdom of God. Blessed are

you who are hungry now, for you shall be satisfied. Blessed are you who weep now, for you shall laugh. Blessed are you when people hate you and when they exclude you and revile you and spurn your name as evil, on account of the Son of Man! Rejoice in that day, and leap for joy, for behold, your reward is great in heaven; for so their fathers did to the prophets. But woe to you who are rich, for you have received your consolation. Woe to you who are full now, for you shall be hungry. Woe to you who laugh now, for you shall mourn and weep. Woe to you, when all people speak well of you, for so their fathers did to the false prophets.

(Luke 6:20–26)

"The kingdom of God" is named in the first sentence (verse 20). The English word *kingdom* makes us think of a country, but the Greek word used refers not so much to a realm as to a *reign*, a way of administering and arranging a society of people. If a new head comes into your department over you or a new coach takes over your team, you'll find that things are being done differently. The new leader has a different set of values, priorities, and emphases. So Jesus is saying, "When you believe in me, you enter into my kingdom, and I will now tell you the values of my kingdom, as opposed to the kingdom of this world." He lays out four values of each:

THE WORLD— GOOD THINGS		JESUS'S KINGDOM— HARD THINGS	
Rich	Power	*Poor*	Weakness
Full	Comfort	*Hungry*	Deprivation
Laugh	Success	*Weep*	Loss
All speak well	Recognition	*Hated*	Exclusion

Let's look at the world's set of values first. Jesus speaks of people who are rich, full, laughing, and popular ("all people speak well of you"). The first term designates power, because in the end that is what levels of wealth and poverty boil down to—different degrees of power to affect and control others. The second refers to comfort. These are people who are full: they have all they desire—eating at the best restaurants, wearing the best clothes, living in the most beautiful homes. The third word, *laugh*, is the Greek word for gloating. Jesus is referring not so much to happiness as to success. These are people who have competed and won and who gloat about it. They take full credit for their high standing. They look down on others and say: "I won; you didn't." Finally, Jesus designates people who are "well spoken of by all." These are people who have achieved acclaim, recognition, and perhaps celebrity.

Then Jesus makes a list of the values of his kingdom. The people who are "blessed" have lives going exactly the opposite of those of the world. We can paraphrase them like this—the kingdom of God is marked by weakness, deprivation, loss, and exclusion. These are the conditions of people who lack—power, satisfaction of material desires, achievement, and popularity.

These lists were dumbfounding to Jesus's hearers, but they are no less startling to us today. Who wants to join a kingdom like this? At first glance it seems Jesus is saying that anyone who is successful cannot be part of Jesus's kingdom and only the failed, deprived, and impoverished can. But as we have seen, God calls and includes the rich in his kingdom. Think of Abraham and Job in the Old Testament and Joseph of Arimathea in the New Testament. Michael Wilcock, in his commentary on Luke, sums up the teaching of Luke 6 nicely:

> In the life of God's people will be seen first of all a remarkable *reversal of values* (Luke 6:20–26). They will prize what the world calls pitiable, and suspect what the world thinks desirable.[4]

Jesus is not urging us to actively seek out weakness, deprivation, or exclusion. Nor is he saying that we should be unwise and passive toward all the forces in the world that can hurt us. The book of Proverbs urges us to avoid the kinds of behavior that can lead to poverty, disappointment, and loss. Rather, Jesus is telling us that weakness, deprivation, or exclusion will find us soon enough, because that is the world we live in. But when they come to us, we must respond in a way that brings blessing out of curses and life out of death.

GOOD THINGS AND HARD THINGS

One way to understand Jesus's teaching is to think of these two lists as "good things" and "hard things." Wealth, satisfaction, success, and recognition are indeed good things, and their opposites are hard to bear. But the people of the world look to these things as their deepest "consolation" (verse 24), a Greek word, *paraklesis*, that also refers to the comfort and fulfillment that the Holy Spirit, the "Paraklete," gives us (John 14:26, 15:26, 16:7). Of course, believers and nonbelievers both seek successful careers, but in the world's understanding of reality, life without them is completely meaningless and unbearable. Their hearts and identities rest completely in them—they are what they boast in (Jeremiah 9:23–24) and what they get their greatest meaning and comfort in. So when the good things go and the hard things come in their place, life is basically over.

One example of this is Jesus's parable of Lazarus and the rich man (Luke 16:19–31). Lazarus (a name that means "God helps me") is the only figure in any of Jesus's parables given a name. Jesus does so to point to an invisible reality that only becomes visible in the afterlife. In the world's view, it is the poor who are part of a nameless mass and whose burial places are lost to history, while the wealthy person makes a name for him- or herself and is buried in a monumental tomb. Yet after death, Lazarus ascends to heaven and the rich man goes to hell, which "reverses the normal anonymity of poverty and the individuating significance of wealth."[5] It also makes a point vividly. The rich man has no name because that was all he was. He had built an identity around his power. He was a rich man or nobody. Without his wealth—without good things—there was no self left. Lazarus, however, had a life full of hard things but had evidently become a man of faith and virtue. It may be that the hard things drove him toward God, where he found himself.

Good things, if received without faith in God, will enslave or disappoint or turn out to be a snare in some way. As David Foster Wallace has said, if you worship something besides a real God, "it will eat you alive."[6] When the Bible says we were made in God's "image" (Genesis 1:27), it means among other things that we were made like a mirror to face and reflect God's glory, to grow into his likeness as we worship, serve, and please him. That is what we were designed for. If instead our souls "face" anything else, if we love anything more than God, we go against our own design and against, as it were, the grain of the universe. The result is always the reverse of what the world expects and seeks. Power ends up being weakness; success without God is really failure, and time will reveal this. "He has filled the hungry with good things but has sent the rich away empty" (Luke 1:53).

HARD THINGS AND BEST THINGS

Good things received without God will become a curse. On the other hand, people who receive hard things *with* faith in God will discover that the seeming curses will turn out to be blessings. In many cases that reversal does not happen within the confines of this life (as Luke 16 teaches us). And yet most Christians can look back on their hard things and see how God worked his blessing into their lives through weakness and trouble. So Christians see hard things as indeed hard and not to be sought, but we have been armed with this great truth, namely that when received with faith in God, hard things lead to the best things.

J. K. Rowling's Harvard commencement address, "The Fringe Benefits of Failure," traces out an often-seen dynamic, that it is only through failure that we learn crucial lessons—about human nature, about our own strengths and weakness, about the craft in which we work—that are the basis for future success. But the promise of the kingdom is for far more than that.

Jesus's promise is that, for his followers living by faith, the hard things will lead to the best things. He names them.

HARD THINGS	BEST THINGS
Weak	*Kingdom of God*
Hungry	*Filled*
Weeping	*Laugh*
Hated	*Reward is great in heaven*

The first best thing Jesus names is the kingdom of God itself. Citizenship in the kingdom happens the moment you put your faith in Christ (Colossians 1:13; Ephesians 2:9; Philippians 3:20). This means, as 1 Peter 1:4 says, we have an "inheritance" of glory waiting for us. Paul says that our afflictions in this world, our hard things, are renewing us inwardly, spiritually, and are "preparing for us an eternal weight of glory beyond all comparison" (2 Corinthians 4:17, RSV). The language is tantalizing. "Glory" in the Bible includes beauty, importance, greatness, and power. Our hard things move us to greater dependence on God, which refines us even now into greater love, joy, peace, patience, kindness, humility, and self-control. So even here there is a foreshadowing of our future glorious beauty of character. And that future glory, which Paul says beggars our imaginations ("incomparable" to anything we know), is guaranteed to members of the kingdom of God.

The last of the best things Jesus mentions is, to the persecuted, that "great will your reward be in heaven." Here we burst the bounds of the ordinary wisdom of the world that "failures teach us lessons" and "in every cloud there is a silver lining." Those common sayings simply don't work in the face of the many horrible tragedies that come to people every day. Not only do such statements trivialize the suffering, but the fact is that many hard things that we experience are too terrible to ever be balanced out in a this-world cost-benefit analysis. But what if there is a heaven, a heaven that is "a world of love," infinitely more fulfilling and glorious than the most wonderful moment of your earthly life? The well-known quote by Teresa of Ávila does the calculus: "From heaven even the most miserable life will look like one night in an inconvenient hotel."[7] She could have as easily said "a thousand miserable lives."

Not only will many horrendous evils be made up for after this life is over but, as the principle holds, all hard things, embraced in faithfulness to the one who did the same for us, will issue in greater good and glory. Through experiences of weakness we grow into a strength we would never have had otherwise, shedding enslaving allegiances and finding a new freedom. We will only have perfect joy ("laughter" and "fullness") the day we see him face to face, and yet even in this life we experience new and deeper satisfaction the more we live for Christ and others rather than ourselves. C. S. Lewis believes that a

> principle runs through all life from top to bottom. Give up yourself, and you will find your real self. Lose your life and you will save it. Submit to death, death of your ambitions and favorite wishes every day and death of your whole body in the end: submit with every fiber of your being, and you will find eternal life. Keep back nothing. Nothing that you have not given away will be really yours. Nothing in you that has not died will ever be raised from the dead. Look for yourself, and you will find in the long run only hatred, loneliness, despair, rage, ruin, and decay. But look for Christ and you will find Him, and with Him everything else thrown in.[8]

Christians then see that in Jesus, the way up is down, the way to true power is to give up power in order to serve, the way to true riches is to be radically generous with all you have, and the way to lasting happiness is to not seek your own happiness so much as the happiness of others. That was how he saved the world and changed your life, and now it becomes our way of seeing and living.

God Meant It for Good

Jesus's sermon is not the only place that the resurrection is applied in order to help us face the reversals and difficulties of life. The stories of Jacob and Joseph that take up a large section of the book of Genesis are two of the best illustrations of the Bible's most famous promise that "all things . . . work together for good to those who love God" (Romans 8:28, NASB).

Jacob had suffered under his father's clear favoritism for his brother, Esau. In an effort to acquire the love and inheritance that came with his father's blessing, Jacob resorted to lying, scheming, and other ways of getting power over others. When he established his own family, however, he inflicted the same pain on his own children, showing obvious favor and greater love to his son Joseph over his eleven brothers. This led the brothers to deep resentment and envy, but it also distorted Joseph's self-view. His arrogance and self-importance came out in dreams of his supremacy, dreams that offended even his father (Genesis 37:10).

JOSEPH AND THE REVERSALS OF GOD

Finally his brothers secretly sold Joseph as a slave to Arab traders, who sold him in Egypt to the captain of Pharaoh's bodyguard. And there he was falsely accused of rape, so he became not only a slave but a prisoner in the king's dungeon in fear for his life. But deep in that dark place, Joseph was changing. "During his imprisonment, the word of the Lord refined Joseph. . . . (Psalm 105:19,22). Thus God used Joseph's circumstances to cause him to trust God."[9] The arrogance that would have destroyed his life and those around him was broken.

Joseph's ability to interpret Pharaoh's dream led to his release from prison and his elevation to first minister in the Egyptian kingdom. From there he mounted a hunger relief program that not only saved thousands of citizens from starvation in the great famine but also saved the lives of his own family. In the process of his confrontation with his brothers, recounted in Genesis 42–45, they were brought to repentance and there was a reconciliation.

After Jacob's death, his brothers came to him in fear that Joseph continued to bear a grudge against them, but he replied to them:

> Don't be afraid. Am I in the place of God? You intended to harm me, but God intended it for good to accomplish what is now being done, the saving of many lives.
>
> **(Genesis 50:19–20)**

Joseph did not make excuses for his brothers—their sin was deliberate. They "intended" to destroy him. But in the economy of God, the harm they inflicted was actually a means for healing Joseph's ruined character and making him someone great. Their actions were also used by God to remove Joseph from Canaan and put him where he could do the most good for the world in general and for his family in particular. Like Jesus, Joseph "overcame by being overcome."[10] The "resurrection" of Joseph to a place of greatness and redemptive influence ("the saving of many lives") could have come only through the death of all his original hopes and happiness in the dungeons of Egypt.

Joseph summed up his entire life by saying: "You meant it for evil but God meant it for good." When he did so, he unwittingly applied the pattern of Jesus's salvation to himself. We, however, know that when we believe in Jesus, we are united by faith with his death and his resurrection (Colossians 2:12; Romans 6:4; Ephesians 2:6), and so the paradoxical pattern of Jesus's life becomes the key to understanding our own lives and histories.

Consider for a moment what a resource this can be for us. If we climb up to a high point on a mountainside, we can get a far better picture of where we have been. Down on the floor of the valley we may have gotten turned around and become lost, but from above we see exactly where we have been and where we need to go. Down "in the valley" of our lives it is hard to see what is going on, especially when disappointments, failures, and suffering come to us. There is a tendency to deal with them along a spectrum from optimism to pessimism. The optimists look at troubles as temporary anomalies. They are sure that things will turn around, that basically the world is a safe place, that if you live right, things will go well. They tend to "hold their breath," as it were, until things turn around. The pessimists see the world as a bleak place. Their view of life is "Life is pain. . . . Anyone who says differently is selling something"[11] and "People will stab you in the back. You can't trust people. You can't trust life." The pessimists look at the troubles of life not as anomalies but as normal. Down "in the valley" of life, without the perspective that the gospel brings, our attitude toward suffering runs back and forth along that spectrum. It's either/or. Either life is going good and therefore God is good or life is bad and therefore God is bad or he's not there.

But Joseph had, with God's help, climbed up out of the valley, and he could see that both optimists and pessimists are partly right but most fundamentally wrong. Suffering is *not* normal. God *is* a good God, as the optimists sense. The Lord made the world originally without evil, suffering, and death, and he is moving history back to making all things right. He was willing to pay an infinite price on the cross to bring that about. On the other hand, suffering is *not* anomalous. Because of humanity's turn away from God, the world is now a very dark place, as the pessimists sense. People living good lives should not expect a life of good circumstances any more than Jesus did.

Joseph's divinely inspired perspective held two things together that the merely human perspective cannot. He says, in effect: "Life is filled with pain," and yet he also says, "God is good." He knows this because God's goodness, in general, comes to us through experiences of difficulty and weakness, and some day will end suffering and evil forever.

JACOB AND THE CROSSED ARMS OF GOD

Near the end of the story of Joseph, we also witness the end of Jacob's life. Just before his father died, Joseph brought his two sons to him. He asked Jacob to give the elder, Manasseh, and the younger, Ephraim, his blessing (Genesis 48:1–22). The two boys were born in Egypt to an Egyptian woman, and after the deaths of Jacob and Joseph, it was likely that other Israelites would say that Joseph's children should not be among the legal heirs of Jacob. Joseph wanted Jacob to bless them in order to put that matter beyond doubt. When Joseph and the boys came to him, Jacob recounted the covenant of God, who promised to give Jacob's descendants a land and a blessing (verses 3–4). Then Jacob said that, though Manasseh and Ephraim were born in Egypt, they shall be numbered among his descendants and receive a portion of his inheritance (verses 5–7). This is what Joseph wanted and he was pleased.

Then Joseph approached his father with his sons, leading Manasseh toward Jacob's right hand and Ephraim toward his left. The right hand was considered the place of greater honor. Joseph expected the older child to get the greater blessing and the headship of the family. To everyone's surprise, Jacob deliberately crossed his arms to put his right hand on Ephraim's head (verse 14). This displeased Joseph, but he assumed that his father was simply making a mistake due to his failing eyesight or, perhaps, declining mental faculties. So Joseph responded, to paraphrase him: "Father, you are confused—*this* is the son who gets the bigger blessing. This is the right one and that is the wrong one" (verse 18). But Jacob retorted, in effect: "I know *exactly* what I am doing, Joseph. The son you think is the wrong son is actually the right son" (see verse 19). Jacob resisted both family pressure and cultural norms and blessed the younger boy over the older.

Of course, Jacob was operating on prophetic insight from God, because he said, "Nevertheless, his younger brother will be greater than he, and his descendants will become a group of nations" (verse 19). But it is important to notice that Hebrews 11:21 selects Jacob's blessing of Joseph's sons as the premier act of faith in his life ("By faith Jacob, when he was dying, blessed each of Joseph's sons, and worshiped as he leaned on the top of his staff.") That means that much more is going on here than merely a prophecy about the future of two boys.

Jacob has finally recognized the "crossed-arms" approach of God, the way the Lord turns the world's understanding of greatness and status upside down. When he refused to bless the father's pride and joy, Jacob was pointing to God's "crossed-arms" method of grace and salvation, which always contradicts the world's way. In the world's economy, the first shall be first and the last shall be last; in the gospel's economy, the first shall be last and the last shall be first. That is the secret to understanding the ways of God in the world, and it is utterly foolish to human thinking. Over and over again, God chooses to work in the world through what the world thinks of as weaker.

This is not merely because "God likes underdogs"—it speaks to something deep in God himself, and in how he will redeem the world. In the gospels, when Jesus the Messiah comes, he is born in a feed trough to poor parents. He has no political party and no military might. Over and over again, Jesus chooses the marginal, the prostitute, the tax collector, the pagan, the women and children to be his disciples and rejects the social insider, the moral, the religious, and the upstanding. And finally, in his greatest act of salvation, he gives himself to be beaten and to die. In every case, salvation is accomplished in exactly the opposite way to the world's logic. God is always acting against expectations, putting his hands on the "wrong son," bucking the world's system.

And this is indeed the high point of Jacob's faith and life. He finally (as Joseph did) looked back on his life and saw the paradoxical pattern of strength out of weakness and how God had always been with him, even when he had seemed absent. One commentator writes about the Genesis 48 passage: "There is gentle irony in the fact that this is just such a situation as the one on which he had exercised his guile in his youth. Once more the firstborn's blessing is destined for the younger brother, but now there is no faithless scheming or bitter after taste. It is an object-lesson in quiet responsiveness and faith."[12]

Throughout his life Jacob had felt the need to "help" God in his purposes by scheming and lying and seeking to get leverage and power, all in order to get the blessing of his father. Now Jacob saw that this was completely wrong, that God gives us blessing through faithfulness in weakness.

So at the very end of his life, Jacob gently instructed Joseph to accept God's ways of free grace and counterintuitive salvation. He looks back on his life and no longer says, "Everything is against me!" as he once did (Genesis 42:36). That was tantamount to saying, "All things are working together for evil for me." It seemed to him that God was behind the scenes, working at every point to hurt him and make him miserable. Now he says that God has been his shepherd "all my life to this day" (Genesis 48:15), and he even says that the Angel of the Lord "delivered me from all harm" (Genesis 48:16). This is the complete opposite of his previous statement. Now, as he remembers his sufferings (the flight from his homeland, the deception of Laban, the early death of Rachel, the loss of Joseph), he has the audacity to say that he was being "shepherded" and "kept from all harm" in every one of them. He sees that God was working behind the scenes for his good, out of love.

Joy through Suffering

DON'T WASTE YOUR SORROWS

The Great Reversal pattern is also evident in the Psalms.

The Old Testament is filled with assurances that God will not abandon his people in times of stress and suffering. Psalm 30:1–5 is typical. The psalmist wrote, "I called to you for help, and you healed me" (verse 2). He then turned to the congregation and told them to "sing the praises of the Lord," because with God "weeping may stay for the night, but rejoicing comes in the morning" (verses 4–5). He assured them that joy will come after sorrow.

But there are hints in the Old Testament of something else, of a joy that comes *through* sorrow, not just in spite of it. In Psalm 126 we read, "Those who sow with tears will reap with songs of joy. Those who go out weeping, carrying seed to sow, will return with songs of joy, carrying sheaves with them" (verses 5–6). The imagery is striking. The seed being sown consists of *tears* and *weeping*. They are planting their tears and receiving a harvest of joy.

This suggests that there is a way to weep and there is sorrow that bears fruit, fruit that includes a deeper happiness. It is inevitable in this world that we should weep—but do we *sow* our tears? Do we waste our sorrows or do we know how to weep? If a sower were to simply dump all his seed in one spot, there would be no harvest. So simple venting of grief may not produce fruit in our lives or the lives of those around us. To "go out weeping, carrying seed to sow" means something more than just pouring out our sorrow. We are called to sow our tears, not waste them.

Psalm 126 does not spell out exactly how to sow our tears, but perhaps it does not need to. The entire Psalter is filled with prayers called "laments." It gives us numerous examples of people taking their pain and suffering to God, praying through it in his presence, and thereby avoiding the anger, self-pity, and despair that can poison hearts and make us bitter and harder rather than wiser and better.

So the teaching is that there is a sorrow that *produces* joy. It is in the New Testament that it becomes clear why and how this can be.

JOY UNSPEAKABLE

The biblical book that perhaps most clearly applies this pattern to suffering is Paul's second letter to the Corinthians. In the first chapter Paul spoke of the great trials and difficulties he and his companions had suffered in Asia.

> We do not want you to be uninformed, brothers and sisters, about the troubles we experienced in the province of Asia. We were under great pressure, far beyond our ability to endure, so that we despaired of life itself. Indeed, we felt we had received the sentence of death. But this happened that we might not rely on ourselves but on God, who raises the dead.
>
> **(2 Corinthians 1:8–9)**

Out of this weakness had come new strength, the new confidence, courage, and the peace that comes from relying on God rather than on one's own abilities. But that is not the only fruit that has grown out of Paul's tears. He told his readers that "the God of all comfort . . . comforts us in all our troubles so that we can comfort those in any trouble with the comfort we ourselves receive from God" (2 Corinthians 1:3–4). Only because Paul suffered was he able to receive divine comfort, "a concrete manifestation of the grace of God, a divine intervention,"[13] elsewhere referred to as "the peace . . . which transcends all understanding" (Philippians 4:7). Only troubles can drive us to rely on God in such a way as to trigger the coming of this comfort. And that comfort is the Holy Spirit bringing the declarations and promises in his Word home to the heart, so as to make God's presence, love, and power real to us (cf. John 16:12–14). But this comfort, when we receive it, is not to be kept to ourselves. "If we are distressed, it is for your comfort . . . which produces in you patient endurance of the same sufferings we suffer" (2 Corinthians 1:6). Paul could go so far as to conclude that one of the reasons that bad things happen to him is so that God can use him in the lives of others, helping them find the same life-changing, refining, enriching comfort of God. Out of Paul's weakness came strength not just for him but for countless others.

Then in 2 Corinthians 4:8–9, Paul went deeper to explain how the sorrow can produce joy under the hand of God. He wrote: "We are hard pressed on every side, but not crushed; perplexed, but not in despair; persecuted, but not abandoned; struck down, but not destroyed." Where does this remarkable resilience come from?

> So we do not lose heart. Though our outer self is wasting away, our inner self is being renewed day by day. For this light momentary affliction is preparing for us an eternal weight of glory beyond all comparison, as we look not to the things that are seen but to the things that are unseen. For the things that are seen are transient, but the things that are unseen are eternal.
>
> **(2 Corinthians 4:16–18, ESV)**

Even though outwardly his body was aging and "wasting away," nevertheless inwardly he was being renewed and strengthened every day, and this is especially *through* afflictions. We know something of Paul's "light" troubles from his listing of them in 2 Corinthians 11:23–29. They include imprisonment, public floggings (at least five of them), and beatings. They were only "momentary" and "light" in comparison with the eternal and infinitely solid glory that he knew was in store for him.

However, there are two reasons he never lost heart in the face of his sufferings. One is that they were *renewing* him. They were making him more like Christ, finding his joy in God, his peace in God's love, his meaning in God's calling. More and more his heart was anchored in things that could not be shaken or taken away. He was growing in love, joy, peace, patience, humility, self-control, and the fruit of the Spirit (Galatians 5:22–23), and nothing was increasing those things in him more than his afflictions and the self-knowledge and God-reliance they brought.

But in addition, they were *preparing* him for this future, eternal glory. The word translated as "preparing" does not mean that sufferings earn the glory. Rather it is a word that means a process of cultivation, a means by which someone is better and better prepared to experience and receive something. Paul is saying that his sufferings are not only inwardly strengthening him now but preparing him for an unimaginable joy and glory. How so? The next verse tells us. This renewal and preparation happen as we look not to the things that are seen but to "the things that are unseen."

This ties back to what Paul has been saying in 2 Corinthians 3:18: that by faith, not with our literal eyes (cf. 2 Corinthians 5:7), we can nonetheless behold "the glory of God in the face of Jesus Christ" as we consider all he has done for us in the gospel (2 Corinthians 4:6, ESV). And the more we wonder and adore his beauty and glory, the more that changes us into his "image from one degree of glory to another" (2 Corinthians 3:18, ESV). When we do this in the midst of suffering, looking not to the seen (where the evil is) but to the greatness and glory of Christ and what he has done for us, that changes us into his image. It grows a joy within not based on changing circumstances.

We have looked at how John Owen expounded on these passages in 2 Corinthians, explaining that it is possible to have a "faith-sight" of Jesus's glory here and now. John Owen had at least as many afflictions in his life as did Paul. He had eleven children and outlived every one of them, as well as his first wife. In the "Great Ejection" of 1662 he, along with other Puritan ministers, was turned out of his church and employment. During all his trials he was sustained by the promises of 2 Corinthians 3 and 4. He found that his weaknesses drove him into prayer, where he found delight and joy that he would never have known otherwise. He wrote: "If we are satisfied with vague ideas about him we shall find no transforming power communicated to us. But when we cling wholeheartedly to him and our minds are filled with thoughts of him and . . . delight . . . in him then spiritual power will flow from him to purify our hearts, increase our holiness, strengthen our graces, and sometimes fill us with joy inexpressible and full of glory."[14]

Here indeed is joy out of sorrow. Owen knows that this is the promise of Psalm 126. He adds: "No thoughts of Christ, then, proceeding from faith, accompanied with love and delight, shall be lost. They that sow this seed shall return with their sheaves."[15]

MY POWER IS MADE PERFECT IN WEAKNESS

By the end of this letter, Paul insisted not only that sorrow could produce greater joy and weakness could produce greater strength but also that there was no other way to get these good things. Paul spoke of some unnamed chronic and painful reality in his life, his "thorn," and of how he had asked God to remove it. But God answered, "My grace is sufficient for you, for my power is made perfect in weakness" (2 Corinthians 12:9). Looking back, Paul realized that his suffering was the only thing that kept him from becoming "conceited" (verse 7), and inner humility, wisdom, joy, and strength are unavailable except through experiences of weakness that finally bring us to rely on God's grace.

So sorrow can produce joy and weakness produce strength. Nice idea! But how is Paul sure that this will work? He tells us in the very middle of chapter 4 of 2 Corinthians. After speaking of all their trials, he says that he and his ministry companions are

> always carrying in the body the death of Jesus, so that the life of Jesus may also be manifested in our bodies. For we who live are always being given over to death for Jesus's sake, so that the life of Jesus also may be manifested in our mortal flesh. So death is at work in us, but life in you. . . . *knowing that he who raised the Lord Jesus will raise us also with Jesus and bring us with you into his presence.*
>
> **(2 Corinthians 4:10–14, ESV)**

The principle of joy produced by sorrow and strength out of weakness is operative because Jesus was raised from the dead. Paul says because the resurrection of Jesus happened, it's the very meaning of history that redemption comes out of injustice; that life comes out of death.

The answer for a Christian is much clearer than it could have been for the psalmists. In the central event in the history of the world, Jesus's suffering did not just give way to joy, it produced it. His agony and weeping were substitutionary. He took our punishment. Thus his weeping was the ultimate sowing in tears and produced the ultimate reaping in joy. His tears and blood redeemed us. Remembering his tears and suffering for us, we now will weep and grieve differently.

We won't grieve in unresolved guilt. ("I know that though I'm suffering, this is not God's abandoning me, since Jesus was abandoned *for* me on the cross.")

We won't grieve in deep self-pity and anger. ("I know that he took far worse grief on himself than I will ever know, and undeserved—and all for me! So I can bear this smaller amount of suffering for him.")

We won't grieve impatiently. ("I know his suffering and death did not make sense to his followers, and this suffering does not make sense to me. But you were working in that to bring joy and redemption, and somehow I know you are working in this.") It is by watching how his tears produced joy that we will be able to avoid having our griefs crush us, embitter us, and destroy us. And thus our griefs will produce in us character, patience, humility, love, and wisdom (cf. Romans 5:1–5).

Just as Jesus's weakness and shame are the only way to real strength and glory, so our repentance and acknowledgment of guilt and sin are the only way to the highest confidence and honor, the knowledge that in Christ we are accepted and delighted in by the Lord of all.

CHAPTER 12

HOPE FOR THE FUTURE

The stone the builders rejected
has become the cornerstone;
the Lord has done this,
and it is marvelous in our eyes.

—PSALM 118:22–23

How can we have hope in times of fear? This book is being written in the midst of COVID-19, but many people think that a number of "epic crises" are happening together.[1] The pandemic is only one. To remove the virus as a major threat to life will require overcoming many hurdles and may take years—if another pandemic doesn't intrude before this one is over. Globalization and technology only increase the danger of these epidemics. And even though this book will be read years from now, when the fears of this time will have likely receded, there will be other times of crises ahead. There are cyclical economic recessions or depressions. In most Western nations political polarization has become more intense than ever and promises to remain that way for decades. Waves of protest against racial injustice and calls for social change have never been stronger. But as we have seen, there is little consensus on the way forward.

I write this book with the expectation that the sense of fear, pessimism, and anxiety that our world is experiencing now is not likely to be dispelled anytime soon.

No one can live without hope, but how do we get it? This is not just an issue for individuals. How does a society live without hope for its future? For several centuries Western culture has had significant hope for the future, a strong belief in historical progress that has been a great aid to the flourishing of its civilization. But recently that hope has been waning, and the implications are serious.

The Rise of Cultural Hope

The American belief has long been that each generation will have a better life—economically, technologically, socially, personally—than the previous one. But this idea of linear historical progress did not exist in most other cultures. All ancient cultures—Chinese, Babylonian, Hindu, Greek, and Roman—had different views. Some saw history as cyclical and others saw history as a slow decline from past golden ages.

The cyclical model was very common. In this view history went through rhythmic rounds that ended in a conflagration and then a starting over. The Greeks described these with the word *palingenesia*. Norse mythology believed in Ragnarok, a great future battle in which many of the gods and all human beings would die and then the world start over with a new set of gods and a new human race. Confucianism saw the world as constantly re-creating itself through the interaction of the two primordial energies— yin and yang. Many of the ancient poets, such as Hesiod and Ovid, spoke of human history as one of long-term decline, from a golden age to a silver age and so on down to the present.

The idea that history was moving in the direction of continual progress and improvement in the human condition simply did not exist.[2]

Then, however, came Christianity. As Robert Nisbet writes in his book *History of the Idea of Progress*, Christian thinkers gave "to the idea of progress a large and devoted following in the West and a sheer power that the idea could not have otherwise [in the absence of Christian beliefs] acquired."[3] The Greeks thought that the accumulation of human knowledge led to a mild, temporary improvement in the human condition—but only between conflagrations. But Christian philosophers "endowed the idea of progress with new attributes which were bound to give it a spiritual force unknown to their pagan predecessors."[4]

These new attributes were powerful and lasting. Christians believed in the unity of humankind, that the human race was moving toward a common and glorious destiny. Christians also did not believe in multiple restarts of the world. They believed that there would be one final judgment, after which all things would be put right. This wonderful end point was one of historical necessity, because it was the climax of "an unfolding through long ages of a design present from the very beginning of man's history," all under a sovereign God who was directing all of the ages toward it. Finally, and perhaps most important, Christians had a "confidence in a future that [was] . . . *this*-worldly in orientation as compared with *next*-worldly." They did not merely believe in heaven or an afterlife like other religions. Uniquely, they expected a "golden age of happiness *on earth* . . . with the returned Christ as ruler."[5]

It was only in the Western world, then, that the idea of historical progress took a deep root and animated people's thinking and living.

The next crucial stage in the history of the idea of progress happened in the European Enlightenment when the Christian hope became secularized. From approximately 1750 to 1900 many of the leading thinkers of Western culture turned away from religion in general and from Christianity in particular. Yet they did not turn away from belief in historical progress. Thinkers as diverse as the Marquis de Condorcet, Auguste Comte, Karl Marx, John Stuart Mill, and Herbert Spencer began a process of the "secularization of the idea of progress—detaching it from its long-held relationship with God, making it a historical process activated and maintained by purely natural causes."[6]

In the short run, this pulling of historical hope out of its Christian belief setting seemed to strengthen it. The Bible taught that history was under God's control and he was guiding it toward an end in complete peace and justice, joy, and life. But it did not teach that every successive generation of people would experience greater prosperity, peace, comfort, and well-being than previous generations. The "linear" nature of Christian hope is not an unbroken succession of better and better eras. The secularized version of historical hope did, however, promise that.

Perhaps the height of the secular idea of progress was reached in the thought of three nineteenth-century figures. Georg Wilhelm Friedrich Hegel saw world history as a series of great ascending stages. Each new stage comes about through a synthesis of competing forces from the previous era. When two warring forces from one age are reconciled, it leads to a new age that is related to the past "as the man is related to the child and the plant to the seed."[7] Karl Marx also saw history as moving inevitably toward more justice for greater numbers of people through the class struggle of the workers (the proletariat) and the owners (the bourgeoisie). Finally, Charles Darwin taught that all life forms were making progress through a process of biological adaptation. It made sense to infer from this idea (and most people did at the time) that society itself was evolving and getting better and better.[8]

And so Western societies cruised into the early twentieth century with a confident hope for history. People believed that the future would be better than the past and that life would be better for their children than it had been for their parents.

The Loss of Cultural Hope

But from the beginning of the twentieth century into our own time the secular idea of progress has been on the wane. Nisbet explained that the secular hope for history had been based on several premises, including the "conviction of the nobility, even superiority of Western civilization" as well as "faith in reason and in the kind of scientific and scholarly knowledge that can come from reason alone."⁹ These beliefs, however, were sorely tested from the beginning of the century.

The period from 1900 to 1950 saw not only two world wars but a worldwide flu pandemic and the Great Depression. These were things that the progress of human reason and advancing Western civilization were supposed to stop, but they did not. Many thinkers of the Enlightenment had turned toward science and away from religion because, it was thought, religious faith led to dogmatism, strife, wars, and violence. Through reason and science we would come to consensus on how to live good lives together. The thinkers of the Enlightenment believed that to go to war and to exploit races and classes was simply irrational, and that all reasonable people would see that and agree. But after two world wars and repeated episodes of ethnic genocide it became clear that reason and science were not able to change whatever it was within human nature that led to violence and oppression.

The loss of faith in the secular idea of progress took two world wars for some. H. G. Wells, a well-known British writer, wrote *A Short History of the World* in 1922. World War I had already shaken the faith of many, but Wells maintained his hope in reason and science by arguing that the same science that gave us the ability to destroy one another would also give us the ability to use these powers to promote peace and justice.

> Science has brought [humanity] such powers as he never had before. And the scientific method of fearless thought, exhaustively lucid statement, and exhaustively criticized planning, which has given him these uncontrollable powers, gives him also the hope of controlling these powers. . . . As yet we are hardly in the earliest dawn of human greatness. . . . Can we doubt that presently our race will more than realize our boldest imaginations, that it will achieve unity and peace, that . . . the children of our blood and lives will live, in a world made more splendid and lovely than any palace or garden that we know, going on from strength to

strength in an ever widening circle of adventure and achievement?[10]

Wells brushes aside the failure of science and reason to avoid World War I by arguing that the solution is simply more scientific method. He ends the book with the lyrical passage above, which perfectly expressed the secular faith in human reason, goodness, and therefore inevitable progress.

But by 1939 Wells had finally begun to lose his faith, in light of what he saw as overwhelming evidence against it. He wrote:

> The wanton destruction of homes, the ruthless hounding of decent folk into exile, the bombings of open cities, the cold-blooded massacres and mutilation of children and defenseless gentle people, the rapes and filthy humiliations and, above all, the return of deliberate and organized torture, mental torment and fear to a world from which such things had seemed wellnigh banished— has come near to breaking my spirit altogether.[11]

And in 1945, just before he died in August of that year, Wells wrote his last, brief book, *Mind at the End of Its Tether*. Most of the horrors of the Second World War, including the dropping of the atomic bomb and the Nazi death camps, had not come to light when he penned the essay. Yet the burden of his book was that humankind had failed as the highest species on the planet and that the future would be bleak for many centuries until some other species took our place. "A series of events has forced upon the intelligent observer the realization that the human story has already come to an end and that *Homo sapiens*, as he has been pleased to call himself . . . is played out. . . . He has to give place to some other animal better adapted to face the fate that closes in more and more swiftly on mankind."[12]

Even though no World War III arrived, the midtwentieth century saw growing skepticism about the idea of progress. Literature became darker about human prospects, as seen in the work of existentialist writers such as Jean-Paul Sartre and Albert Camus, whose novel *The Plague* depicts human life as going down to a never-ending defeat in the struggle against death.

A new school of thought developed by the early 1960s called "poststructuralism" or "postmodernism." Perhaps the single best book summarizing the postmodern turn among Western intellectuals is Jean-François Lyotard's *The Postmodern Condition*. Lyotard argued that our age no longer accepted "metanarratives"—"master discourses" that purport not only to explain everything that happens but also to provide answers to all our problems. In Lyotard's view, the fundamental metanarrative of Western culture has been emancipation through science but, he rightly argued, even though this narrative can take both a liberal form that leads toward socialism and a conservative form that leads toward fascism, the twentieth century has revealed it to be, in any guise, a failure.[13]

Lyotard, however, did not stop with the secular hope of scientific progress. He went on to criticize the belief in progress of any kind as just a way that people in power maintain it. "The State resorts to the narrative of freedom every time it assumes direct control over the training of 'the people' . . . in order to point them down the path of progress."[14] Nisbet agreed: "[T]he same idea of inexorable, unfolding, necessary progress . . . could also be made to serve the ends of absolute power, utopian, political, racist."[15]

For example, liberals who take control of public education and insist that every person should be able to define and express themselves sexually are imposing a very white, Western, individualistic understanding of identity on everyone. In doing so they will marginalize more traditional understandings of humanity and sexuality as "psychologically unhealthy" and "socially oppressive." What is this but a strong move of power on the part of the state, lifting up favored groups and marginalizing disfavored groups—all in the name of scientific progress? And of course if we do all this using the idea that such historical progress is inevitable because history is inexorably moving in this direction, then our accrual of power seems justified. We are only going along with the flow of progress.

Lyotard was one of a whole generation of postmodern thinkers who saw atrocities of both the Left and the Right (e.g., the Soviet Union and Nazi

Germany) all done under the claim of historical progress. Michel Foucault, in works such as *History of Madness in the Classical Age* (1961) and *The Order of Things* (1966), completely broke with Hegel and Marx and their progressivism. Foucault saw not a sequence of ascending stages but a series of ruptures in which a new era is different from the previous—particularly different in who has more power and who has less—but not necessarily better.[16]

A Revival of Hope?

While most academics and intellectuals in the West were losing their hope in historical progress, there was something of a revival of it at the popular level in two social arenas in particular. The first arena was in the realm of liberal politics. Over the last two decades many on the left side of the political spectrum have rejected the term *liberal* and adopted the term *progressive* to describe themselves. Especially Democrats in the U.S. began to justify their policies, or their opposition to policies, on the assumption that there was an unstoppable movement of history toward their vision of a just society.

During an address on terrorism, President Barack Obama said: "My fellow Americans, I am confident we will succeed in this mission because we are on *the right side of history*."[17] In an *Atlantic* article about this usage, David Graham pointed out that Obama used the phrase "right side of history" fifteen times and "the wrong side of history" at least thirteen times. His staff and press secretaries used the phrases another sixteen. President Clinton used the phrases "right side" and "wrong side" of history twenty to thirty times, and his staff added more. Politicians do not use such language unless they have evidence that it appeals to people. At the left end of the political spectrum the idea of historical progress toward a more free and just society was reasserting itself. Democratic leaders spoke of policies that they did not like as "regressive" and spoke of thinkers they liked as "ahead of their time."[18] All this language seeks to revive the secular belief, without

God or any divine influence, that history was inevitably, on its own, moving toward greater freedom, prosperity, and enlightenment.

The other arena besides politics that has sought to revive the secular idea of progress is the world of technology. Margaret O'Mara wrote in *The New York Times* of "The Church of Techno-Optimism." By that she means "the belief that technology and technologists are building the future. . . . Place a computer on every desk and enable networked communication, [Silicon Valley] believed, and you could remedy society's failures and injustices."[19] A survey of technology companies' marketing presentations of their products will find innumerable confident claims of "changing the world" and quite a few defiant statements that the changes they were bringing could not be resisted because they were part of the inevitable path of progress.

But these voices are being challenged by many, not by pointing to the world wars and the Holocaust as in midcentury, but by pointing out how many of our current intractable problems are *caused* by technological advancement. One of those is looming climate change. Another is the prospect that fast-moving, destructive pandemics are more likely because of the globalization of our economy through technology. What if in the next pandemic—and other ones likely to come—the fatality rate is 10 percent rather than the far lower rate of COVID-19?

In their article "The Un-Easy Case for Technological Optimism," James Krier and Clayton Gillette point out that modern technology brings in changes so quickly that their bad effects cannot be discovered before they are irreversible, and so sweepingly that their effects are catastrophic. They mention carcinogens and climate change as just two examples.[20] Technology critics such as Kara Swisher of *The New York Times* are pointing out other dangers of social media and "big tech." She regularly expresses alarm at how the biggest companies have decimated the news business and created a cultural situation in which citizens do not know whom to believe. They have also provided all the tools for a complete loss of privacy and a surveillance state, as well as altering many retail industries in the direction of putting more wealth in the hands of the few.[21]

And so as we near the end of the first quarter of the twenty-first century, despite the rhetoric in the areas of politics and technology, the cultural loss of hope is palpable and growing. Sci-fi movies no longer provide us with optimistic scenarios of the future. Younger adults are far less likely to marry or have children or vote—all of these are indicators of hope loss. All studies of the members of Generation Z indicate that they are far more pessimistic about the future and about themselves than older generations.

The eminent Harvard scientist Harlow Shapley, who died in 1972, listed five factors that could destroy Western civilization.[22] Four of them were nuclear war or terrorism, famine or food shortages, climatic or topographical catastrophe, and plague or pandemic. He points out that technological advancement has helped us only with the issue of food—in the other three areas, as Krier and Gillette predicted, our technological advances have actually worsened our perilous future prospects.

Interestingly, Shapley listed "boredom" as the fifth factor that could destroy us. Nisbet explains that boredom increases as we lose hope for progress, but then that boredom becomes one of the things that further erodes progress. "What this state of mind [boredom] means in social and cultural terms is increasingly widespread and chronic indifference to ordinary values, pursuits, freedoms, and obligations. The present becomes a scene composed of the absurd, the irrelevant, and the demonic. So, necessarily does the past and of course, the future." Nisbet then adds: "As G. K. Chesterton wrote . . . the result of ceasing to believe in God is not that one will then believe nothing; it is that one will believe anything."[23]

The Critique of Secular Hope

Why did the secular hope in progress—once so powerful and such a driving force in our culture—fail? There were two design flaws in the Western idea of progress that doomed it. I will call one the problem of human nature and the other the problem of ultimate oblivion.

The first is the problem of human nature. Western progressives reasoned that as knowledge increased, life would get better. But that assumed that human beings would use that knowledge properly, for the good of everyone. The secular hope for the future assumed that advances in knowledge would never be used to increase one group's or nation's power and wealth at the expense of others. It presupposed the basic goodness of human nature. H. G. Wells was a prime avatar of this premise. He acknowledged that in World War I the fruits of the scientific method were used to harm others. What did he say was the solution? It was a *more* rigorous scientific method. His assumption was that the violence of World War I was just irrational behavior, a lack of clear, reasoned thinking, and that increased use of reason and education would solve it. No wonder World War II "broke his spirit," because the Germans were considered to be both culturally and scientifically advanced, the creators of the modern research university, yet they used their superior knowledge to destroy.

One way to reveal the flaw in secular reasoning is to look at the horrors of Auschwitz and ask, "Why did this happen? Why did the Nazis do what they did?"

H. G. Wells's view (at least in 1922) was that the Nazis failed to follow the scientific method and the dictates of human reason. That answer—that they were the victim of irrational thinking—however, trivializes the evil of what happened. A variation on this same basic view is the Marxist one. Karl Marx believed we are the product of social forces, of structural power, and that people who are criminals are so because of systemic injustice that causes them to act as they do. Marx believed that crime and poverty would end when all people equally owned the means of economic production.[24] But again, to say that the massive genocide at Auschwitz was caused by people who were victims of social forces is to minimize the evil of what happened. Indeed, it is to lose a category for human evil.

A second possible answer is that the Nazis were simply more evil people than others. They were morally inferior to the rest of us. *We* would be too good and decent to do anything like that. They are, then, beneath us, subhuman. But as soon as such words are out of our mouths, we realize that this is exactly how the Nazis justified their slaughter of the Jews. They dehumanized them in their minds, seeing them as an inferior, wicked group of people, and thus they legitimized the violence they visited upon them. As soon as we say that the perpetrators of Auschwitz are morally inferior to us, we begin the same process of dehumanization that led them to exclude, marginalize, and destroy the Jews.

The only viable answer to the question is this: Auschwitz happened because of something profoundly wrong with human nature. There is something warped and wrong within us. We are prone to self-centeredness and capable of great cruelty. Lord David Cecil summed up this tragic flaw when he said after World War II: "The jargon of the philosophy of progress taught us to think that the savage and primitive state of man is behind us. . . . But barbarism is not behind us, it is [within] us."[25]

A novelistic version of this verdict can be seen in the post–World War II novel by William Golding, *Lord of the Flies* (1954). It is the story of a group of British schoolboys who are stranded on an uninhabited island. Earlier novels such as *The Coral Island* (1857), still operating on the optimistic premises of secular hope, had depicted shipwrecked boys creating a kind of idyllic paradise away from the corrupting influences of society. Golding, who explicitly referenced *The Coral Island* in his novel, paints a very different picture. The boys in his story descend into tribalism and violence—they kill one another and hunt one another down. The novel was a refutation of the view of Jean-Jacques Rousseau, so dominant in the West for so many years, that we are in ourselves pure and good, and it is only society that ruins us, teaching us to exploit. No, says Golding, the evil we see in society is the outworking of what is already in our nature. If we start a new society from scratch, we will only bring the corruption with us.

C. E. M. Joad was a socialist, an atheist professor of philosophy, and a regular on the BBC wartime radio program *Brain Trust*. He came to faith in Christ after World War II. In his book *The Recovery of Belief* he described how he and all his colleagues had explained evil human behavior with recourse either to Marx or to Freud. Human cruelty was psychological and sociological "maladjustment." Within his intellectual circles words such as "evil, sinful, wicked [were] sedulously avoided" in favor of descrip-

tions such as "ill-adjusted behavior" or "aggressive instincts." Human beings could be rehabilitated away from selfish and cruel behavior if you
could just change their circumstances. In full agreement with Rousseau or
Marx, Joad believed that if you took a man and could "place [him] in an
approved environment . . . make him feel important but not too important,
refrain from oppressing or restricting him, carefully avoid inculcating feelings of guilt or inferiority, and he will grow up into a . . . healthy, cheerful,
effective, balanced, and fearless adult."[26]

Joad says that this view, "so pervasive in modern thought," failed to prepare anyone for World War II. The modern view of human evil that he had
"adopted unthinkingly as a young man" was perhaps plausible in "the first
fourteen years of this century when . . . the state of mankind seemed to be
improving," but now this view of human goodness, reason, and progress
had "been rendered utterly implausible by the events of the last forty
years."[27] He realized that science did not improve human beings but only
improved their ability to get what they want. "Science . . . is not an end but
a means, a means to the furtherance of man's desires."[28]

Finally, Joad adds a personal note:

> It is because we rejected the doctrine of original sin that we on
> the Left were always being disappointed; disappointed by the re-
> fusal of people to be reasonable . . . by the failure of true Social-
> ism to arrive, by the behavior of the nations and politicians . . .
> above all, by the recurrent fact of war.[29]

In short, the secular idea of progress assumed that the barriers to progress
that faced the human race were outside of us, and we only needed sufficient
technological knowledge, education, and social policy to control the natural world and to overcome disease, famine, war, poverty, racism, and depression. But history has shown us that increasing knowledge can be used
in terrible ways to worsen our situation, because the greatest barrier to
progress is actually within us.

There is a second major problem with the secular idea of progress. The original Christian idea of historical progress was that history was moving not just to an ending, but to something good beyond history. God's renewed world will be the culmination and fulfillment of all the best of humanity's aspirations and hopes throughout history. But the secular idea of progress believes in nothing at all beyond this material world. This means not only that when we die as individuals we go to nothing, but also that human civilization itself will eventually disappear without a trace. In other words, the secular hope is only for a progress that is very temporary. It assumes that the actual destiny of human history is complete oblivion.

C. S. Lewis penned a brief essay, "On Living in an Atomic Age," in 1948, when the possibility of a nuclear war loomed. He wrote that many people were frightened that the atomic bomb could "totally destroy civilization itself." He responded: "What were your views about the ultimate future of civilization *before* the atomic bomb . . . ? What did you think all this effort of humanity was to come to in the end? The real answer is known to almost everyone who has even a smattering of science. . . . The whole story is going to end in NOTHING."[30] He added: "If Nature is all that exists—that is, if there is no God and no life of some quite different sort somewhere outside Nature," then all of human civilization will eventually die with the death of the sun, and so humanity will turn out to have been "an accidental flicker . . . infinitesimally short in relation to the oceans of dead time which precede and follow it . . . and there will be no one even to remember it."[31]

Brian Greene, in his book *Until the End of Time: Mind, Matter, and Our Search for Meaning in an Evolving Universe*, has the same message. Greene, unlike Lewis, is a secular man, but his message is the same. How can you live a meaningful life if you know that human life is the tiniest blip in the history of the universe and that nothing we do here at all—whether good or cruel—will make any final difference? Greene recalls in the movie *Annie Hall* the nine-year-old character Alvy Singer who, once he realizes that the universe will break down and all human civilization will be destroyed, decides that there is no reason to do his homework. Of course, audiences are meant to laugh at this point in the movie, but Greene won't let us off the hook. He believes the point is no laughing matter. He reasons that, if you knew you were going to die tomorrow, then doing your homework would certainly be pointless. And if we knew that the world was about to be incinerated, it would make all the things we think of as so significant—art, politics, rearing a family—pointless and futile. He then argues that "if the immediate demise of humanity would render life meaningless, then the same should be true even if the end is far off."[32] We try to take comfort in "symbolic transcendence"—the idea that what we do will live on in our works or in the lives of our children. But the reality is that, in the end, whether you live a life of goodness or of cruelty will make no final difference at all. The knowledge of ultimate oblivion, even when somewhat repressed, seeps in and robs life of significance. If Foucault is right, history lurches from one disjunction to the next, never improving, until it ends with our solar system, or sooner through some climate or nuclear disaster. History is indeed "a tale told by an idiot, full of sound and fury, signifying nothing."[33]

Greene and Lewis are making the point that, if this material world is all that exists, ultimately all our loves, persons, and accomplishments will come to nothing. But Lewis, unlike Greene, is pushing us toward this conclusion so that we might begin to question it. He writes:

> You can't go on getting any very serious pleasure from music if you know and remember that its air of significance is a pure illusion, that you like it only because your nervous system is irrationally conditioned to like it. You may still, in the lowest sense, have a "good time" . . . [but] you will be forced to feel the hopeless disharmony between your emotions and the universe in which you really live.[34]

When Lewis speaks of the disharmony between our emotions and our view of the universe, he is pushing us to see that the secular worldview is not actually something that, deep down, anyone can truly hold. He reminds us that, if everything within us has a material cause, then love and even our moral convictions are really just the product of biological forces that helped us survive. But does anyone really believe that? Indeed, *can* anyone believe that? Lewis goes on: "You can't, except in the lowest animal sense, be in love with a girl if you know (and keep on remembering) that all the beauties both of her person and of her character are a momentary and accidental pattern produced by the collision of atoms and . . . from the behavior of your genes."

Lewis is arguing that, at the practical level, no one can live consistently with the belief that we are only matter and that our ultimate end is oblivion. So we have no hope.

Unless.

Unless there is a God who has promised to guide history not to an end but to a new beginning, to a world in which finally death and evil are completely destroyed and justice and peace reign supreme, the sign of which is the resurrection.

Christian Resources for Cultural Hope

Christianity offers unparalleled resources for cultural hope. We are not for the moment talking about individual hope—hope for life after death. We are talking about corporate hope, social hope, hope for the future of society, of the human race—hope for a good direction to history. As Nisbet and others have shown, the original wellspring of the idea of historical progress and hope was Christianity. Cut off from this source, Western society is understandably growing in cynicism and boredom. Let's look at what Christianity offers that could renew hope in our culture. Christian resources for hope are uniquely reasonable, full, realistic, and effective.

CHRISTIAN HOPE IS REASONABLE

First, as discussed at some length in the first chapter, there is formidable historical evidence that the resurrection of Christ actually happened. This makes Christian hope different from any other variety.

N. T. Wright explains that the resurrection of Christ presents evidence that demands explanation from historians and scientists. It can't simply be dismissed. He writes: "Insofar as I understand scientific method, when something turns up that doesn't fit the paradigm you're working with, one option . . . is to change the paradigm." We are not to exclude the evidence just because our old paradigm can't account for it, but we are to include it within a new paradigm, "a larger whole."[35] A failure to provide a historically plausible alternative explanation for the eyewitness accounts and the revolutionary, overnight worldview change of thousands of Jews is not being more scientific—it is being less so.

So as Wright points out, faith in Jesus's resurrection "is not blind belief that rejects all history and science [or] that . . . inhabits . . . a separate watertight compartment," a kind of faith that is completely impervious to empirical realities. Rather, "faith in Jesus risen from the dead *transcends but includes* what we call history and what we call science."[36]

Various kinds of Western progressivism believe history is moving toward more individual freedom or class equality or economic prosperity or technologically acquired peace and justice. But all of these views are not hypotheses that anyone can test. They are "hope so" hopes—beliefs that are not rooted in the empirical realm. The resurrection of Christ, however, includes powerful evidence from the empirical realm and, while still requiring faith, provides a highly reasonable, rational hope that there is a God who is going to renew the world.

CHRISTIAN HOPE IS FULL

Every religion has offered people a hope for a life after death. They variously teach that our souls will live in paradise or that our spiritual essence will pass into the All-Soul of the world or that we will continue in some other mode of spiritual existence. So while the physical world ends in oblivion, we continue. Our secular culture, in radical contrast, is the first in history to tell its members that *both* individuals and world history will end in ultimate oblivion. In the end, we go to nothing, both as a civilization and as persons.

Other religions are ultimately "Spirit-tist" in the sense they teach that matter is unimportant and in the end all that will exist is Spirit. Secularism, of course, is materialist in its belief that there is no soul or supernatural reality, that everything has a scientific, physical cause. Christianity differs from both. It does not merely offer the prospect of a wholly spiritual future in heaven. The resurrection of Jesus is *arrabon*, a down payment, and *aparche*, firstfruits of a future physical resurrection in which the material world will be renewed. It will be a world where justice dwells, in which every tear will be wiped away, in which death and destruction are banished forever, in which the wolf will lie down with the lamb—these are lyrical, poetic ways of saying that *this* world will be mended, made new, liberated from its bondage to death and decay (Romans 8:18–23).

No other faith says not only that we will be resurrected as individuals but that the material world will be renewed as well. And so human society is destined not for ultimate oblivion but for the longed-for goal of perfect prosperity, love, justice, and peace. And this hope is not wishful thinking but is grounded in history, the sign of which is the risen Christ. The risen Jesus said he was not "a ghost" (Luke 24:39); our future is not an ethereal existence in some other world but a renewed, resurrected existence in this one.

This is the fullest possible hope. The resurrection of Christ promises us not merely some future consolation for the life we lost but the *restoration* of the life we lost and infinitely more. It promises the world and life that we have always longed for but never had.

CHRISTIAN HOPE IS REALISTIC

Hegel's philosophy was highly influential for Western thought, and he taught that history was proceeding through a "dialectic" in which, in each age, conflicting forces reached a new, greater synthesis. This meant that every age was better than the one before and history was moving upward in a series of unbroken steps. That, as we have seen over the last century, is simply unrealistic. Christianity offers an infinitely greater and more wonderful destiny for human history and society, but it does so realistically.

If we look to the death and subsequent resurrection of Jesus, we see a very different divine model. The Bible "offers us a paradigm for understanding world history that resolves neither to Hegelian dialectic nor to a Nietzschean/Foucauldian disjunctive succession. . . . The Bible offers us a nonlinear, v-shaped account of history, the pattern of which is the incarnation, death, and resurrection of Jesus Christ."[37]

Jesus came to earth, but his life was not a series of upward steps. He emptied himself of his glory and came and died, yet this descent led to an ascent to even greater heights, because now he rules not only the world in general but a saved people. It was only through his suffering and descent that he was able to save us and ascend. This is not the Hegelian merger of equal and opposite forces. Jesus did not "synthesize" holiness with sin or life with death. He defeated sin and death *through* death. But neither is Jesus's life and career the random sequence of ruptures described by the postmodernists. Jesus goes through darkness to eventually bring us to greater light. History *is* moving toward a wonderful destiny, but not in a series of successively better and better eras, going from strength to strength. That is not how God works.

And that is not how human life works either. It is often seen that it is through hardship and difficulty that we grow, we finally see truths about ourselves, we finally become all we should be. That is true not just individually but socially as well. It is "through many tribulations we enter the kingdom of God" (Acts 14:22 ESV).

The secular idea of progress was naive and unrealistic. It is wrong to base a society on the assumption that every generation will experience more prosperity, peace, and justice than the one before. But the postmodern alternative robs us of any hope. Christianity, however, gives us a noncynical but realistic way to see history.

CHRISTIAN HOPE IS EFFECTIVE

Finally, Christian hope works at the life level, the practical level.

The New Testament uses the word *hope* in two ways. When it comes to hoping in human beings and ourselves, our *hope* is always relative, uncertain. If you lend to someone, you do so in the hope that they will pay you back (Luke 6:34); if we plow and thresh, we do so in the hope that there will be a harvest (1 Corinthians 9:10).[38] We choose the best methods and wisest practices in order to secure the outcome we want. We insist to ourselves and others that "we have it sorted" and under control. But we do not—we never do. This is relative, "hope so" hope.

But when the object of hope is *not* any human agent but God, then hope means confidence, certainty, and full assurance (Hebrews 11:1). To have hope in God is not to have an uncertain, anxious wish that he will affirm your plan but to recognize that he and he alone is trustworthy, that everything else will let you down (Psalms 42:5,11, 62:10), and that his plan is infinitely wise and good. If I believe in the resurrection of Jesus, that confirms that there is a God who is both good and powerful, who brings light out of darkness, and who is patiently working out a plan for his glory, our good, and the good of the world (Ephesians 1:9–12; Romans 8:28). Christian hope means that I stop betting my life and happiness on human agency and rest in him.

How do we do that? A person who gets a diagnosis of cancer will rightly put his relative hope in doctors and medical treatment. But his main dependence must be in God. He can have certainty that his plan and will for him is always good and perfect (Romans 8:28) and that the inevitable destiny is resurrection. If he puts his heart's main hope in medicine, then an unfavorable report will be devastating. But if his heart's main hope is in the Lord, he will be like a mountain that cannot be shaken or moved (Psalm 125:1). Isaiah 40:31 says that those who "hope in the Lord" are not anxiously holding on but always "renewing their strength" and even "soaring." Hope in God leads to "running and not growing weary" and "walking and not being faint."

J. R. R. Tolkien explains this difference between defiance and true hope in a passage in the last volume of his trilogy *The Lord of the Rings*. Sam Gamgee has been guarding his master, Frodo, during a harrowing journey through a deadly, evil country. At one point he rescued Frodo from a prison tower out of sheer force of will. Later he is falling asleep and sees a white star twinkling in the sky:

The beauty of it smote his heart, as he looked up out of the forsaken land, and hope returned to him. For like a shaft, clear and cold, the thought pierced him that in the end the Shadow was only a small and passing thing: there was light and high beauty forever beyond its reach. His song in the Tower had been defiance rather than hope; for then he was thinking of himself. Now, for a moment, his own fate, and even his master's, ceased to trouble him. He crawled back into the brambles and laid himself by Frodo's side, and putting away all fear he cast himself into a deep untroubled sleep.[39]

This perfectly captures the difference between relative hope in human agency and infallible hope in God. In the tower, Sam had put his hope in his plan and his prowess. And certainly stoicism or powerful anger can get us through some crises, temporarily. But real courage comes with self-forgetfulness based on joy. It comes from a deep conviction that we here on earth are trapped temporarily in a little corner of darkness, but that the universe of God is an enormous place of light and high beauty and that is our certain, final destiny. It is so because of Jesus. He was so committed to bringing us into that light and beauty that he lost all glory and gladness and was plunged into the depths so that we can know that "weeping may stay for the night, but rejoicing comes in the morning" (Psalm 30:5).

Jesus has secured this for us by his death and resurrection. When this assurance abides in us, our immediate fate—how the current situation turns out—can no longer trouble us. Defiance comes from looking at ourselves. Hope comes from looking at him.

THE BUILDING BLOCK
AND THE DARKNESS

**The building block that was rejected
became the cornerstone of a whole new world**

└─NOEL PAUL STOOKEY (1977)

P salm 118:22–23 uses a striking metaphor that has reverberated through the centuries:

> *I will give you thanks, for you answered me;*
> *you have become my salvation.*
>
> *The stone the builders rejected*
> *has become the cornerstone;*
>
> *the Lord has done this,*
> *and it is marvelous in our eyes.*

Psalm 118, like so many other psalms, is a call for God's salvation from a man who is surrounded by a ring of enemies (verses 11–14). In this case the foes were "builders"—men of power in Israel, "the movers and shakers."

They rejected a "stone," which may have been the king of Israel, or the Lord himself, or perhaps it was the truth of God's Word. Isaiah 28:15–16 speaks of the leaders and rulers rejecting God's "tested stone" for a pack of lies.

But when we get to the New Testament, the apostles make it clear that all this foreshadowed Jesus Christ (Romans 9:30–32), who was rejected by the rulers and powers yet who, through his rejection and death, became the cornerstone of a new, living spiritual house in which dwells the Spirit (1 Peter 2:6–10; Ephesians 2:20). This living temple contains the power of the new creation. It is a counterculture, an alternate humanity. It will grow until the entire earth is filled with God's glory and is renewed (Revelation 21–22). God's "marvelous" vindication of Jesus, the rejected stone, is the resurrection, as implied by Peter in Acts 4:10.[1]

Noel Paul Stookey based a 1977 song on this powerful idea, writing, "The building block that was rejected became the cornerstone of a whole new world."[2] That, in a nutshell, is the theme of this book and, I have argued, the essence of the message of the Bible. Jesus brings his salvation through rejection, weakness, and sorrow. Yet not despite his weakness but through it he brings the presence of the future and begins to build a whole new world through us.

Stookey rightly sees that this message of the Great Reversal, of light out of darkness and blessing out of curse, is something that can support us through dark times of fear and grief.

> *When all your dreams have been connected*
> *And your vision has been returned*
> *Remember, love, you are protected*
> *By the truth your heart has learned.*
>
> *The building block that was rejected*
> *became the cornerstone of a whole new world*[3]

The gospel does not promise us that we will conquer the world with our faith. This is not a message of "Onward, Christian soldiers, marching as to war."[4] A hymn more in keeping with the Great Reversal is "Not with swords loud clashing, nor roll of stirring drums, (but) with deeds of love and mercy, the heavenly kingdom comes."[5]

Another place where the Bible points us to the resurrection for our hope is what has been called the darkest of all psalms—Psalm 88.

> *I cry to you for help, Lord;*
> *in the morning my prayer comes before you.*
> *Why, Lord, do you reject me*
> *and hide your face from me?*
> *From my youth I have suffered and been close to death;*
> *I have borne your terrors and am in despair.*
> *Your wrath has swept over me;*
> *your terrors have destroyed me.*
> *All day long they surround me like a flood;*
> *they have completely engulfed me.*
> *You have taken from me friend and neighbor—*
> *darkness is my closest friend.*

(Psalm 88:13–18)

Most psalms that are laments and cries of pain end on at least some note of hope. But Psalm 88 recounts all the writer's griefs and his imminent death and ends by saying that God has abandoned him and that "darkness is my closest friend" (verse 18). In fact, in the middle of the psalm he actually asks bitterly, "Do their [the dead's] spirits rise up and praise you? Is your love declared in the grave?" (verses 10–11). He is in despair. But the New Testament answers with the Great Reversal. Do the dead rise up to praise? Yes! Is your love declared in the grave? Oh yes!

Here's your hope.

Jesus was truly abandoned so that you only feel abandoned but you're not. When Jesus Christ was in the garden of Gethsemane and the ultimate darkness was coming down on him and he knew it was coming, he didn't abandon you; he died for you. If Jesus Christ didn't abandon you in *his* darkness, the ultimate darkness, why would he abandon you now, in yours?

Because it can be said truly of Jesus Christ that, on the cross, darkness was his only friend, and so he paid for your sins—then you can know that in your darkness God is still there as your friend. He hasn't abandoned you. He's not going to take two payments for the same debt. Jesus paid for your sins, and now he loves you.

If you know—and keep on remembering—that resurrection is coming, then you won't be in utter darkness. I know a chronically ill woman who, whenever somebody says to her, "Oh, you seem like you're suffering so much; how do you feel?" always says, "Nothing the resurrection won't cure." She's right. If you know the resurrection is coming, it's impossible to be in utter darkness.

There's a man who wrote a commentary on Psalm 88, and he concludes the commentary with "This [darkness] can happen to a believer, [this psalm] says. It doesn't mean you're lost. It can happen to someone who does not deserve it; it does not mean you have strayed. It can happen at any time as long as this world lasts; only in the next will such things be done away with. And it can happen without you knowing why. [But] there are answers, there is a purpose, and eventually you will know."[6]

ACKNOWLEDGMENTS

It seems overly pious to start by acknowledging the help of God, but I must. I believe, of course, that every book or sermon I have ever written and delivered was part of God's plan and that, without violating our responsible agency, he "works out everything in conformity with the purpose of his will." (Ephesians 1:11) God has millions of good but usually hidden reasons for everything that happens, but some of those reasons were easier to see than usual in this case. My publisher, Brian Tart, suggested a book on Easter that would be something of a companion book to *Hidden Christmas*. So I began a book on the resurrection and then the COVID-19 pandemic struck and I was diagnosed with pancreatic cancer. Such things, as Samuel Johnson says, "concentrate the mind wonderfully." Writing in such dark times helped me see in the resurrection new depths of comfort and power. This is not to claim that this is a better book than others I have written. Let readers be the judge of that. But it is the one in which I felt the most divine guidance and help.

With every book my appreciation and gratitude grows for the circle of friends and colleagues who have made my writing possible over the years. There are those who gave Kathy and me great places and spaces to work, including Ray and Gill Lane of Ambleside, Cumbria, UK, and Janice Worth of Palm Beach Gardens, Florida. On the publishing side, David McCormick and Brian Tart have been the team whose editorial and literary guidance through over twenty Penguin titles (!) has made it all work. You two are an author's dream team.

NOTES

PREFACE

1. Martin Luther King Jr., "I Have a Dream" (speech, Washington, DC, August 28, 1963), www.americanrhetoric.com/speeches/mlkihaveadream.htm.

INTRODUCTION

1. See chapter 12 ("Hope for the Future") for more on how this optimism and hope about the future developed historically in the West.

2. Pew Research Center, "Once Again, the Future Ain't What It Used to Be," May 2, 2006, 1, www.pewresearch.org/wp-content/uploads/sites/3/2010/10/BetterOff.pdf.

3. Steven Pinker, *The Better Angels of Our Nature: Why Violence Has Declined* (New York: Viking Books, 2011); and *Enlightenment Now: The Case for Reason, Science, Humanism, and Progress* (New York: Viking Books, 2018).

4. Yuval Noah Harrai, *Homo Deus: A Brief History of Tomorrow* (New York: Harper, 2017), 1–2. Find this excerpt at https://medium.com/thrive-global/the-new-human-agenda-d0ae506779a.

5. Pew Research Center, "Once Again, the Future Ain't," 1–2.

6. Kim Parker, Rich Morin, and Juliana Horowitz, "Looking to the Future, Public Sees an American Decline on Many Fronts," Pew Research Center, March 21, 2019, https://tinyurl.com/yxcdd4vw.

7. Andrew Sullivan, "The World Is Better Than Ever. Why Are We Miserable?" *New York*, March 9, 2018, https://nymag.com/intelligencer/2018/03/sullivan-things-are-better-than-ever-why-are-we-miserable.html.

8. Jürgen Habermas, *An Awareness of What Is Missing: Faith and Reason in a Post-Secular Age* (Malden, MA: Polity Press, 2010). See especially pages 18–19.

9. Rod Dreher, "The Germs That Destroyed an Empire," *The American Conservative*, April 24, 2020, www.theamericanconservative.com/dreher/roman-empire -plague-germs-kyle-harper.

10. Richard Gaffin gives a survey of standard, traditional systematic theologies to show how the cross and the atonement receive far more treatment than the resurrection. See the lengthy footnote 2 on page 12 of Richard B. Gaffin, *Resurrection and Redemption: A Study in Paul's Soteriology* (Phillipsburg, NJ: Presbyterian and Reformed, 1987).

11. Sam Allberry, *Lifted: Experiencing the Resurrection Life* (Phillipsburg, NJ: Presbyterian and Reformed, 2012), 15–16.

12. Christopher Watkin, *Michel Foucault* (Phillipsburg, NJ: Presbyterian and Reformed, 2018), 81.

13. From J. R. R. Tolkien, *The Silmarillion* (Boston: Houghton Mifflin, 1977), 31. These words describe Gandalf, one of several recognizable "Christ figures" in this popular mythology.

CHAPTER 1: CERTAIN HOPE

1. H. Richard Niebuhr, *The Kingdom of God in America* (Middletown, CT: Wesleyan University Press, 1988), 193. For an extensive and trenchant critique of liberal Christianity as a significantly different religion from historical Christianity, see J. Gresham Machen, *Christianity and Liberalism* (1923; new ed., Grand Rapids, MI: Wm. B. Eerdmans, 2009).

2. For a recent example, see Eliza Griswold, "Richard Rohr Reorders the Universe," *The New Yorker*, February 2, 2020, www.newyorker.com/news/on-religion/richard -rohr-reorders-the-universe.

3. John Updike, "Seven Stanzas at Easter," *Collected Poems 1953–1993* (1993; repr., New York: Alfred A. Knopf, 2012), loc. 769– 787, Kindle.

4. See James D. G. Dunn, *Jesus Remembered: Christianity in the Making*, vol. 1 (Grand Rapids, MI: Wm. B. Eerdmans, 2003), 855.

5. Tom Holland, *Dominion: How the Christian Revolution Remade the World* (New York: Basic Books, 2019), 6.

6. N. T. Wright, *The Resurrection of the Son of God: Christian Origins and the Question of God*, vol. 3 (Minneapolis: Fortress Press, 2003). The Greeks understood the physical body to be the prison-house of the soul, which was liberated at death, and so the afterlife was a "One-Way Street." Souls did *not* return to bodies—the dead did not rise again. (See pages 81–84.) For an extensive survey of "Second Temple Judaism"—the Jewish beliefs of Jesus's time, see pages 85–208.

7. Wright, *The Resurrection of the Son of God*, 699–700. "Jewish resurrection belief rule[s] out any possibility that the belief [in Christ's resurrection] could have generated spontaneously from within its Jewish context. When we ask the early Christians themselves what had occasioned this belief, their answers home in on two things: . . . Jesus's tomb being empty . . . him appearing to people, alive again" (686). "[M]any of the messianic movements between roughly 150 BC and AD 150 ended with the violent death of the founder. When this happened, there were two options open to any who escaped death: they could give up the movement, or they could find themselves another Messiah. The followers of a dead prophet could of course go on believing that he was a true prophet. . . . But with a would-be Messiah, who was supposed to be inaugurating the kingdom, it was impossible. Nobody, after all, believed that the Messiah would be raised from the dead; nobody was expecting any such thing. Clinging to the belief that the recently executed person was after all the Messiah was simply not an option" (700).

8. "This addition to line 1, 'and that he was buried' . . . emphasizes the fact that a dead corpse was laid in the grave, so that the resurrection that follows will be recognized as an objective reality, not merely a 'spiritual' phenomenon. Therefore, even though the point is incidental to Paul's own concern, this very early expression of Christian faith also verifies the reality of the empty tomb stories." Gordon D. Fee, *The First Epistle to the Corinthians* (Grand Rapids, MI: Wm. B. Eerdmans, 1987), 725.

9. See Craig A. Evans, *Jesus and the Remains of His Day: Studies in the Evidence of Material Culture* (Peabody, MA: Hendrickson, 2015), 109–45.

10. Peter J. Williams, *Can We Trust the Gospels?* (Wheaton, IL: Crossway, 2018), 134.

11. Williams, *Can We Trust the Gospels?*, 134–35.

12. See Josephus, *Jewish Antiquities* 4.219, cited in Williams, *Can We Trust the Gospels?*, 134n7.

13. Some writers have indeed implausibly claimed that hundreds of people can have a hallucination at once, but see Gary Habermas, "Explaining Away Jesus's Resurrection: The Recent Revival of Hallucination Theories," *Christian Research Journal* 23, no. 4 (2001): 26–31, 47–49, www.researchgate.net/publication/228846841_Explaining_Away_Jesus'_Resurrection_the_Recent_Revival_of_Hallucination_Theories.

14. Wright, *The Resurrection of the Son of God*, 413. For another major work that organizes and presents the considerable historical evidence for the resurrection, see Michael R. Licona, *The Resurrection of Jesus: An New Historiographical Approach* (Nottingham, UK: Apollos, 2010).

15. Wright, *The Resurrection of the Son of God*, 707, n63.

16. John Polkinghorne, *The Faith of a Physicist* (Princeton, NJ: Princeton University Press, 2016), 115.

17. Wright, *The Resurrection of the Son of God*, 605.

18. Polkinghorne, *Faith of a Physicist*, 114.

19. N. T. Wright, *Surprised by Scripture: Engaging Contemporary Issues* (New York: HarperOne, 2014), 46.

20. For a good summary of the evidence based on the portrait of Jesus in the resurrection narratives, and its incommensurability with any existing worldview, see N. T. Wright, "Resurrection Narratives," in *Dictionary for Theological Interpretation of the Bible*, ed. Kevin J. Vanhoozer (Grand Rapids, MI: Baker Books, 2005), 675–766.

21. Wright, *Surprised by Scripture*, 46, 50.

22. Wright, *Surprised by Scripture*, 59.

23. Wright, *Surprised by Scripture*, 58.

24. See Alister E. McGrath, *The Territories of Human Reason: Science and Theology in an Age of Multiple Rationalities* (Oxford: Oxford University Press, 2019).

25. An interesting case study is the twentieth-century orthodox Jewish scholar Pinchas Lapide. After looking at the evidence for the resurrection, he concluded, "I accept the resurrection of Jesus not as an invention of the community of disciples, but as a historical event." Even though he concluded that the resurrection actually happened, Lapide did not convert to Christianity. See the quotation in Pinchas Lapide, *Jewish Monotheism and Christian Trinitarian Doctrine* (Eugene, OR: Wipf and Stock, 2003), 59. See also Pinchas Lapide, *The Resurrection of Jesus: A Jewish Perspective* (Minneapolis: Augsburg Fortress, 1982).

26. Gustav K. Wiencke, *Luther's Works*, vol. 43, *Devotional Writings II* (Philadelphia: Fortress Press, 1968), 133–34.

27. Wiencke, *Luther's Works*, 123.

28. In a remarkably modern-sounding passage, Luther writes: "If in the Old Testament God himself ordered lepers to be banished from the community and compelled to live outside the city to prevent contamination [Leviticus 13–14], we must do the same with this dangerous pestilence so that anyone who becomes infected will stay away from other persons, or allow himself to be taken away and given speedy help with medicine. Under such circumstances it is our duty to assist such a person and not forsake him in his plight, as I have repeatedly pointed out before. Then the poison is stopped in time, which benefits not only the individual but also the whole community, which might be contaminated if one

person is permitted to infect others. Our plague here in Wittenberg has been caused by nothing but filth. The air, thank God, is still clean and pure, but some few have been contaminated because of the laziness or recklessness of some. So the devil enjoys himself at the terror and flight which he causes among us. May God thwart him! Amen." Wiencke, *Luther's Works*, 133–34.

29. Wiencke, *Luther's Works*, 121.

30. Wiencke, *Luther's Works*, 121.

31. Wiencke, *Luther's Works*, 121.

32. Wiencke, *Luther's Works*, 137.

CHAPTER 2: FUTURE HOPE

1. The central thesis of this book is that Jesus's resurrection was not just a dramatic miracle but the initiation of God's future kingdom, in which everything will be made subservient to the glory of God and thus will be renewed and healed—"a new creation." There are two "axes" to this kingdom. It means that the glory of God in the realm of heaven has now come to earth, not merely in episodic appearances or even within an inner sanctuary of the temple, but into the people of God. Second, it means that when Jesus rose, he brought the future new creation into the present world, so that the old world and the age of sin and death now overlaps with the new (Ephesians 1:21). The two ages—this present age of darkness and sin and the age to come, full of light and goodness—now exist together in human history. Every human being can either continue to be under the control of this present age (Ephesians 2:1) or be transferred into the age to come (Galatians 1:4; Colossians 1:13). The kingdom has come now—and yet will come in its fullness at the end of history. When we unite with the risen Christ by faith, we are "raised with Christ" by faith and we participate partially but substantially in that heavenly presence and that future kingdom power and life. So to understand the resurrection is to understand how this new life comes in and (a) changes us individually, (b) creates a new "kingdom community" called the church, and (c) enables us to bring some reordering and renewal of the world even now.

While not every part of the Bible speaks of "kingdom come yet still coming" as often as the synoptic gospels, nevertheless this basic understanding of the structure of salvation history is there in other biblical authors' writings as well. While the Gospel of John hardly uses the term *kingdom,* it repeatedly speaks of Jesus bringing eternal life—which is essentially the resurrection life that the Jews expected at the end of time being brought into history now. While Paul doesn't use the word *kingdom* a great deal in his letters, he speaks of this present "age," which continues while Christ has already begun his rule in the "age . . . to come" (Ephesians 1:21). Paul says that we who believe are delivered from this present age

(Galatians 1:4), and we become the new creation that derives from the age to come (2 Corinthians 5:17; 6:2). He teaches, therefore, "the overlap of the ages." In other words, all New Testament writers assume this fundamental fact, that the kingdom of God is "already" here but also "not yet" here in its world-renewing fullness.

This understanding of Christian salvation as not merely about individual pardon but also wholistic and world-renewing was developed especially by the Dutch theologians Geerhardus Vos and Herman Ridderbos in the early and mid-twentieth century. I note this because in the last couple of decades writers such as N. T. Wright have popularized this understanding of biblical teaching, and many readers have come to believe that it is only these recent writers who discovered this structure of biblical thought and the older theologians had missed the mark. Actually, the classic statements about this structure of biblical thought in Paul can be found in Geerhardus Vos, *The Pauline Eschatology* (1930; repr., Grand Rapids, MI: Wm. B. Eerdmans, 1972), especially 36–39. See also Geerhardus Vos, *The Kingdom of God and the Church* (Nutley, NJ: Presbyterian and Reformed, 1971), especially the "Recapitulation" at 102–103. For an extensive study of Paul's thought about the two "ages," see Herman Ridderbos, *Paul: An Outline of His Theology*, trans. John Richard DeWitt (Nutley, NJ: Presbyterian and Reformed, 1972), especially 44–90. For a study of the teaching of the kingdom of God in the synoptic Gospels, see Herman Ridderbos, *The Coming of the Kingdom* (Philadelphia: Presbyterian and Reformed, 1962), and George Eldon Ladd, *Jesus and the Kingdom* (New York: Harper and Row, 1964). I cite these earlier works not because there are not more good recent works that explain this same structure but because, unlike many of the older works by Vos and Ridderbos, they often pit the concept of kingdom and new creation against the Reformation teaching of penal substitutionary atonement and forensic justification. For a thorough explanation of why we do not need to pit these traditions against each other, see the important work by Michael Horton, *Justification: New Studies in Dogmatics*, vols. 1 and 2 (Grand Rapids, MI: Zondervan Academic, 2018).

2. Geerhardus Vos, *The Kingdom of God and the Church*, 102.

3. These "maps" of the structure of the kingdom were, from what I can tell, originally drawn by Geerhardus Vos in his book *The Pauline Eschatology*. My diagrams are heavily based on his. See Geerhardus Vos, *The Pauline Eschatology* (1930; repr., Grand Rapids, MI: Wm. B. Eerdmans, 1972), 38. This basic structure is crucial for understanding the Bible, and it is assumed throughout the New Testament even though different authors use different words to describe it. In the synoptic Gospels, the word *kingdom* is central, while Paul uses the word *aeon* or *age* to convey the same teaching, namely, that between the first and second comings of Christ the ages overlap. Vos's classic statement of Paul's doctrine of the two ages is found in *The Pauline Eschatology*, 36–41.

4. See Francis Schaeffer, *True Spirituality* (Wheaton, IL: Tyndale, 1971), 134.

5. See John Stott, "The Now and the Not Yet," in *The Contemporary Christian* (Downers Grove, IL: InterVarsity Press, 1992), 375–92.

6. To call risen Jesus the "firstfruits" is to declare that "Christ's resurrection is not an isolated event but *guarantees* something even more stupendous." (Italics are mine.) This quote and the others in this paragraph not from the Bible are from Roy E. Ciampa and Brian S. Rosner, *The First Letter to the Corinthians*, The Pillar New Testament Commentary (Grand Rapids, MI: Wm. B. Eerdmans, 2010), 761.

7. For the ideas in this section, see the crucial work by Herman Ridderbos, *Paul: An Outline of His Theology* (Grand Rapids, MI: Wm. B. Eerdmans, 1975). For Jesus as the firstfruits/firstborn of the new creation, see 53–57. "In Paul's proclamation the resurrection of Christ in fact means the breakthrough of the new aeon in the real, redemptive-historical sense of the word, and therefore cannot be understood only in forensic, ethical, or existential categories" (55).

8. John White, *The Fight: A Practical Handbook for Christian Living* (Downers Grove, IL: InterVarsity Press, 1976), 88–89. The quote is from a hymn by Samuel W. Gandy.

9. Jonathan Edwards, "Heaven Is a World of Love," in *The Sermons of Jonathan Edwards: A Reader*, ed. Wilson H. Kimnach, Kenneth P. Minkema, and Douglas Sweeney (New Haven, CT: Yale University Press, 1999), 242–72.

10. "Time" (1633) by George Herbert. See *The English Poems of George Herbert*, ed. Helen Wilcock (Cambridge, UK: Cambridge University Press, 2007), 432.

11. Douglas J. Moo, *The Letters to the Colossians and to Philemon*, The Pillar New Testament Commentary (Grand Rapids, MI: Wm. B. Eerdmans, 2008), 216.

12. Rebecca Manley Pippert, *Out of the Saltshaker and Into the World*, 2nd ed. (Downers Grove, IL: InterVarsity Press, 1999), 52–54.

13. "[F]alse teachers in Colossae, feeding on a widespread ancient fear of various celestial spirits, insisting that believers needed to follow their own rules-oriented procedure for finding freedom from the power of these spirits." In response, Paul insists that God, by sending Christ to the cross as the final and definitive means to take care of the sin problem, has removed any power that these evil spirits might have over us. This victory, celebrated and displayed in the resurrection and ascension of Christ, is what believers need to grasp as their own. Moo, *Letters to the Colossians*, 216.

14. Horton, *Justification*, vol. 2, 257, 275.

15. John Bunyan, *The Pilgrim's Progress: A Norton Critical Edition*, ed. Cynthia Wall (New York: W. W. Norton, 2009), 32–33.

16. John Murray, *The Epistle to the Romans* (Grand Rapids, MI: Wm. B. Eerdmans, 1968), 156–57.

17. Murray, *Epistle to the Romans*, 156–57.

18. Eric Nelson, *The Hebrew Republic: Jewish Sources and the Transformation of European Political Thought* (Cambridge, MA: Harvard University Press, 2011). Nelson disproves the common idea that democratic republics arose as a result of secularization. Rather, sixteenth- and seventeenth-century Christian scholars began to study the constitution of Israel looking for political ideas for their own time. From the Harvard University Press description: "Nelson identifies three transformative claims introduced into European political theory by the Hebrew revival: the argument that republics are the only legitimate regimes; the idea that the state should coercively maintain an egalitarian distribution of property; and the belief that a godly republic would tolerate religious diversity."

19. C. S. Lewis, *Present Concerns: Ethical Essays* (London: Fount Paperbacks, 1986), 20.

20. C. S. Lewis, "The Invasion" in *Mere Christianity* (New York: MacMillan, 1958), 56.

CHAPTER 3: GLORIOUS HOPE

1. See Gordon J. Wenham, "Sanctuary Symbolism in the Garden of Eden Story," in *I Studied Inscriptions from Before the Flood*, ed. Richard S. Hess and David Toshio Tsumura (University Park, PA: Eisenbrauns, 1994), available online at www .godawa.com/chronicles_of_the_nephilim/Articles_By_Others/Wenham -Sanctuary_Symbolism_Garden_of_Eden.pdf.

2. Augustine, *Confessions* 1:1.

3. C. S. Lewis, *Perelandra* (New York: Macmillan, 1965), 19.

4. Alec Motyer, *Philippian Studies: The Richness of Christ* (Chicago: InterVarsity Press, 1966), 58.

5. Jeremy Treat, *Seek First: How the Kingdom of God Changes Everything* (Grand Rapids, MI: Zondervan, 2019), 19–20.

6. Treat, *Seek First*, 20–21.

7. Information on this case study is found in Barry Hankins, *Francis Schaeffer and the Shaping of American Evangelicalism* (Grand Rapids, MI: Wm. B. Eerdmans, 2008), especially the chapters "The Making of an American Fundamentalist," "The Making of a European Evangelical," and "L'Abri," 1–73; and in Charles E.

Cotherman, *To Think Christianly: A History of L'Abri, Regent College, and the Christian Study Center Movement* (Downers Grove, IL: IVP Academic, 2020), 13–47.

8. Cotherman, *To Think Christianly*, 17.

9. Frank Schaeffer, *Crazy for God: How I Grew Up as One of the Elect, Helped Found the Religious Right, and Lived to Take All (or Almost All) of It Back* (Cambridge, MA: Da Capo Press, 2007), 21.

10. Francis Schaeffer, "Revolutionary Christianity," in *The Church at the End of the 20th Century* (Wheaton, IL: Crossway, 1994), 100–101.

11. Schaeffer, *Crazy for God*, 21–22.

12. Geerhardus Vos, *Kingdom of God and the Church* (Nutley, NJ: Presbyterian and Reformed, 1971), 87.

13. Vos, *Kingdom of God and the Church*, 87–88. Geerhardus Vos teaches that since the resurrection of Christ, "the kingdom-forces . . . are at work, [and] the kingdom-life . . . find[s] expression in the kingdom-organism of the visible church" (87). The main place that the supernatural forces of the kingdom are manifest in the world is within the church. And yet Vos goes on, "From this, however, it does not necessarily follow, that the visible church is the only outward expression of the invisible kingdom." He argues that since the purpose of the kingdom is to renew the entire world, then it is "intended to pervade . . . the whole of human life" (87). He hastens to say emphatically that Jesus's teaching was *not* "that this result should be reached by making human life in all its spheres subject to the visible church." Rather, he says, "there is a sphere of science . . . of art . . . of the family . . . of the state . . . of commerce and industry," and when individual Christians do their work in such a way that "the sphere comes under the controlling influence of the principle of the divine . . . glory . . . there we can truly say that the kingdom of God has become manifest" (87–88). "While it is proper to separate between the visible church and such things as the Christian state, Christian art, Christian science, etc., these things, if they truly belong to the kingdom of God, grow up out of the regenerated life of the invisible church" (88–89).

14. Vos, *Kingdom of God and the Church*, 89.

15. Michael Horton, "N. T. Wright Reconsiders the Meaning of Jesus's Death," The Gospel Coalition, October 10, 2016, www.thegospelcoalition.org/reviews/the-day-the-revolution-began.

16. When Isaiah sees the holiness and glory of God, he says he is "undone" (King James Version) or "ruined" (New International Version) or "lost" (English Standard Version). The Hebrew word literally means to be destroyed.

17. C. S. Lewis, "The Weight of Glory," *Theology*, November 1941, www.wheelers
burg.net/Downloads/Lewis%20Glory.pdf.

CHAPTER 4: SUBVERSIVE HOPE

1. This is the subtitle to a book by Gregory K. Beale, *Redemptive Reversals and the
Ironic Overturning of Human Wisdom* (Wheaton, IL: Crossway, 2019). Beale's
book is crucial for the arguments of this chapter. See also Christopher Watkin,
"Introducing the Cruciform 'Great Reversal,'" in *Michel Foucault* (Phillipsburg,
NJ: Presbyterian and Reformed, 2017), 77–138.

2. Beale, *Redemptive Reversals*, 21.

3. Beale, *Redemptive Reversals*, 22.

4. See Robert Alter, *The Art of Biblical Narrative*, 2nd ed. (New York: Basic Books,
2011). "Indeed . . . the entire book of Genesis is about the reversal of the iron law
of primogeniture" (5).

5. Beale, *Redemptive Reversals*, 91.

CHAPTER 5: THE GREAT REVERSAL

1. Richard B. Hays, *The Moral Vision of the New Testament: A Contemporary Introduction to New Testament Ethics* (New York: HarperCollins, 1996), 89.

2. Hays, *Moral Vision of the New Testament*, 89–90.

3. Hays, *Moral Vision of the New Testament*, 90.

4. Hays, *Moral Vision of the New Testament*, 90.

5. "At its core 'irony is saying one thing and meaning another.' All ironies are composed of three basic elements: (1) two or more layers of levels of meaning (one to
the observer and one to the victim). (2) One layer has an opposite meaning to that
of the other layer (respectively, what is apparent is the opposite of what is reality).
(3) Either the observer or the victim is . . . surprised by it." Gregory K. Beale, *Redemptive Reversals and the Ironic Overturning of Human Wisdom* (Wheaton, IL:
Crossway, 2019), 22.

6. Since "God's manner of revelation is characterized by hiddenness, reversal, and
surprise . . . there can be no place for smugness or dogmatism." He concludes: "If
our sensibilities are formed by this narrative . . . we will learn not to take ourselves
too seriously . . . [and to] be self-critical." Hays, *Moral Vision of the New Testament*, 90.

7. For a good summary (from which many references in this chapter are taken), see Donald Guthrie, *New Testament Introduction* (Downers Grove, IL: InterVarsity Press, 1970), 90–91.

8. Simon Gathercole, "The Gospel of Paul and the Gospel of the Kingdom," in *God's Power to Save: One Gospel for a Complex World?*, ed. Chris Green (Leicester, UK: InterVarsity Press, 2006), 138–54.

9. Gathercole, "Gospel of Paul," 143. See notes 14 and 15 on this page as well.

10. Gathercole, "Gospel of Paul," 149.

11. Okay, you guessed it. This is a true story about me.

12. Joseph Haroutunian, ed., *Calvin: Commentaries*, The Library of Christian Classics (Philadelphia: Westminster Press, 1958), 69.

CHAPTER 6: PERSONAL HOPE: 1

1. I explore other aspects of Jesus's encounter with Mary in John 20 in my book *Encounters with Jesus: Unexpected Answers to Life's Biggest Questions* (New York: Dutton, 2013). See "The First Christian," 82–102.

2. Josiah Conder, "'Tis Not That I Did Choose Thee" (hymn), 1836.

3. The interpretive path I take with these verses is summarized well in Andreas J. Köstenberger, *John*, Baker Exegetical Commentary on the New Testament (Grand Rapids, MI: Baker Academic, 2004), 569: "Her reaction is entirely natural; yet, once again, it reveals misunderstanding. Apparently, Mary is determined not to lose a second time what it cost her such effort to find again; yet she must not cling to the unascended Jesus, for 'his permanent abiding with her is to be not in the flesh as she supposes . . . but in the Spirit' (Lee 1995: 42)."

4. The traditional argument for the gospel's Johannine authorship has a strong foundation. The earliest church leaders unanimously attributed the gospel to the apostle John, including Ireneaus, whose mentor Polycarp had been a disciple of John. Many modern scholars differ with this view. We can't go into those debates here. For a good summary and a defense of the traditional view, see D. A. Carson, *The Gospel According to John* (Grand Rapids, MI: Wm. B. Eerdmans, 1991), 68–81. For our purposes it is important to note that even some who deny that the apostle John wrote the gospel nonetheless believe it was written by an eyewitness to the events. (See Richard Bauckham, *The Testimony of the Beloved Disciple: Narrative, History, and the Theology of the Gospel of John* [Grand Rapids, MI: Baker Academic, 2007].)

5. Sir Arthur Conan Doyle, "The Sign of the Four," in *Sherlock Holmes: The Complete Illustrated Novels* (New York: University of Life Library, Carlisle Media, 2018), 170.

6. As anyone with an internet browser will quickly discover, this story is told about Charles Blondin, the French tightrope walker who crossed Niagara Gorge on a rope on June 30, 1859. I have not been able to confirm that this incident actually happened. The wide variations in the story are some indication that they did not come from any authoritative historical source. Nevertheless the story serves perfectly well as an illustration of the difference between mental belief and heart trust.

7. Bruce Milne, *The Message of John: Here Is Your King!*, The Bible Speaks Today (Downers Grove, IL: IVP Academic, 1993), 302.

8. Milne, *Message of John*, 302.

9. Richard Bauckham, *Jesus and the Eyewitnesses: The Gospels as Eyewitness Testimony*, 2nd ed. (Grand Rapids, MI: Wm. B. Eerdmans, 2017).

10. Leon Morris, *The Gospel According to John*, The New International Commentary on the New Testament (Grand Rapids, MI: Wm. B. Eerdmans, 1995), 753.

11. C. S. Lewis, *The Horse and His Boy* (1954; illustrated ed., New York: HarperCollins, 2002), 175–76.

CHAPTER 7: PERSONAL HOPE: 2

1. See Richard Bauckham, *Jesus and the Eyewitnesses: The Gospels as Eyewitness Testimony*, 2nd ed. (Grand Rapids, MI: Wm. B. Eerdmans, 2017), 170. Bauckham cites R. T. France and R. E. Brown as also supporting this interpretation.

2. Miroslav Volf, *Exclusion and Embrace: A Theological Exploration of Identity, Otherness, and Reconciliation* (Nashville: Abingdon Press, 1996), 95–96.

3. See Equal Justice Initiative, *Lynching in America: Confronting the Legacy of Racial Terror*, 3rd ed. (no date), https://eji.org/reports/lynching-in-america.

4. J. R. R. Tolkien, *The Two Towers*, (New York: Houghton Mifflin Company, 1987), 848.

5. Billy Graham, *Just as I Am: The Autobiography of Billy Graham* (San Francisco: HarperSanFrancisco, 1997), 25.

6. Graham, *Just as I Am*, 27.

7. Graham, *Just as I Am*, 29. "The 180-Degree Turn" is the name of the chapter in Graham's autobiography that describes his conversion under the ministry of evangelist Mordecai Ham.

8. I have personally heard Billy Graham explain this about his wife. The quotation from Ruth Bell Graham can be found in many places on the internet. Here is one: faithinwriting.com/Tradition/Family/index.htm.

9. Huxley adds: "For myself, the philosophy of meaninglessness was essentially an instrument of liberation, sexual and political." Aldous Huxley, *Ends and Means* (London: Chatto and Windus, 1946), 273.

10. C. S. Lewis, "The Invasion," in *Mere Christianity* (New York: MacMillan, 1958), 33.

11. The corresponding paragraph is based on D. A. Carson's July 22 meditation on Acts 9 in *For the Love of God*, vol. 1 (Wheaton, IL: Crossway Books, 1998).

12. Martin Luther, *The Freedom of a Christian*, trans. Mark D. Tranvik (Minneapolis: Fortress Press, 2008), 62–63.

13. See D. Bruce Hindmarsh, *The Evangelical Conversion Narrative: Spiritual Autobiography in Early Modern England* (Oxford, UK: Oxford University Press, 2008); and D. Bruce Hindmarsh, *The Spirit of Early Evangelicalism: True Religion in the Modern World* (Oxford: Oxford University Press, 2017).

14. D. M. Lloyd-Jones, "Introduction," in William Williams, *The Experience Meeting* (Vancouver, BC: Regent College Publishing, 2003), 5.

15. I have modernized the language of these questions. The original questions can be found in William Williams, *The Experience Meeting*, 34–36, 39–41.

CHAPTER 8: HOPE FOR YOU

1. D. Martyn Lloyd-Jones, *God's Ultimate Purpose: An Exposition of Ephesians 1:1 to 23* (Grand Rapids, MI: Baker Book House, 1978), 71. For many of the thoughts in this entire chapter, see these sermons by Lloyd-Jones, as well as D. Martyn Lloyd-Jones, *God's Way of Reconciliation: Studied in Ephesians Chapter 2* (Grand Rapids, MI: Baker Book House, 1972).

2. This illustration is from Lloyd-Jones, *God's Way of Reconciliation*, 90.

3. Lloyd-Jones, *God's Way of Reconciliation*, 103.

4. Isaac Watts, "Come Ye That Love the Lord" (hymn), 1649.

5. Archibald Alexander, *Thoughts on Religious Experience* (Edinburgh: Banner of Truth Trust, 1967), xvii.

6. For much more on Christian experience through prayer, see Timothy Keller, *Prayer: Experiencing Awe and Intimacy with God* (New York: Penguin Books, 2014), 143–86.

7. Suzanne MacDonald, "Beholding the Glory of God in the Face of Jesus Christ: John Owen and the 'Reforming' of the Beatific Vision," in *The Ashgate Research Companion to John Owen's Theology*, ed. Kelly M. Kapic and Mark Jones (Surrey, UK: Ashgate, 2012), 142.

8. The key text is John Owen, *Meditations and Discourses on the Glory of Christ* (1684). This was Owen's last publication. As he was weakening and dying, he turned to the promise and practice of beholding Christ's glory to prepare himself for death. I am doing the same thing. The best versions of this work are John Owen, *The Glory of Christ: His Office and Grace* (Fearn, Ross-shire, Scotland: Christian Heritage Books, 2015) (an unabridged text with modernized English); John Owen, *The Glory of Christ*, abridged by R. J. K. Law (Edinburgh: Banner of Truth, 1994) (an abridged and modernized version); and the original text, John Owen, *The Works of John Owen*, vol. 1, ed. William H. Goold (Edinburgh: Banner of Truth, 1965), 274–464.

9. Owen, *Glory of Christ: His Office and Grace*, 44–45.

10. Owen, *Glory of Christ: His Office and Grace*, 44–45.

11. Owen, *Glory of Christ: His Office and Grace*, 49.

12. Owen, *Glory of Christ: His Office and Grace*, 49.

13. See the classic sermon by Thomas Chalmers, "The Expulsive Power of a New Affection," found at www.monergism.com/thethreshold/sdg/Chalmers,%20 Thomas%20-%20The%20Expulsive%20Power%20of%20a%20New%20Af.pdf.

14. The classic text on what we have been calling the "killing" stroke is John Owen, "On the Mortification of Sin in Believers," in *The Works of John Owen*, vol. 6, ed. William H. Goold (Edinburgh: Banner of Truth, 1967), 2–88. The classic texts on what we have been calling the "raising" stroke are John Owen, "On the Grace and Duty of Being Spiritually Minded," in *The Works of John Owen*, vol. 7, ed. William H. Goold (Edinburgh: Banner of Truth, 1967), and Owen, *Meditations and Discourses*.

15. See John Owen's example of how to meditate on Jesus as the "altogether lovely one" (Song of Solomon 5:16) in John Owen, *Communion with the Triune God*, ed. Kelly M. Kapic and Justin Taylor (Wheaton, IL: Crossway, 2007), 181–82.

16. Richard B. Hays, *The Moral Vision of the New Testament: A Contemporary Introduction to New Testament Ethics* (New York: HarperOne, 1996), 1–2.

17. All the quotes in this paragraph are from Hays, *Moral Vision of the New Testament*, 2.

18. Hays, *Moral Vision of the New Testament*, 209. Hays's four "hermeneutical modes of moral appeal" are named "rules," "principles," "paradigms," and "symbolic

world." He defines the "symbolic world" as how the Bible "creates the perceptual categories through which we interpret reality," in particular, how it represents the human condition and nature and how it depicts the character of God (209). I will use the term *worldview* in place of *symbolic world* because I believe it is a more recognizable term.

19. Hays, *Moral Vision of the New Testament*, 197–98.

20. Elisabeth Elliot, *Passion and Purity* (Grand Rapids, MI: Baker, 2013), 73.

21. Elliot, *Passion and Purity*, 73.

22. Hays, *Moral Vision of the New Testament*, 202.

23. Hays, *Moral Vision of the New Testament*, 203.

24. Hays, *Moral Vision of the New Testament*, 197.

25. Hays, *Moral Vision of the New Testament*, 197.

26. Another thinker who saw the Great Reversal as the basis for ethics was the late Duke University professor Allen Verhey. [See Allen Verhey, *The Great Reversal: Ethics and the New Testament* (Grand Rapids, MI: Wm. B. Eerdmans, 1984).] But the most prominent and influential thinker on the significance of the resurrection for Christian morality is Oliver O'Donovan, especially in his classic *Resurrection and Moral Order: An Outline for Evangelical Ethics*, 2nd ed. (Grand Rapids, MI: Wm. B. Eerdmans, 1994). O'Donovan's basic thesis is that "Christian ethic depends upon the resurrection of Jesus Christ from the dead" (13), and this keeps us from becoming either "moralists or antinomians" (11), nor does it offer some kind of abstract "middle ground" (12). The raising and redemption of Jesus's body—rather than just taking Jesus's spirit to heaven—is a new affirmation of the created order. "It might have been possible, before Christ rose . . . for someone to wonder whether creation was a lost cause. If the creature consistently acted to uncreate itself, and with itself to uncreate the rest of creation, did this not mean that God's handiwork was flawed beyond hope of repair? It might have been possible before Christ rose from the dead to . . . hope for redemption *from* creation rather than for the redemption *of* creation. . . . When the gospel is preached without out a resurrection . . . the cross and ascension, collapsed together without their center, become symbols for a gnostic other-worldliness. [But after the resurrection, we know] man's life on earth is important to God: he has given it its order. . . . Once we have grasped that, we can understand how . . . this requires . . . both a denial of all that threatens to become disordered and a progress toward a life which goes beyond this order without negating it" (14–15). O'Donovan goes on to argue that a resurrection-centered ethic avoids the grave errors of both Enlightenment rationalism and religious dualism. The Enlightenment project was the effort to *not* look to faith or revelation to discern moral norms. Rather we were to

use our reason to examine the natural world and discern moral principles (sometimes called "natural law"). But we cannot simply read moral values out of nature in its present, fallen condition. Annie Dillard's *Pilgrim at Tinker Creek* (New York: HarperCollins, 1974) vividly depicts animal cruelty and the violent nature of ordinary evolutionary process. We cannot discover a "moral order" inductively simply by looking at nature with unaided human reason. On the other hand, much of religion is dualistic, seeing the spiritual as good and the material as evil. In dualism salvation is conceived as escaping this material world permanently into a wholly spiritual paradise forever. Instead, the resurrection affirms the goodness of the original creation and gives us the power of the Spirit so that, as we obey God's moral directives, we partially but genuinely begin to heal the ruptured relationships of the fallen world.

CHAPTER 9: HOPE FOR RELATIONSHIPS

1. I am aware of the argument that "race" is a modern construct, one that takes up the older concept of ethnicity and subsumes it under headings of the races—"whiteness," "blackness," "brownness"—in order to set them in a hierarchy from superior to inferior. I believe that this scholarship has much to teach us. But some have, on the basis of such scholarship, argued that we cannot speak of any biblical writers or figures being "racist" as we understand the word today. In their view, racism is a modern invention and can't be applied to any part of the Bible. Despite great respect for the concept that modernity has forged a peculiarly culturally powerful form of racism, Bill Melone argues racism and "racializing" did exist in ancient times, and specifically that Peter was indeed guilty of racism in Galatians 2. (See Bill Melone, "The Tribe of Ishmael: Whiteness and Christian Identity," *Mere Orthodoxy*, March 24, 2020, https://mereorthodoxy.com/whiteness-christian -identity.) Melone argues: "The concept of race is fundamentally characterized by hierarchical, absolute and disembodied categories, so to racialize people groups is to (1) see those groups according to a scale of supremacy to inferiority, and to (2) organize those groups into categories that are completely separate from each other and cannot be mixed, all through (3) the work of reimagining identities as disconnected from real bodies. So can we say that Peter 'racialized' the Gentiles by seeing them according to these three elements?" He goes on to answer "yes."

2. Herman N. Ridderbos, *The Epistle of Paul to the Churches of Galatia*, The New International Commentary on the Old and New Testament (Grand Rapids, MI: Wm. B. Eerdmans, 1953), 226.

3. John Oswalt, *The Book of Isaiah 40–66* (Grand Rapids, MI: Wm. B. Eerdmans, 1998), 547–48.

4. Grant R. Osborne, *Revelation* (Grand Rapids, MI: Baker, 2002), 763.

5. Larry W. Hurtado, *Destroyer of the Gods: Early Christian Distinctiveness in the Roman World* (Waco, TX: Baylor University Press, 2016), 93.

6. See Irwyn Ince, *The Beautiful Community: Unity, Diversity, and the Church at Its Best*, InterVarsity Press, 2020; Manuel Ortiz, *One New People: Models for Developing a Multiethnic Church* (InterVarsity Press, 1996); George Yancey, *One Body, One Spirit: Principles of Successful Multiracial Churches* (InterVarsity Press, 2003); and Efrem Smith, *The Post-Black and Post-White Church: Becoming the Beloved Community in a Multi-Ethnic World* (Josey-Bass, 2012).

7. See David Swartz, *Culture and Power: The Sociology of Pierre Bourdieu* (Chicago: University of Chicago Press, 1998); and David Swartz, *Symbolic Power, Politics, and Intellectuals: The Political Sociology of Pierre Bourdieu* (Chicago: University of Chicago Press, 2013).

8. Joel B. Green, *The Gospel of Luke*, The New International Commentary on the New Testament (Grand Rapids, MI: Wm. B. Eerdmans, 1997), 550–51.

9. "Recognition of the structure of the beatitude, or pronouncement of blessing, of v 14a is critical. According to Jesus, the state of blessedness resides in the fact that one has given without expectation (or hope!) of return. It is true that, according to v 14b, blessedness will take the eschatological form of divine 'repayment,' but Jesus does not advise people to engage in guileless generosity *in order that* one might receive divine benefaction. Luke has already established that human generosity flows from an appreciation of the expansive mercy of God (6:36); to this he now adds that genuine, uncalculating generosity toward those of low status will not go unrewarded." Green, *Gospel of Luke*, 554.

10. See N. T. Wright, "Resurrection of the Dead," in *Dictionary for the Theological Interpretation of the Bible*, ed. Kevin J. Vanhoozer (Grand Rapids, MI: Baker Books, 2005), 676–78.

11. Gordon D. Fee, *The First Epistle to the Corinthians*, The New International Commentary on the New Testament (Grand Rapids, MI: Wm. B. Eerdmans, 1987), 233–34.

12. Kyle Harper, *From Shame to Sin: The Christian Transformation of Sexual Morality in Late Antiquity* (Cambridge, MA: Harvard University Press, 2013), 89.

13. Hurtado, *Destroyer of the Gods*, 155–75.

14. Harper points out that the inclusion of porneia in the Apostolic Decree of Acts 15 shows the importance and "uncanny power of the term to condense a whole bundle of expectations about the use of the body." Harper, *From Shame to Sin*, 90.

15. C. S. Lewis, *Mere Christianity* (New York: MacMillan, 1958), 81.

16. Anthony C. Thiselton, *The First Epistle to the Corinthians: A Commentary on the Greek Text*, New International Greek Testament Commentary (Grand Rapids, MI: Wm. B. Eerdmans, 2000), 474.

17. "The love felt by the Jewish god for his chosen people—so unlike anything displayed by the heedless gods of [paganism] had long aroused in Gentiles emotions of envy. . . . Now . . . with the coming of Christ . . . no longer were the Jews alone the 'children of God.'" Tom Holland, *Dominion: How the Christian Revolution Remade the World* (New York: Basic Books, 2019), 86. Holland throughout his book shows that the love relationship between God and his people was something Eastern religions did not offer (since God is essentially impersonal) and Western religions did not either (since the gods were too fickle and uncaring about human concerns).

18. C. S. Lewis, *The Problem of Pain* (New York: HarperCollins, 1996) 157.

19. Lewis, *Problem of Pain*, 157–58.

CHAPTER 10: HOPE FOR JUSTICE

1. See Jonathan Edwards, "Sermon Fifteen: Heaven Is a World of Love" in *The Works of Jonathan Edwards*, WJE Online, Jonathan Edwards Center, Yale University, http://edwards.yale.edu/archive?path=aHR0cDovL2Vkd2FyZHMueWFsZS5lZHUvY2dpLWJpbi9uZXdwaGlsby9nZXRvYmplY3QucGw/Yy43OjQ6MTUud2plbw==.

2. This is one of the main themes of the writing of I. Lillias Trotter. See her *Parables of the Cross* (Orland Park, IL: Oxvision Books, 2014).

3. Jonathan Edwards, "Christian Charity or The Duty of Charity to the Poor, Explained and Enforced," Bible Bulletin Board, www.biblebb.com/files/edwards/charity.htm.

4. J. G. McConville, *Deuteronomy: Apollos Old Testament Commentary* (Leicester, UK: 2002), 104.

5. The Mosaic law was intended to enlighten all the nonbelieving nations as to true wisdom and true justice (Deuteronomy 4). That must mean that it has applicability at some level to all cultures and that it therefore reflects God's timeless wisdom and justice. But does that mean that Christians must obey everything in the Mosaic law? Many insist that, after the coming of Jesus, nothing in the Old Testament is binding on believers. Others have read ethics out of the Old Testament as if the advent of Jesus made no difference at all.

    Historically, there may be no better balance struck than that by a seventeenth-century Protestant confessional document, the Westminster Confession of Faith (later adopted by the Church of Scotland and Presbyterian churches around the world). In chapter 19, it speaks of three kinds of law in the Old Testament. There are first broad moral laws, like the Ten Commandments. Second, there are Israel's civil and judicial laws, such as the laws of gleaning or of military service or of payment of wages, and so on. Finally, there are the "ceremonial" laws that had to do with worship in the tabernacle—the animal sacrifices, and the many ceremonial rules that defined "cleanness" and fitness for that worship. The Confession teaches that the ceremonial laws are not binding, having all be fulfilled in Christ. The Confession also concludes that the Ten Commandments still are binding on us, as Romans 13:8–10 and 1 John 2:3–4 and 7 indicate, as well as Jesus's exposition of the Ten Commandments in the Sermon on the Mount. But what about the civil or judicial laws?

The Confession says that these laws were given to Israel "as a body politic, which expired together with the State of that people" (Westminster Confession of Faith 19:4). This does not mean that the Jewish people no longer exist but that the "State"—the specific form of a monarchy using the Mosaic law as its constitution—is no more. Also, the civil and judicial laws were detailed applications of the moral law to an agrarian economy and culture that is also, largely, no more. The Confession says that these laws are "not obliging any other now, further than the *general equity* thereof may require." This is a wonderfully nuanced view. The "judicial law" of Israel in this full, detailed form is not binding on us. But there are general principles of "equity" or justice that lie behind every one of the laws that, as Deuteronomy 4 hints, every century and culture can use to critique its own society.

The Confession cites some New Testament passages where Paul bases his exhortations to Christians on the very civil laws that are no longer binding in their specifics. In 1 Corinthians 9:8–10 Paul uses the basic principle of Deuteronomy 25:4 ("Do not muzzle an ox while it is treading out the grain") to require Christians' support of laborers in the ministry. Another example is 2 Corinthians 8:13–15's application of the basic "equity" of Exodus 16:18—the rules for gathering manna—to how Christians must give sacrificially to those in need. It's fair to surmise that the Confession, as a Reformed and Calvinistic document, was on the Old Testament following the lead of Calvin, who took this same approach to the judicial laws.

Baptists and many others have resisted the way the Presbyterian and Anglican confessions divide the Old Testament law into three distinct categories. With warrant, they complain that the boundaries between these groupings are not always clear. Nevertheless there has been over the last fifty years a consensus among orthodox and conservative biblical scholars across many denominations and traditions that the civil and judicial laws of the Old Testament reflect principles of justice that point forward and that we must find ways of embodying them in our own times and places. For excellent contemporary overviews of this topic, see Walter Kaiser, *Toward Old Testament Ethics* (Grand Rapids, MI: Zondervan, 1983); and Christopher J. H. Wright, *Old Testament Ethics for the People of God* (Downers Grove, IL: InterVarsity Press, 2004). See also William W. Klein, Craig L. Blomberg, and Roberts Hubbard Jr., *Introduction to Biblical Interpretation*, 3rd ed. (Grand Rapids, MI: Zondervan, 2017), 443–51. Klein et al. are Baptists who reject the hard and fast threefold division of the Presbyterians and Anglicans but believe, as Blomberg writes of the Old Testament law, that "its principles should find some application in all cultures" and that we should look for "transcultural values."

If the Jerusalem of the psalmists' and of Moses's time was to be "the joy of the whole earth" because its model of justice and quality of cultural life were crucial to attracting the nations to the glory of God, we can assume that in some ways, fitful and partial, the laws of the earthly Jerusalem were pointing to the perfect justice of the heavenly Jerusalem, the final city of God. So we can look for directions and principles in the Old Testament law—always looking for how it is used in the New Testament—to give us guidance for doing justice today.

6. Craig Blomberg, *Neither Poverty nor Riches: A Biblical Theology of Possessions* (Leicester, UK: Apollos, 1999), 46.

7. The first text from Proverbs is rendered by the Good News Translation (GNT) and the second from Psalms by the English Standard Version (ESV).

8. John B. Taylor, *Ezekiel: An Introduction and Commentary* (London: Tyndale, 1969), 147.

9. Richard Rothstein, "The Black Lives Next Door," *The New York Times*, August 15, 2020, www.nytimes.com/2020/08/14/opinion/sunday/blm-residential-segregation.html.

10. Robert Bellah et al., *Habits of the Heart: Individualism and Commitment in American Life* (Berkeley: University of California Press, 2007). One of Bellah's basic arguments is that it can work for a culture to be officially secular and individualistic if there are large bodies of religious people whose moral convictions can offset the otherwise inevitable erosion of communities and families, and also the trend toward selfishness.

11. Clarence Darrow, "Crime and Criminals: Address to the Prisoners in the Chicago Jail" (speech, 1902), Bureau of Public Secrets, www.bopsecrets.org/CF/darrow.htm.

12. Charles Taylor, *Avenues of Faith: Conversations with Jonathan Guilbault* (Waco, TX: Baylor University Press, 2020), 5–7.

13. For a seminal essay on this subject, see Dutch theologian Herman Bavinck's 1913 *Christian Worldview*, ed. and trans. Nathaniel Gray Sutanto, James Eglinton, and Cory C. Brock (Wheaton, IL: Crossway, 2019)—only recently translated from

the Dutch. Despite writing over a century ago, Bavinck was already facing the twin forces of the scientific materialism of the Enlightenment and the proto-"deconstruction" of the thought of Friedrich Nietzsche. Bavinck argues that all secular worldviews have three characteristics: (1) They are reductionistic or "mechanical," seeking to explain all life in terms of some material condition. (2) They are forced to demonize as the root of evil some good thing in God's creation. (3) They are also forced to valorize or idolize as their salvation some fallen and imperfect part of creation. Bavinck shows how these inadequate explanations fail to unite our head and our heart—how we think about human life from what we know intuitively about it.

14. Proverbs 13:23: "The unplowed field of poor people yields plenty of food but their existence is swept away through injustice." [See Bruce K. Waltke, *Book of Proverbs: Chapter 1–15* (Grand Rapids, MI: Wm. B. Eerdmans, 2004), 549–50.] "The unplowed field . . . yields" refers to land so productive that it produces fruit even when not plowed. "Plenty of food" means that the poor are working hard to harvest it. So then why are they poor? "Their existence is swept away through injustice [Hebrew *lo mishpat*]." Here, then, are three possible causes of poverty—environmental, personal, and social. According to Proverbs, sometimes poverty is caused by poor resources, sometimes by personal irresponsibility. But here we see that poverty can be caused by sheer injustice, without any blame on the poor at all.

15. James Mumford, *Vexed: Ethics Beyond Political Tribes* (London: Bloomsbury, 2020).

16. See Yuval Levin, *A Time to Build: From Family and Community to Congress and the Campus, How Recommitting to Our Institutions Can Revive the American Dream* (New York: Basic Books, 2020). See especially chapter 3, "We the People," 45–68.

17. This chapter should not be used to infer that the job of the gathered church is mainly to do social activism and social service. Rather, the primary tasks of the church include worshipping, teaching the Word and administering baptism and the Lord's supper, and evangelizing and discipling. If the church wins people to faith and disciples them into the biblical belief in the new creation and resurrection, and into all the entailments of the gospel, it will produce a steady stream of believers who serve as "salt and light" in the world (Matthew 5:13–16), doing justice and good works and loving their neighbors as in the parable of the Good Samaritan (Luke 10:25–37). Experience shows that usually local church elders do not have the expertise to both govern a church *and* operate community development corporations, affordable housing corporations, drug rehab centers, schools, and so on. The institutional church's first responsibility is to evangelize and disciple through the Word of God. But that discipling and training must motivate and equip Christians to do justice throughout their city and their world, or it is not true to the Word and the gospel.

18. O'Donovan, *Resurrection and the Moral Order: An Outline for Evangelical Ethics* (Grand Rapids, MI: Wm. B. Eerdmans, 1986).

19. C. S. Lewis, "The Practical Conclusion," in *Mere Christianity* (New York: Mac-Millan, 1958), 50.

20. C. S. Lewis, "The Rival Conceptions of God," in *Mere Christianity*, 31.

21. N. T. Wright, *For All God's Worth: True Worship and the Calling of the Church* (Grand Rapids, MI: Wm. B. Eerdmans, 1997), 65–66.

CHAPTER 11: HOPE IN THE FACE OF SUFFERING

1. Christopher Watkin, *Michel Foucault*, Great Thinkers Series (Phillipsburg, NJ: Presbyterian and Reformed, 2018), 81.

2. See John Stott, *The Message of the Sermon on the Mount: Christian Counter-Culture* (Downers Grove, IL: InterVarsity Press, 1978). The term "counter-culture" is taken from the subtitle.

3. Stott, *The Message of the Sermon on the Mount*, 18–19.

4. Michael Wilcock, *The Savior of the World: The Message of Luke's Gospel*, The Bible Speaks Today (Downers Grove, IL: InterVarsity Press, 1979), 86.

5. John Nolland, *Luke 9:21–18:34*, vol. 35B, Word Biblical Commentary (Dallas: Word, 1993), 828.

6. David Foster Wallace, "Commencement Address" (speech, Kenyon College, Gambier, OH, May 21, 2005), transcript available at https://web.ics.purdue.edu/~drkelly/DFWKenyonAddress2005.pdf.

7. It is impossible to confirm that this quote came from the historical figure Saint Teresa of Ávila (1515–1582). But it is well known and often cited.

8. C. S. Lewis, "The New Men," in *Mere Christianity* (New York: MacMillan, 1958), 174–75.

9. Gregory. K. Beale, *Redemptive Reversals and the Ironic Overturning of Human Wisdom* (Wheaton, IL: Crossway, 2019), 118.

10. Beale, *Redemptive Reversals*, 120.

11. William Goldman, "The Princess Bride," in *Four Screenplays with Essays* (New York: Applause Books, 2000), 324.

12. Derek Kidner, *Genesis: An Introduction and Commentary* (Downers Grove, IL: InterVarsity Press, 1967), 212.

13. Paul Barnett, *The Second Epistle to the Corinthians*, The New International Commentary on the New Testament (Grand Rapids, MI: Wm. B. Eerdmans, 1997), 73.

14. John Owen, *The Glory of Christ*, abridged by R. J. K. Law (Edinburgh: Banner of Truth, 1994), 115.

15. John Owen, "The Grace and Duty of Being Spiritually Minded," in *Works*, ed. W. Goold, vol. 7, *Sin and Grace* (London: Banner of Truth, 1965), 347.

CHAPTER 12: HOPE FOR THE FUTURE

1. David Brooks, "America Is Facing 5 Epic Crises All at Once," *The New York Times*, June 25, 2020, www.nytimes.com/2020/06/25/opinion/us-coronavirus-protests .html.

2. Robert Nisbet, *History of the Idea of Progress* (New York: Basic Books, 1980), 10–46.

3. Nisbet, *History of the Idea of Progress*, 47.

4. Nisbet, *History of the Idea of Progress*, 47.

5. Nisbet, *History of the Idea of Progress*, 47. Italics are mine.

6. Nisbet, *History of the Idea of Progress*, 172.

7. Nisbet, *History of the Idea of Progress*, 277.

8. Nisbet, *History of the Idea of Progress*, 171.

9. Nisbet, *History of the Idea of Progress*, 317.

10. H. G. Wells, *A Short History of the World* (New York: J. J. Little and Ives, 1922), 426–27.

11. H. G. Wells, "The Fate of Man," in *H. G. Wells Non-fiction Trio*, vol. 3, *New Worlds for Old, the Fate of Man, Russia in the Shadows* (CreateSpace Independent Publishing Platform, 2017), 232. "The Fate of Man" was originally published as *The Fate of Homo Sapiens* (London: Secker and Warburg, 1939).

12. H. G. Wells, *The Last Books of H. G. Wells: The Happy Turning: A Dream of Life and Mind at the End of Its Tether* (Rhinebeck, NY: Monkfish, 2006), 54.

13. Jean-François Lyotard, *The Postmodern Condition: A Report on Knowledge*, trans. G. Bennington and B. Massumi (Minneapolis: University of Minnesota Press, 1984). See chapter 9, "Narratives of the Legitimation of Knowledge," 31–37.

14. Lyotard, *Postmodern Condition*, 32.

15. Nisbet, *History of the Idea of Progress*, 318.

16. For an excellent summary and assessment of Foucault by a professor of French studies, from a Christian perspective, see Christopher Watkin, *Michel Foucault* (Phillipsburg, NJ: Presbyterian and Reformed, 2018).

17. David A. Graham, "The Wrong Side of 'the Right Side of History,'" *The Atlantic*, December 21, 2015, www.theatlantic.com/politics/archive/2015/12/obama-right -side-of-history/420462.

18. Charles Taylor, *A Secular Age* (Cambridge, MA: Belknap Press, 2007), 716–17.

19. Margaret O'Mara, "The Church of Techno-Optimism," *The New York Times*, September 28, 2019, www.nytimes.com/2019/09/28/opinion/sunday/silicon-valley -techno-optimism.html.

20. James E. Krier and Clayton P. Gillette, "The Un-easy Case for Technological Optimism," *University of Michigan Law Review* 84 (1985): 405–29, https://repository. law.umich.edu/articles/928/.

21. One example is Kara Swisher, "The Immunity of the Tech Giants," *The New York Times*, May 1, 2020, www.nytimes.com/2020/05/01/opinion/tech-companies-coro navirus.html.

22. Nisbet, *History of the Idea of Progress*, 351.

23. Nisbet, *History of the Idea of Progress*, 351.

24. For an example of this view, see the socialist lawyer Clarence Darrow's address to prisoners at Cook County Jail: "Crime and Criminals: Address to the Prisoners in the Chicago Jail" (speech, 1902), Bureau of Public Secrets, www.bopsecrets.org /CF/darrow.htm.

25. Cited by Dorothy Sayers in *Creed or Chaos?* (New York: Harcourt, 1949), 39.

26. C. E. M Joad, *The Recovery of Belief* (London: Faber and Faber, 1952), 61.

27. Joad, *Recovery of Belief*, 63.

28. Joad, *Recovery of Belief*, 74.

29. Joad, *Recovery of Belief*, 82.

30. C. S. Lewis, "On Living in an Atomic Age," in *Present Concerns* (London: Fount Paperbacks, 1986), 74.

31. Lewis, "On Living in an Atomic Age," 74–75.

32. Brian Greene, *Until the End of Time: Mind, Matter, and Our Search for Meaning in an Evolving Universe* (New York: Alfred A. Knopf, 2020), 321.

33. William Shakespeare, *Macbeth*, act 5, sc. 5.

34. Lewis, "On Living in an Atomic Age," 76.

35. N. T. Wright, *Surprised by Scripture: Engaging Contemporary Issues* (New York: HarperOne, 2014), 61.

36. Wright, *Surprised by Scripture*, 61.

37. Watkin, *Michel Foucault*, 102.

38. Gerhard Kittel, Gerhard Friedrich, and Geoffrey William Bromiley, *Theological Dictionary of the New Testament* (Grand Rapids, MI: Wm. B. Eerdmans, 1985), 231.

39. J. R. R. Tolkien, *The Return of the King* (1955; repr., New York: HarperCollins, 2004), 1148–49.

EPILOGUE: THE BUILDING BLOCK AND THE DARKNESS

1. This interpretation of these verses is based on the exegesis and analysis of Derek Kidner, *Psalms 73–150: An Introduction and Commentary*, vol. 16, Tyndale Old Testament Commentaries (Downers Grove, IL: InterVarsity Press, 1975), 450.

2. Noel Paul Stookey, "Building Block" (song), 1977.

3. Stookey, "Building Block."

4. S. Baring-Gould, "Onward, Christian Soldiers" (hymn), 1609.

5. Ernest W. Shurtleff, "Lead On, O King Eternal" (hymn), 1887.

6. Michael Wilcock, *The Message of the Psalms 73–150* (Downers Grove, IL: InterVarsity Press, 2001), 65.